Street by Street

G000149637

CORNWALL

Enlarged Areas Bodmin, Bude & Stratton, Camborne, Camelford, Carnon Downs, Crantock & Pentire, Falmouth, Fowey, Hayle & Lelant, Helston, Launceston, Liskeard, Looe, Lostwithiel, Marazion, Mevagissey, Millbrook, Newlyn, Newquay, Padstow, Par & St Blazey, Penryn, Penzance, Perranporth, Porthleven, Redruth, St Austell, St Erth, St Ives & Carbis Bay, St Just, St Mawes, Saltash, Tintagel, Torpoint, Truro, Wadebridge

Plus THE EDEN PROJECT

2nd edition May 2008
© Automobile Association Developments Limited 2008

Original edition printed May 2003

 This product includes map data licensed from Ordnance Survey® with the permission of the Controller of Her Majesty's Stationery Office. © Crown copyright 2008. All rights reserved. Licence number 100021153.

The copyright in all PAF is owned by Royal Mail Group plc.

Published by AA Publishing (a trading name of Automobile Association Developments Limited, whose registered office is Fanum House, Basing View, Basingstoke, Hampshire RG21 4EA. Registered number 1878835).

Produced by the Mapping Services Department of The Automobile Association. (A03622)

A CIP Catalogue record for this book is available from the British Library.

Printed by Oriental Press in Dubai

The contents of this atlas are believed to be correct at the time of the latest revision. However, the publishers cannot be held responsible or liable for any loss or damage occasioned to any person acting or refraining from action as a result of any use or reliance on any material in this atlas, nor for any errors, omissions or changes in such material. This does not affect your statutory rights. The publishers would welcome information to correct any errors or omissions and to keep this atlas up to date. Please write to Publishing, The Automobile Association, Fanum House (FH12), Basing View, Basingstoke, Hampshire, RG21 4EA. E-mail: streetbystreet@theaa.com

Ref: ML221z

Mileage chart	ii
Key to county map symbols	1
County map pages	2–7
Eden Project	8
Key to town map symbols	9
Town centre map pages	10–87

Bodmin	10–11	Padstow	48–49
Bude & Stratton	12–13	Par & St Blazey	50–51
Camborne	14–15	Penryn	52–53
Camelford	16–17	Penzance	54–55
Carnon Downs	18–19	Perranporth	56–57
Crantock & Pentire	20–21	Porthleven	58–59
Falmouth	22–23	Redruth	60–61
Fowey	24–25	St Austell	62–65
Hayle & Lelant	26–27	St Erth	66–67
Helston	28–29	St Ives	68–69
Launceston	30–31	St Ives & Carbis Bay	70–71
Liskeard	32–33	St Just	72–73
Looe	34–35	St Mawes	74–75
Lostwithiel	36–37	Saltash	76–77
Marazion	38–39	Tintagel	78–79
Mevagissey	40–41	Torpoint	80–81
Millbrook	42–43	Truro	82–85
Newlyn	44–45	Wadebridge	86–87
Newquay	46–47		

Index - county map	88–89
Index - towns & villages	89–90
Index - streets	91–104
Index - featured places	104–107
Acknowledgements	107

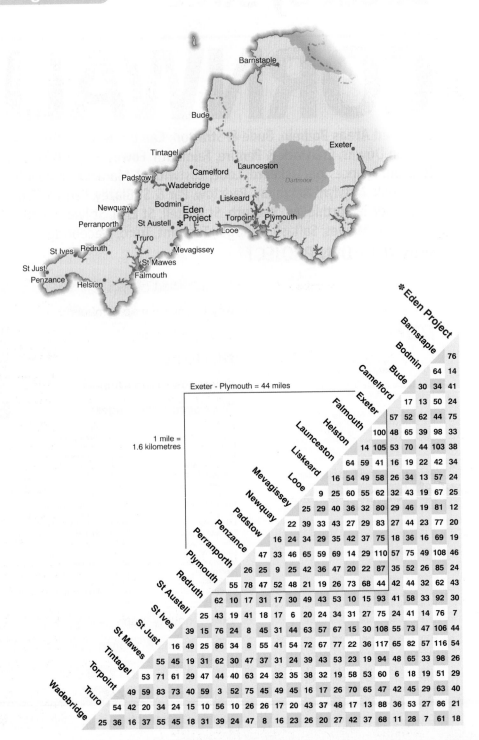

Exeter - Plymouth = 44 miles

1 mile = 1.6 kilometres

M4	Motorway with number
Toll T4 / Toll	Toll motorway with toll station
6	Motorway junction with and without number
3	Restricted motorway junctions
S / Fleet	Motorway service area
	Motorway and junction under construction
A3	Primary route single/dual carriageway
2	Primary route junction with and without number
3	Restricted primary route junctions
S / Grantham North	Primary route service area
BATH	Primary route destination
Truro	Featured place
A1123	Other A road single/dual carriageway
B2070	B road single/dual carriageway
	Unclassified road single/dual carriageway
	Roundabout
	Interchange/junction
	Road under construction
	Road tunnel
	Steep gradient (arrows point downhill)
Toll	Road toll
5	Distance in miles between symbols
V St Malo	Vehicle ferry
	Railway line/in tunnel
o X	Railway station and level crossing
	Tourist railway
	Airport
H	Heliport
★	Major shopping centre
	Viewpoint
P·R	Park and Ride location (at least 6 days)

	City, town, village or other built-up area
628 ▲	Spot height in metres
348 Rannoch Moor	Pass
	River, canal, lake
	Sandy beach
	National boundary
	County, administrative boundary
24	Page continuation
	Enlarged Street by Street mapping area
i	Tourist Information Centre
i	Tourist Information Centre (seasonal)
V	Visitor or heritage centre
ᛘ	Abbey, cathedral or priory
ᛘ	Ruined abbey, cathedral or priory
✗	Castle
🏰	Historic house or building
🏛	Museum or art gallery
⛭	Industrial interest
⊓⊓⊓	Aqueduct or viaduct
✿	Garden
♣	Arboretum
⚘	Vineyard
⚘	Country park
⚑	Agricultural showground
至	Theme park
🐄	Farm or animal centre
🦌	Zoological or wildlife collection
↖	Bird collection
🐟	Aquarium
RSPB	RSPB site
	National Nature Reserves (England, Scotland, Wales)

	Local nature reserve
·············	Forest drive
- - - - -	National trail
♣	Picnic site
⋯	Hill-fort
♠	Roman antiquity
ᛁᚾ	Prehistoric monument
✗ 1066	Battle site with year
🚂	Steam centre (railway)
⌒	Cave
✗	Windmill
🕯	Monument
┏	Golf course
ᛙᛁ	County cricket ground
🏉	Rugby Union national stadium
🏃	International athletics stadium
🐎	Horse racing
🐎	Show jumping/equestrian circuit
▦	Motor-racing circuit
✈	Air show venue
⛷	Ski slope – natural
⛷	Ski slope – artificial
NT	National Trust property
NTS	National Trust for Scotland property
★	Other place of interest
▢	Boxed symbols indicate attractions within urban areas
◉	World Heritage Site (UNESCO)
	National Park
	Forest Park
	Heritage coast

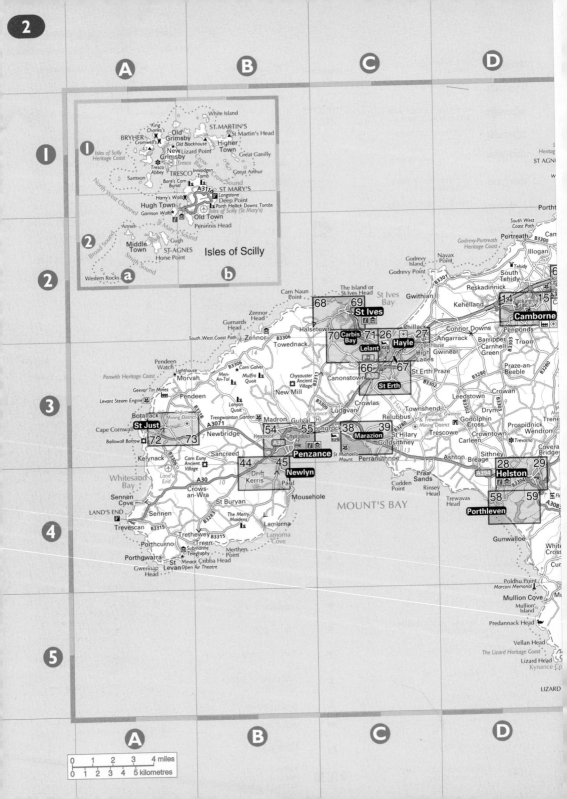

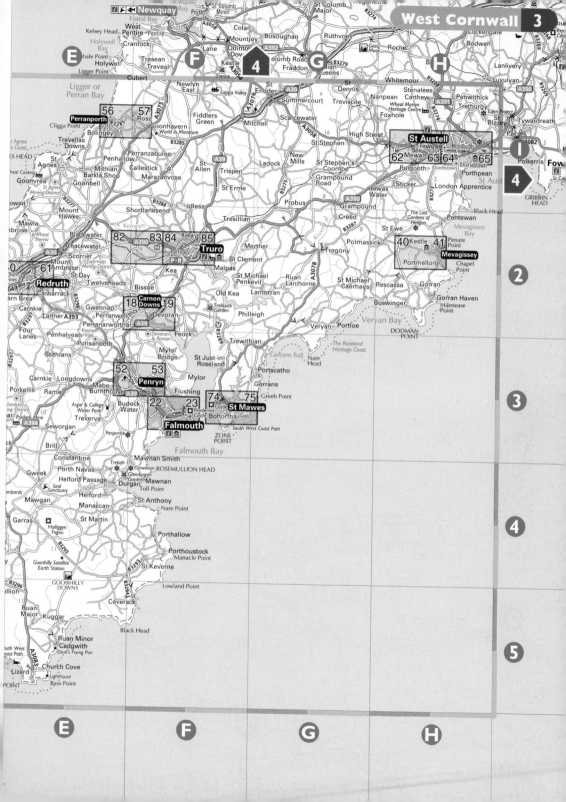

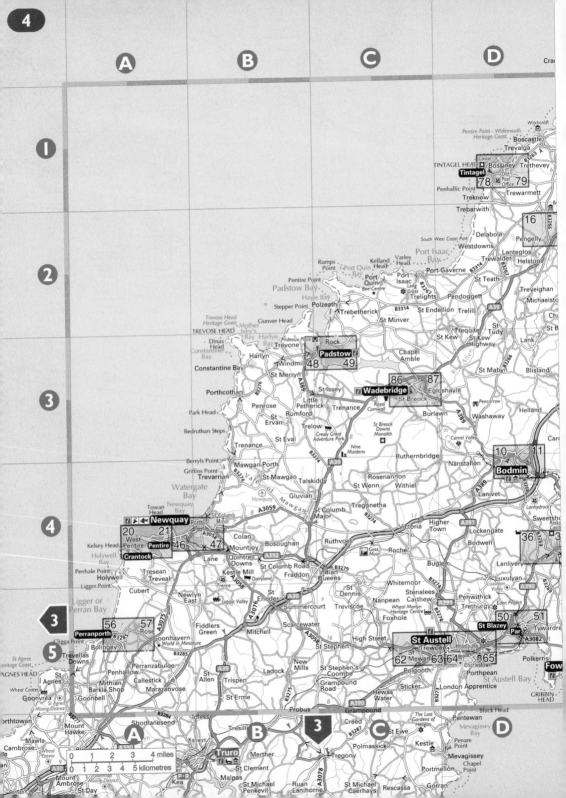

6

North West Point
Lundy Heritage Coast
LUNDY
S42
A
Surf Point
Shutter Point

Bull Point
Lee Bay
Rockham Bay
Damage Cliffs
Morteho
B
C
D
Woolacombe
Tri

Morte Bay

Baggy Point

North Buckla

Croyde Bay
Croyde
Darracot
Knov
B3231
Saunton

Braunton

Braunton Burrows

North Devon Heritage Coast

BARNSTAPLE

OR

BIDEFORD BAY

Westward Ho!
Northam

Crow Point

Appledore
In

Eastleigh

Abbotsham
The Big Sheep
East-the-Wat

HARTLAND POINT
Shipload Bay
Titchberry
Damehole Point
Hartland Abbey & Garden
Stoke
Hartland Quay
Hartland
Spekes Mill Mouth
Milford
Docton Mill Gardens
Philham
B3248
Clovelly
Buck's Mills
Buck's Cross
Milky Way
B3237
Hartland Heritage Coast
Fairy Cross
Ford
Horns Cross
Woodtown
A39
Bideford
Littleham
Landcross
Saltrens

Hardisworthy
Woolfardisworthy
Parkham
Buckland Brewer
Monkleigh
A386
Frithelstock
Frithelstock Stone

Welcombe
Darracott
Ashmansworthy
East Putford
West Putford
Haytown
Langtree
Tor
B3227

Morwenstow
Higher Sharpnose Point
South West Coast Path
Lower Sharpnose Point
Steeple Point
Sandy Mouth
Northcott Mouth
Poughill

Shop Woodford
East Youlstone
West Youlstone
Dinworthy
Gnome Reserve
East Putford
West Putford
Bradworthy
Sutcombe
Sutcombemill
Abbots Bickington
Newton St Petrock
Venngreen
Milton Damerel
Thornbury
Shebbear
Bradford
Sh
Buckland Filleigh
Stibb Cross
Peters Marland
A388

Kilhampton
Stibb
Brocklands
A39
B3254

Dunsdon
Holsworthy Beacon
Chilsworthy
Cookbury
Holemoor
Black
13

Bude Bay
Bude
Flexbury
Stratton
Launcells
12
13
A3072
Grimscott
Kingford
Pancrasweek
10
Holsworthy
Hollacombe
A3072
A3072
Winsford Walled Garden
Halwill Junction
Beaworthy

Widemouth Bay
Budd's Titson
Marhamchurch
Bridgerule
Pyworthy
Chasty
R Claw
Halwill
BRO

Coppathorne
Bangors
19
R Deer

Dizzard Point
Poundstock
Penlean
Tregole
Treskinnick Cross
Whitstone
Week St Mary
Penhallam
North Tamerton
Clawton
A388
Quoditch
Stowford
B
A3079

St Gennys
Coxford
Tetcott
Ashwater
Eworthy
rmansweek
D

Crackington Haven
Cambeak
Sweets
Jacobstow
Southcott
B3254
Luffincott
Chapmans Well
Virginstow
Roadford Reservoir
Bratton
Clovelly
19

Wainhouse Corner
Ma...thy
5
Bennacott
Boyton
Northcott
St Giles-on-the-Heath
Broadwoodwidger

Witchr...
int - Widemouth tage Coast
B3263
Trevalga
0 1 2 3 4 miles
0 1 2 3 4 5 kilometres
South Wheatley
Canworthy Water
Warbstow
Tremaine
North Petherwin
Tamar Otter Sanctuary
Lesnewth
Ottersham

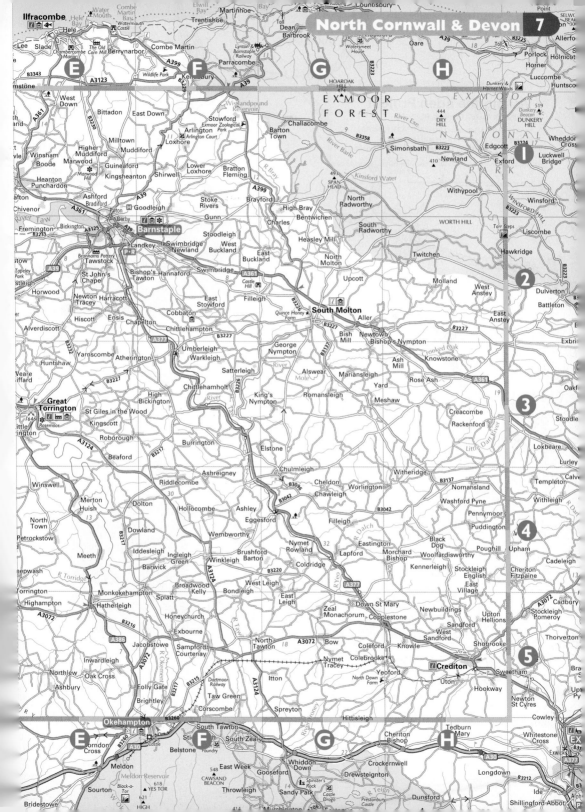

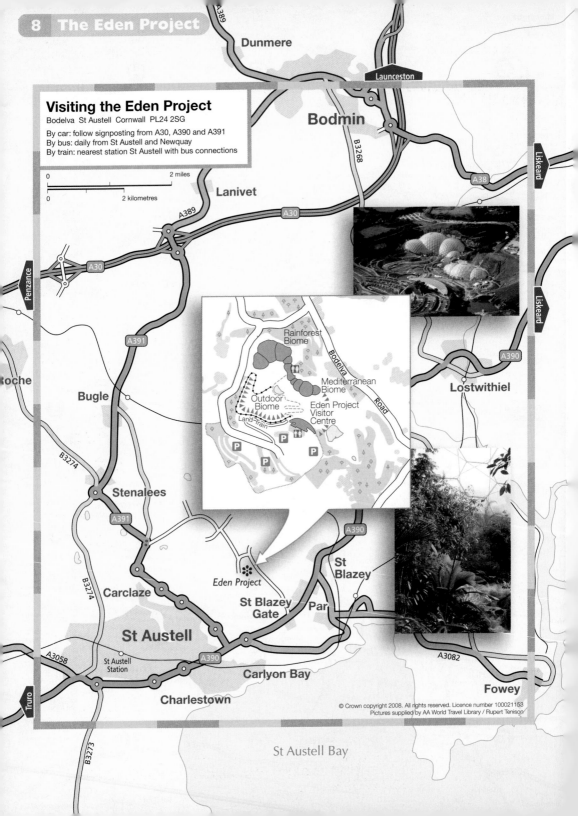

Dunmere

Launceston

Bodmin

B3268

Liskeard

A38

Visiting the Eden Project

Bodelva St Austell Cornwall PL24 2SG

By car: follow signposting from A30, A390 and A391
By bus: daily from St Austell and Newquay
By train: nearest station St Austell with bus connections

0 — 2 miles
0 — 2 kilometres

A389

Lanivet

A30

Liskeard

Penzance

A30

A391

Roche

Bugle

B3274

Stenalees

A391

Rainforest Biome

Bodelva Road

Mediterranean Biome

Outdoor Biome

Eden Project Visitor Centre

Land Train

P   P

P   P

A390

Lostwithiel

A390

B327A

Carclaze

Eden Project

St Blazey Gate

Par

St Blazey

A390

A3058

St Austell Station

St Austell

A390

Carlyon Bay

Charlestown

B3273

A3082

Fowey

St Austell Bay

Junction 9	Motorway & junction	17	Page continuation		Golf course
Services	Motorway service area		River/canal, lake, pier	▲	Camping AA inspected
	Primary road single/dual		Aqueduct, lock, weir		Caravan site AA inspected
Services	Primary road service area	465 ▲ Winter Hill	Peak (with height in metres)		Camping & caravan site AA inspected
	A road single/dual carriageway		Beach		Theme park
	B road single/dual carriageway		Woodland		Abbey, cathedral or priory
	Other road single/dual carriageway		Park		Castle
	Minor/private road, access may be restricted		Cemetery		Historic house or building
←	One-way street		Built-up area	Wakehurst Place NT	National Trust property
	Pedestrian area		Industrial/business building		Museum or art gallery
	Track or footpath		Leisure building		Roman antiquity
	Road under construction		Retail building		Ancient site, battlefield or monument
	Road tunnel		Other building		Industrial interest
P	Parking	Madeira Hotel	Hotel AA inspected		Garden
P+	Park & Ride	A&E	Hospital with 24-hour A&E department		Garden Centre Garden Centre Association Member
	Bus/coach station	PO	Post Office		Garden Centre Wyevale Garden Centre
	Railway & main railway station		Public library		Arboretum
	Railway & minor railway station	i	Tourist Information Centre		Farm or animal centre
	Light railway & station	i	Seasonal Tourist Information Centre		Zoological or wildlife collection
	Preserved private railway		Petrol station, 24 hour Major suppliers only		Bird collection
LC	Level crossing	†	Church/chapel		Nature reserve
	Tramway		Public toilets	V	Visitor or heritage centre
	Ferry route		Toilet with disabled facilities		Country park
	Airport runway	PH	Public house AA recommended		Cave
	County, administrative boundary		Restaurant AA inspected		Windmill
	Mounds		Theatre or performing arts centre		Distillery, brewery or vineyard
	City wall		Cinema		

| 0 | 1/4 | miles | 1/2 | | 3/4 |
| 0 | 1/4 | 1/2 | kilometres | 3/4 | 1 |

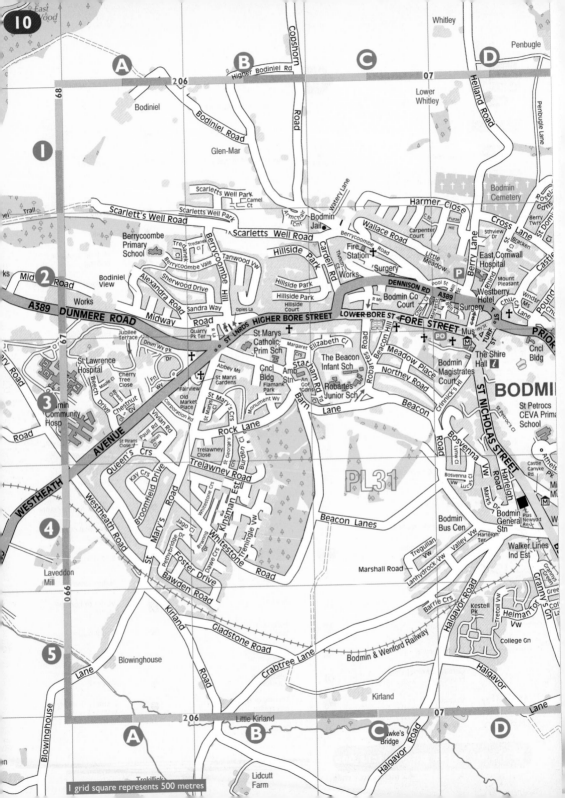

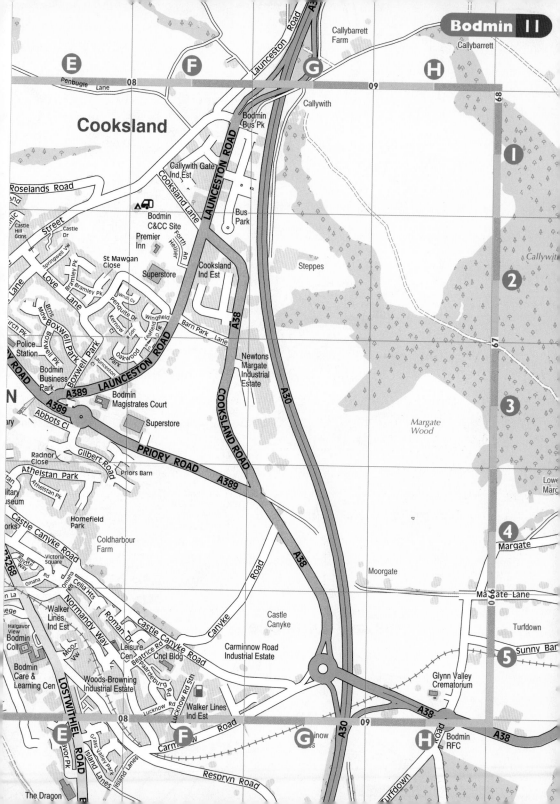

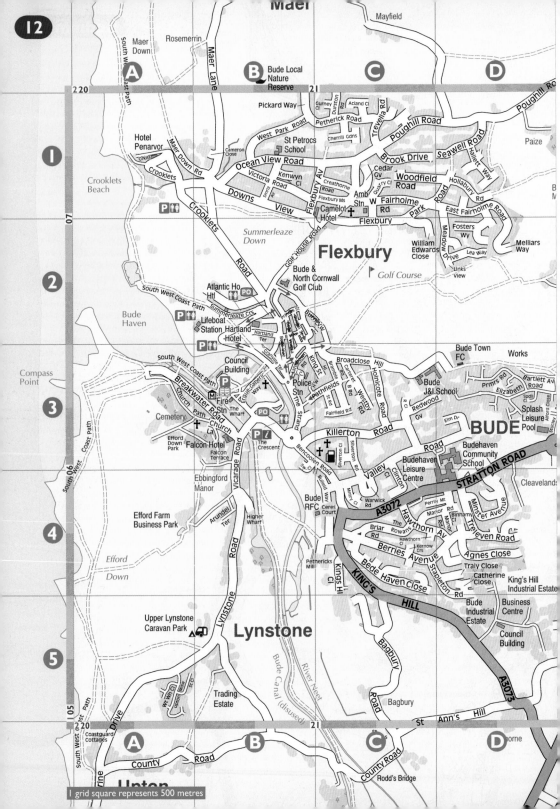

E Poughill

F

G

H

Bs Cl

PO

Broomhill
Lane

Orchard
Close

Stone Hill

22

23

24

Colebrook
Farm

A39

Bush

River Neet

I

Broomhill
Lanor

roomhill
lanor

Broomhill
Lane

Stamford
Hill

Stamford Hill

07

Townsend

Trew
Farm

2

Burn Park

Poundfield

Stratton
Prim Sch

Profrd Hl

STRATTON

Education &
Training Centre

Poundfield
Lane

Malden St

Sanctuary
Lane

Diddies Road

Diddies Lane

Smallridge
La

Smallridge Lane

3

Poundfield
Close

Hosp

Ward Cl

Med
Cen

Union

Bn Dr

Corner
Cotts

Chr St

Fore St

Spicers La

Old
Drovers
Way

Diddies

Superstore

NEW ROAD

HOSPITAL ROAD

HOWELL'S ROAD

Hill

Berkeley Cl

Wdly Cl

Wd Cl

Road

The Leat

Treworden
Close

Parc Fer
Close

A39

A3072

Coast
View

St Michael's

St Peters
Rd

St Alban's

Barnfield
Pk

Howard Lane

STRATTON ROAD A3072

St Olaf's Rd

St Martins
Road

BINHAMY ROAD

90

3

4

EX23

Binhamy

River Neet

Kitts
Farm

A3072

5

Bude-Stratton
Business Park

Howard

Howard Lane

Marsh
Farm

05

22

23

24

E

F

G

H

st
rove

Grove
Park

Cann

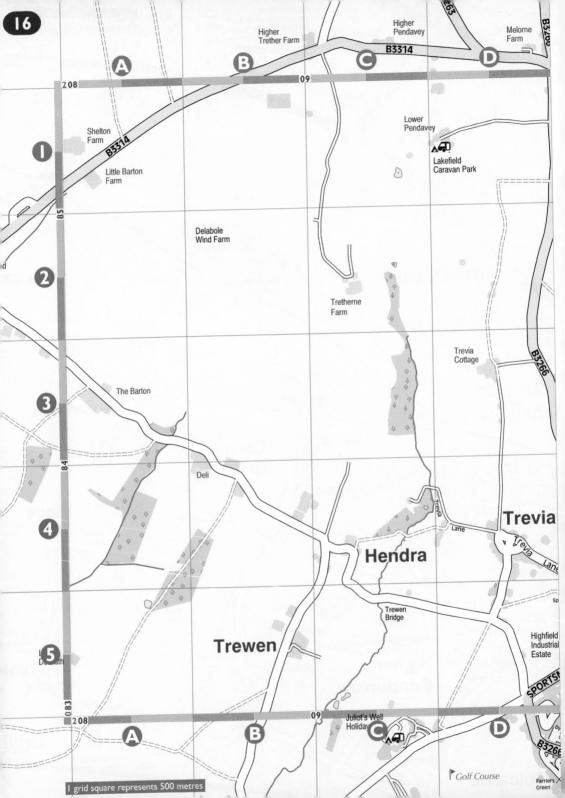

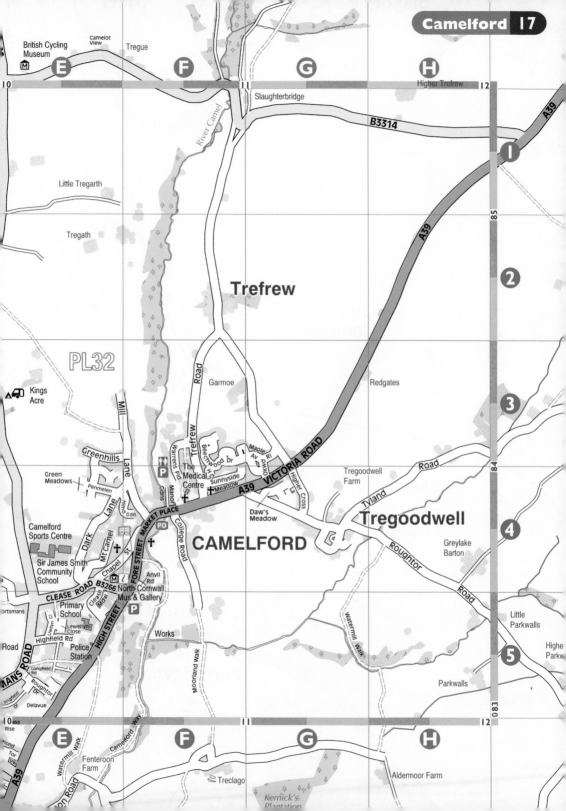

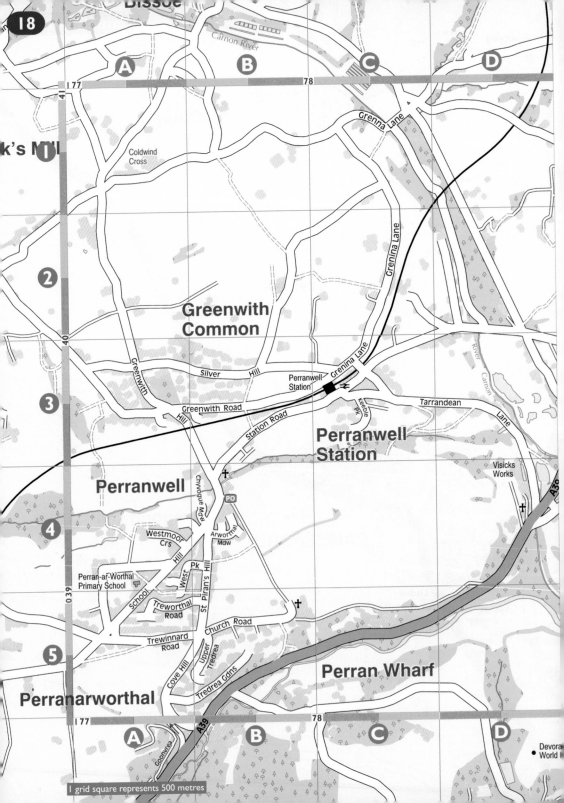

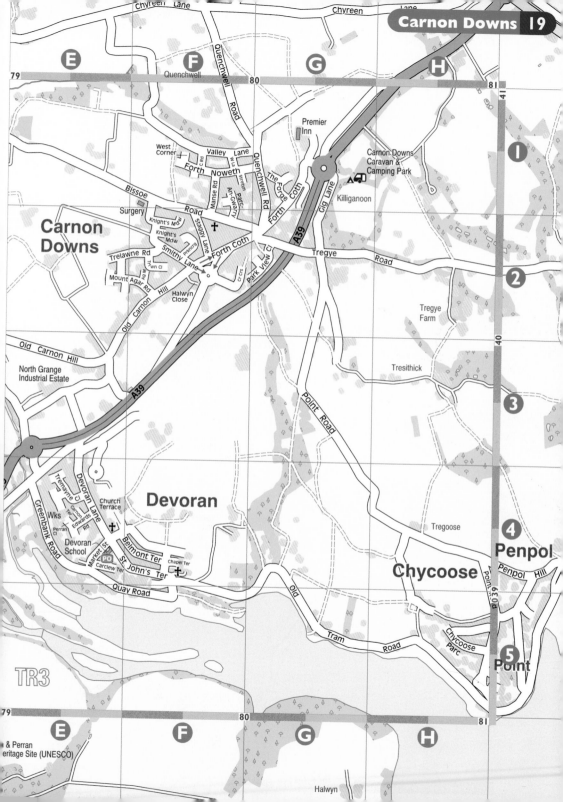

Chyreen Lane

Chyreen Lane

E F G H

79 80 81

Quenchwell

Quenchwell Road

Premier Inn

Carnon Downs Caravan & Camping Park

I

West Corner

Valley Lane

Forth Noweth

The Forge

Killiganoon

Cf Cl Rd

W La

Parc An-Gwarry

Bissoe Road

Surgery

Manse Rd

Quenchwell Rd

Forth

Forth Coth

A39

Knight's Mdw

Knight's Mdw

Gig Lane

Smithy Lane

Pryncry

Staggy Lane

Forth Coth

Tregye Road

2

Carnon Downs

Trelawne Rd

Tn Wn Cl

Park View

Cl Cl

Tregye Farm

Mount Agar Rd

Halwyn Close

Old Carnon Hill

Point Road

Tresithick

Old Carnon Hill

A39

3

North Grange Industrial Estate

A39

Tregoose

4

Penpol

Trenayne Cl

Devoran Lane

Church Terrace

Devoran

Chycoose

Wks

Perran

Carnon Rd

Edwards Rd

Greenbank Road

Devoran School

Belmont Ter

Market St

Chapel Ter

St. John's Ter

Carclew Ter

Penpol Hill

Point Rd

PO

Quay Road

Old

Chycoose Parc

5

Point

Tram Road

TR3

79 80 81

E F G H

& Perran eritage Site (UNESCO)

Halwyn

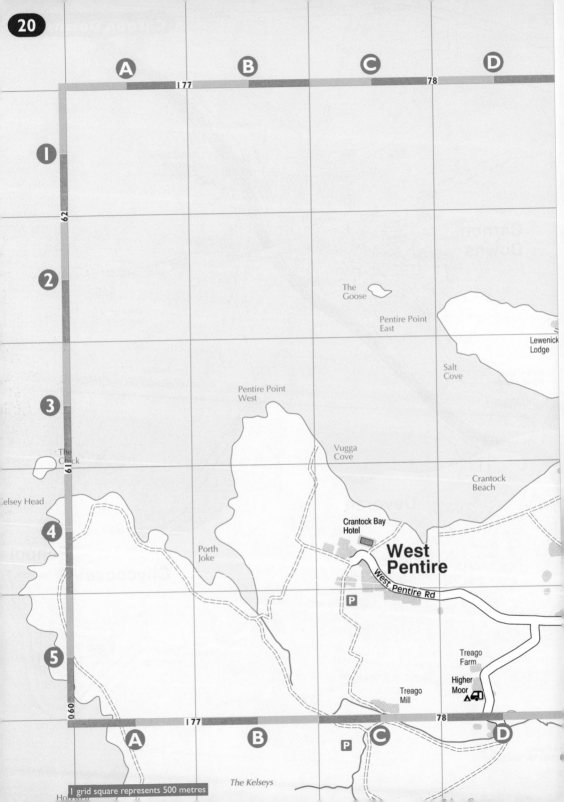

A 1 77 B C 78 D

I

62

2

3

19

The Chick

The Goose

Pentire Point East

Lewenick Lodge

Salt Cove

Pentire Point West

Vugga Cove

Crantock Beach

Kelsey Head

4

Porth Joke

Crantock Bay Hotel

West Pentire

West Pentire Rd

P

5

060

Treago Farm

Higher Moor

Treago Mill

1 77 78

A B P C D

The Kelseys

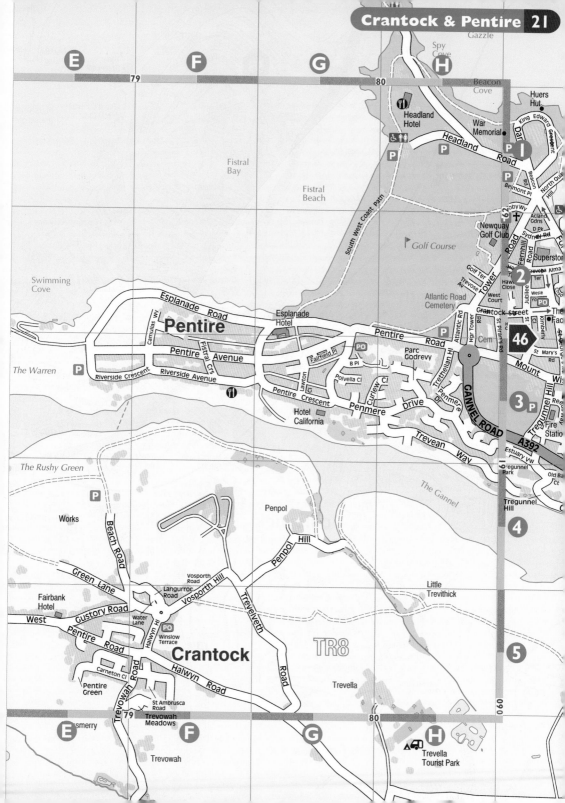

E   F   G   H

79   80

Spy
Cove

Gazzle

Beacon
Cove

Huers
Hut

Headland
Hotel

War
Memorial

Headland Road

King Edward Crescent

North Quay Hill

Fistral
Bay

Fistral
Beach

P

P

P

P

Belmont Pl

Beacon

Toby Wy

Acland
Gdns

D Pk

Sydney Rd

Fernhill
Road

Superstor

South West Coast Path

Golf Course

Newquay
Golf Club

Golf Ter

Trevose
Av

West
Court

Atlantic Road
Cemetery

Trevose
Alma
Ter

Hawk

Jubilee

Wesle

2

The
Fac

Swimming
Cove

Esplanade Road

Pentire

Esplanade
Hotel

Pentire Road

P

Atlantic Rd

Crantock Street

St Piran's Rd

Cem

St Mary's Rd

46

Mount

Wi

The Warren

P

Riverside Crescent

Camullas Wy

Pentire Avenue

Fistral Crs

Riverside Avenue

Fairfield Pl

PO

B Pl

Lawton

Parc
Godrevy

Polvella Cl

Curlew Cl

Penmere Drive

Trethellan Hl

Penmere Dr

Hor Tower

A392

3   P

Fire
Statio

Pentire Crescent

Penmere

Trevean Way

CANNEL ROAD

Estuary Vw

Tregunnel
Park

Old Ba
Ct

Hotel
California

Tregunnel
Hill

The Rushy Green

P

Works

Penpol

The Gannel

4

Beach Road

Green Lane

Fairbank
Hotel

West

Custory Road

Water
Lane

PO

Winslow
Terrace

Vosporth
Road

Languroc
Road

Vosporth Hill

Halwyn Hl

Penpol Hill

Trevelveth Road

Little
Trevithick

TR8

5

Pentire Road

Crantock

Halwyn Road

Trevella

060

Pentire
Green

Carneton Cl

Trevowan Road

St Ambrusca
Road

E   smerry   F   G   H

79   Trevowah
Meadows   80

Trevella
Tourist Park

Trevowah

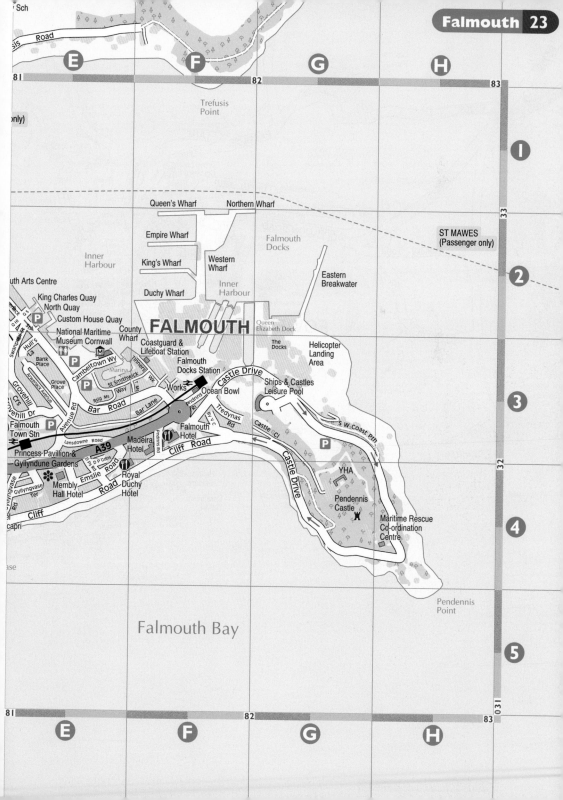

Sch

Road

E

F

G

H

81 82 83

Trefusis
Point

I

33

ST MAWES
(Passenger only)

2

only)

Queen's Wharf   Northern Wharf

Empire Wharf

Falmouth
Docks

Inner
Harbour

King's Wharf

Western
Wharf

Eastern
Breakwater

Duchy Wharf

Inner
Harbour

uth Arts Centre

King Charles Quay

North Quay

FALMOUTH

Queen
Elizabeth Dock

Custom House Quay

County
Wharf

National Maritime
Museum Cornwall

Coastguard &
Lifeboat Station

The Docks

Helicopter
Landing
Area

Bank
Place

Cambeltown Wy

Grove Place

St Smithwick

Falmouth
Docks Station

Way

Works

Ocean Bowl

Ships & Castles
Leisure Pool

Castle Drive

3

32

Grovehill Crs

Grovehill Dr

Bar Road

Bar Lane

Pndns Rd

Tredynas
Rd

Castle Cl

S W Coast Pth

Falmouth
Town Stn

Avenue Rd

Lansdowne Road

Madeira
Hotel

Falmouth
Hotel

Cliff Road

Castle Drive

Princess Pavillion &
Gyllyndune Gardens

A39

D P Gdns

YHA

Gyllyngvase Ter

Emslie Road

Royal
Duchy
Hotel

Road

Pendennis
Castle

Memnbly
Hall Hotel

Maritime Rescue
Co-ordination
Centre

4

Cliff

capri

Pendennis
Point

Falmouth Bay

5

031

81 82 83

E

F

G

H

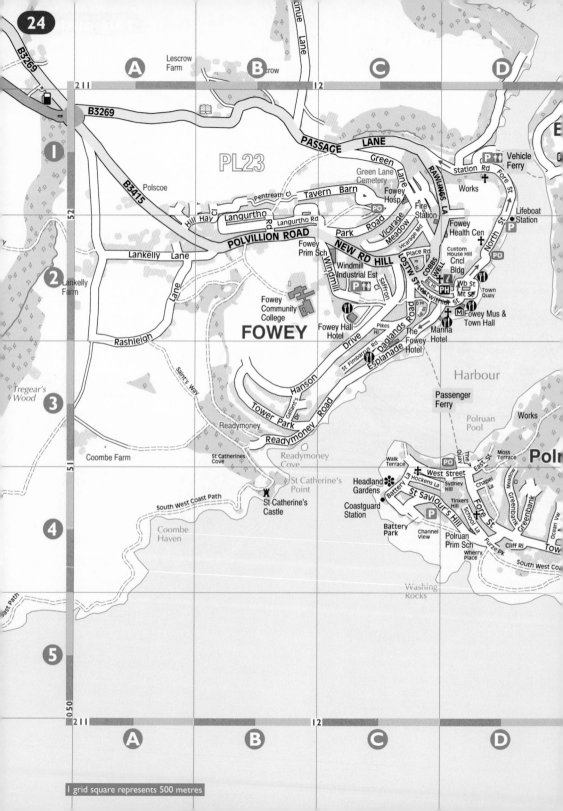

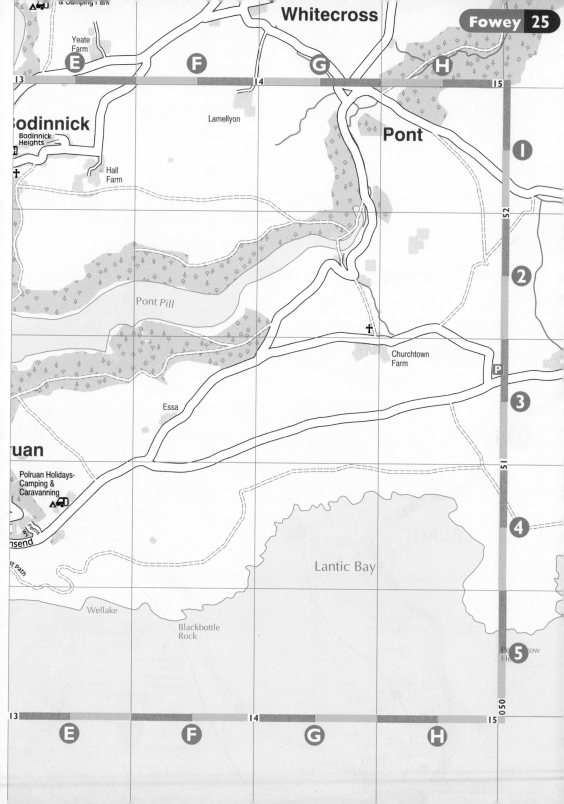

& Camping Park

Yeate
Farm

E

F

G

H

13

14

15

Lamellyon

Pont

I

3odinnick

Bodinnick
Heights

Hall
Farm

52

2

Pont *Pill*

✝

Churchtown
Farm

P

3

Essa

51

ruan

Polruan Holidays-
Camping &
Caravanning

4

Ferris W
nsend

st Path

Lantic Bay

5

Wellake

Blackbottle
Rock

0 50

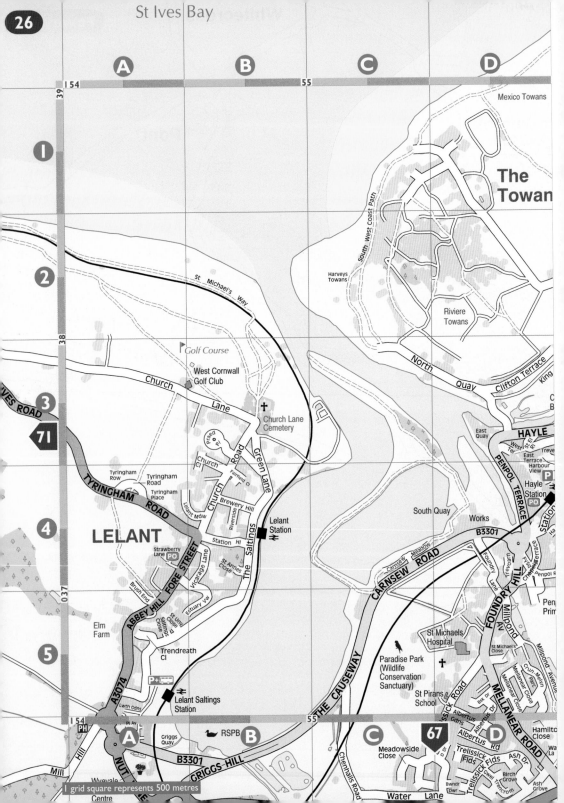

1 grid square represents 500 metres

28

Carnmeal
Farm
Farm

Sithney
Green

A · 163 · B · C · D
29
64

Marsinney
Farm

† Sithney

Wheal Fortune
Farm

1

B3302

Glenardran

Scholar's Lane

Mellangoose
Farm

Mellangoose

Trelissick

Park-an-Ithan

**Sithney
Common**

2

28

Roseladden Mill
Farm

Gipsy Lane

Torleven Rd

A394 SITHNEY COMMON

Antron

Gipsy
Lane

3 394

Little
Antron

Torleven Road

Squires Lane

4

027

St Elvan

Torleven
Road

Lanner Vean

Treza

Praze

Squires Lane

B3304

Torleven Road

Venton
Vedna

Ratcliff

Penventon
Farm

5

Tolponds
Road

St Elvan
Crs
Treza Road
Treza
Rd

Penponds Road
West
VW
South
VW

Penponds
Rd
Praze Rd

The Crs

Mill

Vicarage

163

Old Nursery
Close

Porthleven
School

A

Green
Lane

B

58

C

D

64

PORTHLEVEN

Higher
Lanner

1 grid square represents 500 metres

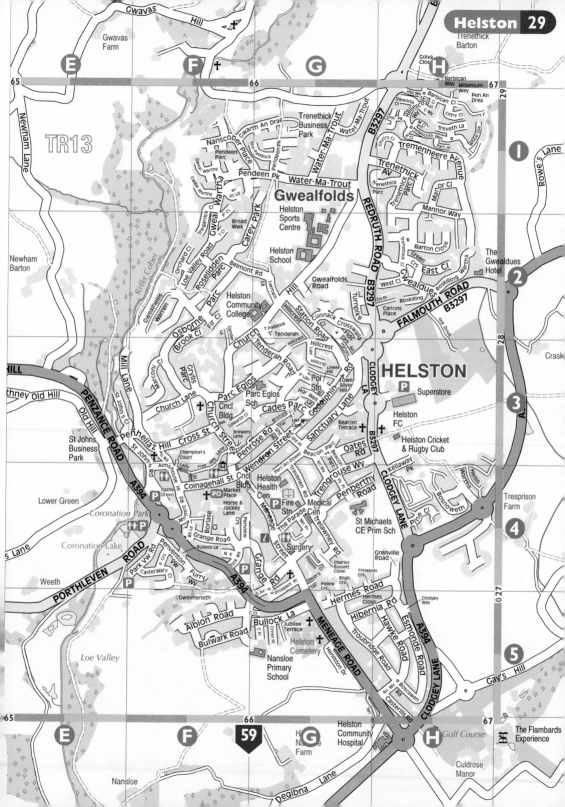

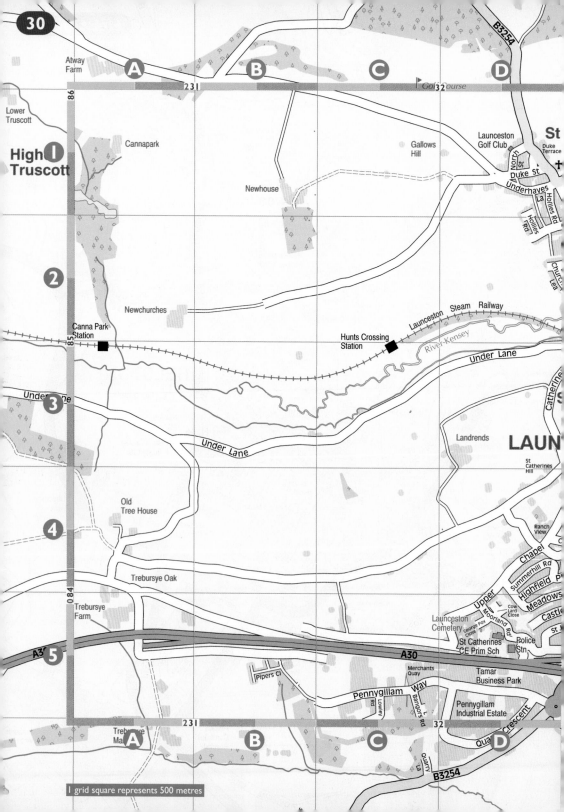

Atway Farm

A

231

B

C

Golf Course

32

D

B3254

Lower Truscott

High Truscott

1

Cannapark

Newhouse

Gallows Hill

Launceston Golf Club

North St

Duke Terrace

St

Duke St

Underhayes

La

Hollies Rd

Hollies Rd

Church Lea

2

Newchurches

Launceston Steam Railway

Canna Park Station

Hunts Crossing Station

River Kensey

Under Lane

Catherine

Under Lane

3

Landrends

LAUN

St Catherines Hill

Old Tree House

Ranch View

4

Chapel

Treburse Oak

Summerhill Rd

Highfield P

Meadows

Upper

Treburse Farm

Moorland Rd

Cow Lard Close

Castle

A30

A30

Launceston Cemetery

George Fox Close

St Catherines CE Prim Sch

Police Stn

St

5

Pipers Cl

Merchants Quay

Tamar Business Park

Pennygillam

Way

Bangors Rd

L Lowley Rd

Pennygillam Industrial Estate

Crescent

Quay

231

A

B

C

32

D

Trebursye Man

B3254

86

85

084

I grid square represents 500 metres

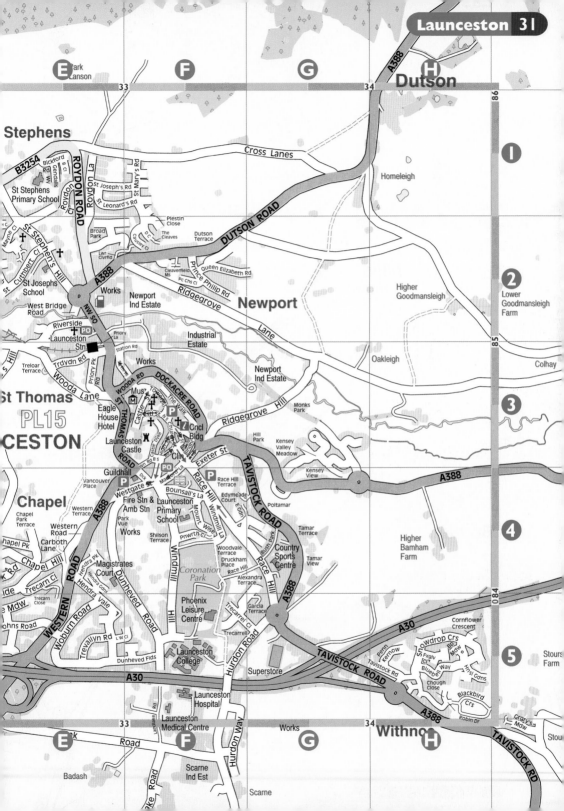

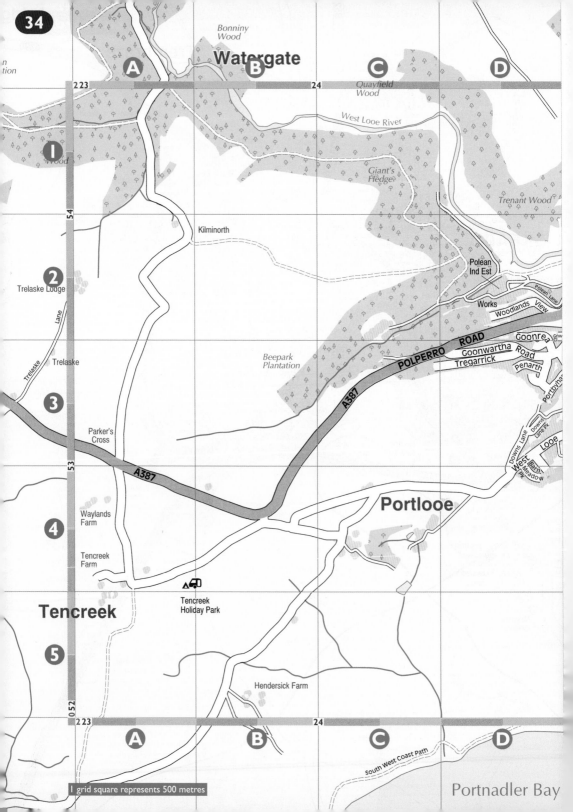

34

Bonniny Wood

Watergate

Quayfield Wood

West Looe River

Giant's Hedge

Trenant Wood

Wood

Kilminorth

Polean Ind Est

Trelaske Lodge

Works

Woodlands View

Polean Lane

POLPERRO ROAD

Goonrea

Goonwartha Road

Tregarrick

Penarth

A387

Beepark Plantation

Trelaske

Trelaske

Parker's Cross

A387

Downs Lane

Downs Lane PK

West Looe

Barn Meadow

Portlooe

Waylands Farm

Tencreek Farm

▲🚐

Tencreek Holiday Park

Tencreek

Hendersick Farm

Portnadler Bay

South West Coast Path

1 grid square represents 500 metres

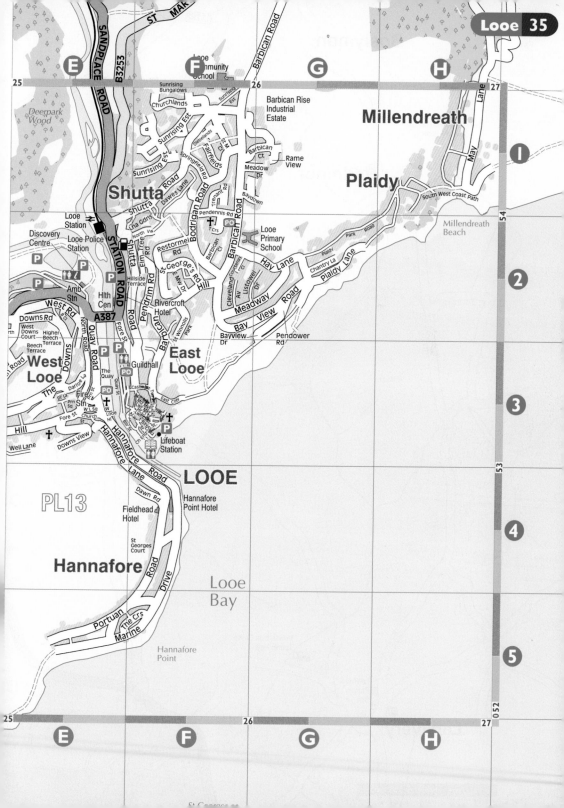

Deerpark Wood

SANDPLACE ROAD

B3253

ST MA

Looe Community School

Sunrising Bungalows

Churchlands

Sunrising Est

Sunrising Est

Barbican Road

Barbican Rise Industrial Estate

Millendreath

Springfield Rd

Fairfields

Barbican Ct

Meadow Dr

Rame View

Baydown

Plaidy

May Lane

South West Coast Path

Shutta

Shutta

Tina Gdns

North Vw

Dawes Lane

Bodrigan Road

Trenant Rd

Pendennis Rd

Crs

PO

Barbican Road

Loe Primary School

Park Road

Plaidy

Chantry La

Millendreath Beach

Looe Station

Discovery Centre

Looe Police Station

STATION ROAD

Shutta

Elm Tree La

Restormel Rd

St George's Hill

Barbican Ct

MW Dr

Hay Lane

Plaidy Lane

Hlth Cen

Hillside Terrace

Pendrim Rd

Rivercroft Hotel

Cleveland Gardens

Listowel Dr

Av

Meadway

Bay View Road

P

Amb Stn

West Rd

Downs Rd

A387

North Road

Quay Road

Fore St

Badrican

St Winnolls Park

Bayview Dr

Pendower Rd

Downs Court

Higher Beech Terrace

West Downs Court

Beech Terrace

West Looe

The Downs

Dance La

Fire Stn

Dr La

Prn Sq

Fore St

Church St

PO

P

The Quay

Quay St

Castle

East Cliff

St Eran

East Looe

Guildhall

PO

Hill

Well Lane

Downs View

W Looe

LOOE

Hannafore Lane

Hannafore Road

Lifeboat Station

Hannafore Point Hotel

PL13

Dawn Rd

Fieldhead Hotel

St Georges Court

Hannafore

Road

Drive

Looe Bay

Portuan

The Crs

Marine

Hannafore Point

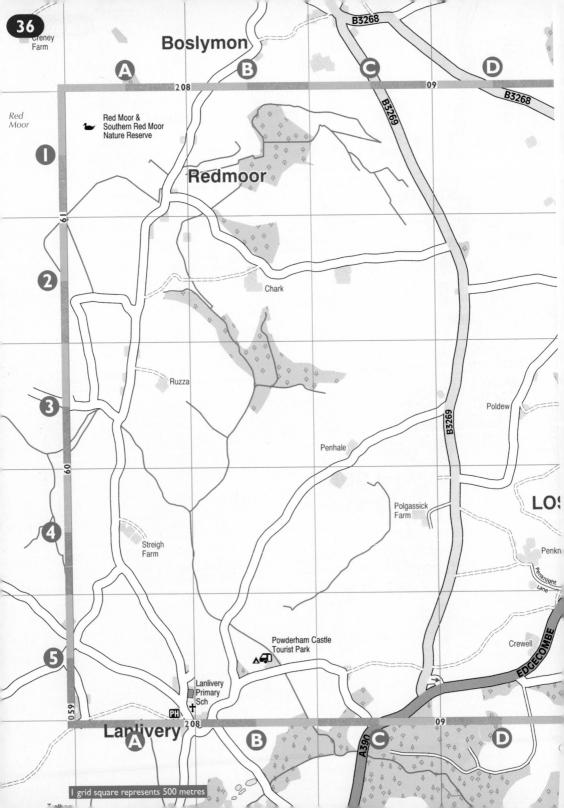

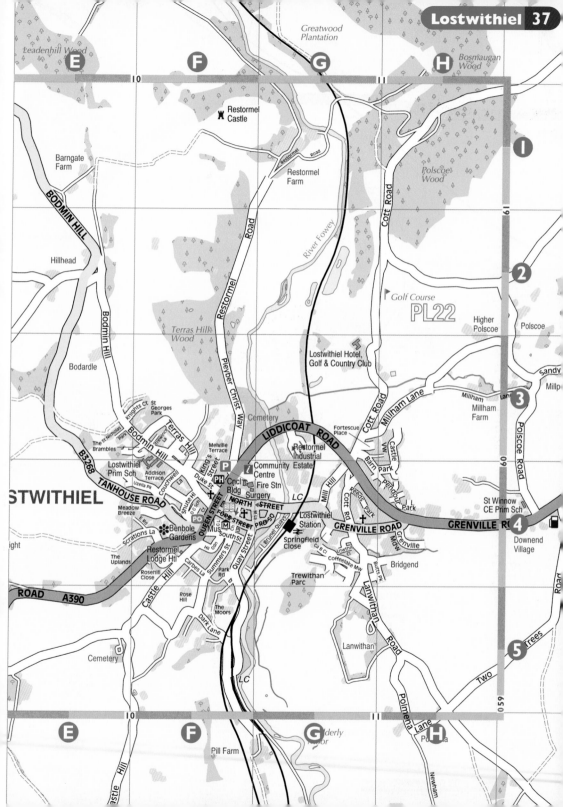

GOLDSITHNEY

St Hilary

Plain-an-Gwarry

Tregurtha Downs

Trevarthian Farm

Tregurtha

Chynoweth

Chynoweth

Trevabyn

Gears Lane

Gears La

Springfield Rd

Orchard Wy

St Aubyns

St Aubyns

WEST END

Trescowe

Bampny Way

Manor Farm Cl

Primrose La

PO

PH

South Road

Cllygr Prc

Primrose

Hill

Boltern Rd

Millet Cl

Coast Path

Trenow Cove

A394

B3280

B3280

A394

Echovean La

Perranuthnoe

St Pirans Wy

PH

Gre Wy

Trebarvah Lane

Dola Lane

Lancamshire La

Well La

Perran Downs

Rosudgeo

Basore Point

Trebarvah

Trevean

Perran Sands

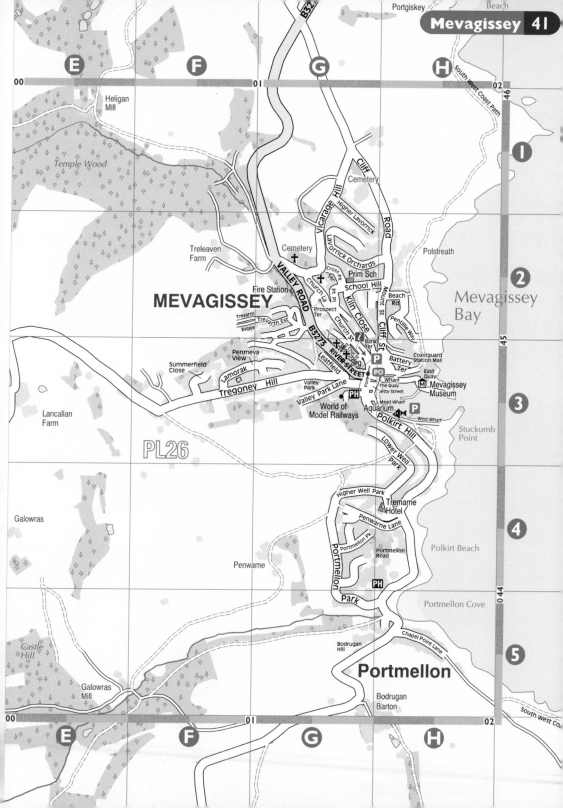

Portgiskey
Beach

E   F   G   H   South West Coast Path

00   01   02   46

I

Heligan
Mill

Temple Wood

Cemetery

Cliff Road

Higher Lavorrick

Lavorrick Orchards

Polstreath

Treleaven
Farm

Cemetery

Vicarage Hill

Cross Pk
Prim Sch

School Hill

Beach
Rd

Mevagissey
Bay

45

MEVAGISSEY

Fire Station

Church La

Prospect Ter

Ph Pl
Pt Pl

Kiln Close

Mount St

Pentille Way

Cliff St

2

Trevarth
Estate

Trevarth Est

Church St

Bank Ter

Battery Ter

Coastguard
Station Mall

Summerfield
Close

Penmeva
View

B3273 RIVER STREET

Leatfield

P

PO

Fore

East
Quay

3

Lamorak Cl

Tregoney Hill

Valley
Park

Valley Park Lane

PH

E. Wharf
The Quay
Jetty Street

M Mevagissey
Museum

Lancallan
Farm

PL26

World of
Model Railways

Aquarium

Mead Wharf

P

West Wharf

Stuckumb
Point

Polkirt Hill

Lower Well Park

4

Galowras

Higher Well Park

Tremarne
Hotel

Penwarne Lane

Polkirt Beach

Penwarne

Portmellon Pk

Portmellon
Road

Portmellon Park

PH

Portmellon Cove

044

Castle
Hill

Bodrugan
Hill

Chapel Point Lane

5

Galowras
Mill

Portmellon

Bodrugan
Barton

South West Co

00   E   F   01   G   H   02

B32

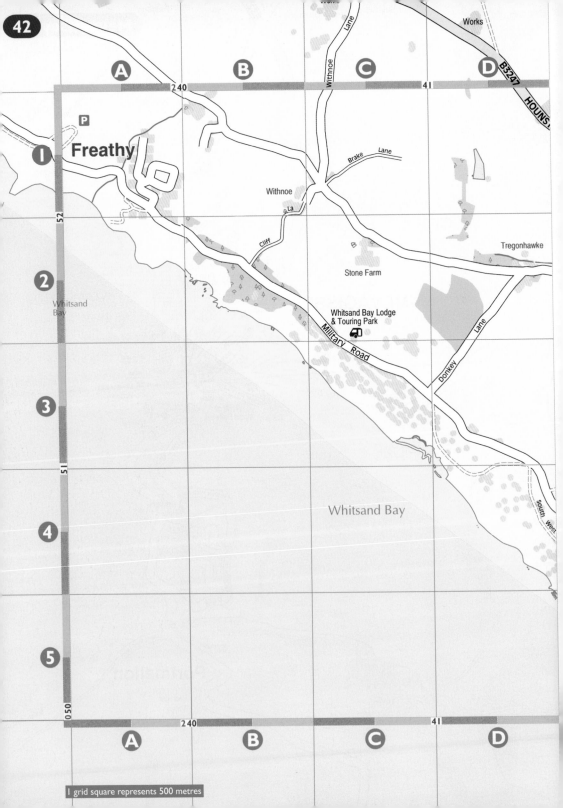

Ⓐ   Ⓑ   Ⓒ   Ⓓ

2 40   41   B3247   HOUNS

Works

Withnoe   Lane

Ⓟ

Freathy

52

Brake   Lane

Withnoe

La

Tregonhawke

Cliff

Stone Farm

Ⓐ

② Whitsand Bay

Whitsand Bay Lodge & Touring Park

Military   Road

Donkey   Lane

③

51

④

Whitsand Bay

South   West

⑤

0 50

2 40   41

Ⓐ   Ⓑ   Ⓒ   Ⓓ

1 grid square represents 500 metres

Insworke

Camperknowle
Close

Heron Cl

Egrt Cl

Millpool Rd

Instwrk

South
Down
Terrace

Silver
Terrace

Calvez Close

St John's Rd

Old Chapel Way

Mnr
Gdns

Welman Rd

Southdown

Road

E

F

G

H

Trefusis Terrace

Spg Cl

Clinton
Terrace

Mill

Road

Blindwell Hill

St John's

Newport Street

Millbrook
CE Primary
School

Molesworth
Terrace

Anderton Road

I

52

Priesthood
Terrace

The Pde

Greenland

Lower

Anderton

Mount
Pleasant

Fore St

New St

Lttl Pnt Crs

Brocks La

Lower Anderton Rd

TER HILL

St Andrew Street

Dwk La

King St

Knill
Cross

Higher

speedwell

Anderton

St Andrew's

WEST ST

West St

Millpool Head

Anderton Road

Anderton

Hounster Dr

P

Radford Lane

Dodbrook

Maker

Lane

MAKER LA

Millbrook

B3247

2

Treninnow

PL10

Fourlanesend County
Primary School

3

Coombe Farm

Earl's

51

Wiggle

Coombe
Park

The
Meadow

4

Coombe Park

Jackman's

Coast Path

Military Road

Trencher Lane

Hat

Lane

New Rd

Close

Fore St

Dart Hl

Kingsw'l

Kingsand

New

Road

Mrk't St

The Cleave

PO

PH

P

The Fort

New Road

St Andrew's St

Garrett Street

5

Forder Hill

Kiln
Cl

P

St Andrew's Pl

Armada Road

Pier La

The Earl's Dr

T Brg

050

Forder

Forder Lane

Cawsand

E

Capt'n
Blake's Point

F

G

H

42

43

South West Coast

Trehill Lane

Rame Lane

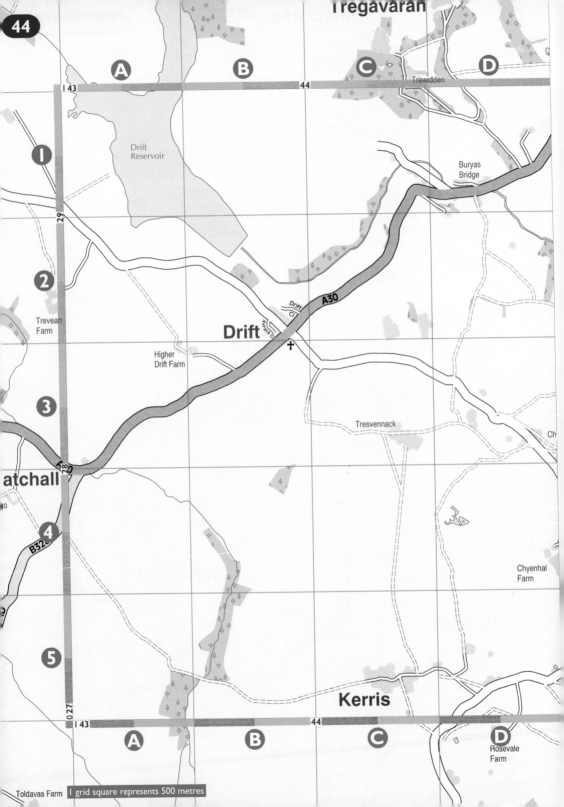

44

Tregavaran

A   B   C   D

I 43   44   Trewidden

I

Drift
Reservoir

Buryas
Bridge

29

2

Trevean
Farm

Drift
Cl   A30

Drift

Higher
Drift Farm

Tresvennack

3

atchall

28

B32

4

Chyenhal
Farm

5

Kerris

027

I 43   44

A   B   C   D

Rosevale
Farm

Toldavas Farm   I grid square represents 500 metres

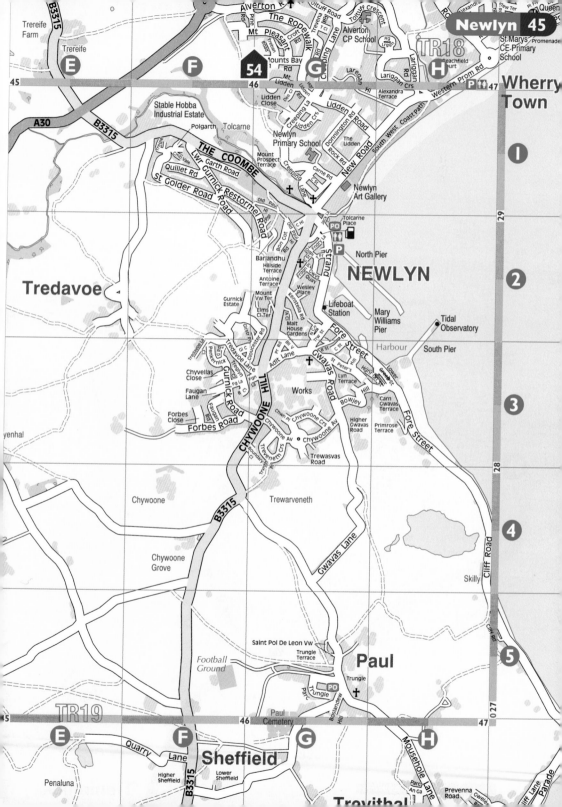

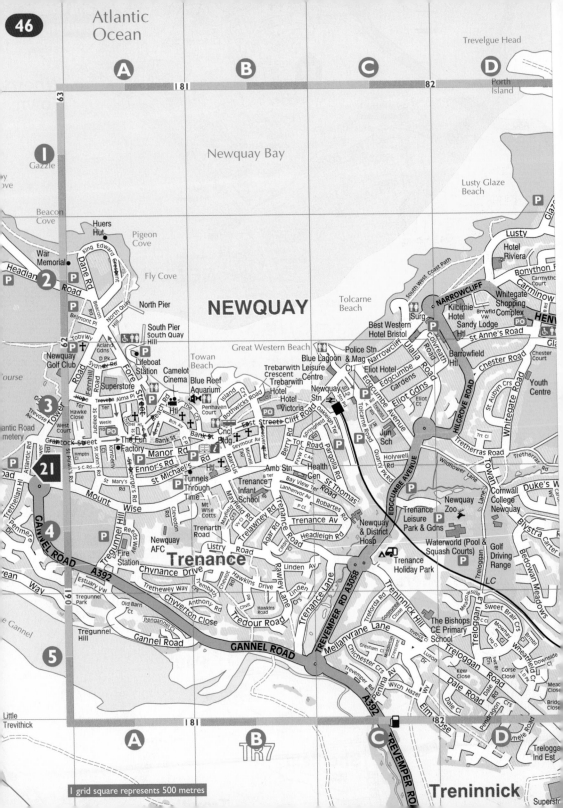

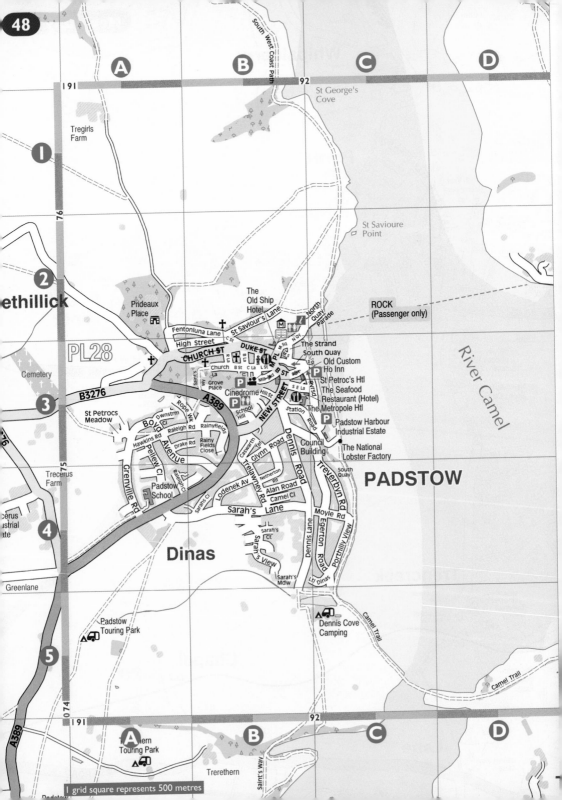

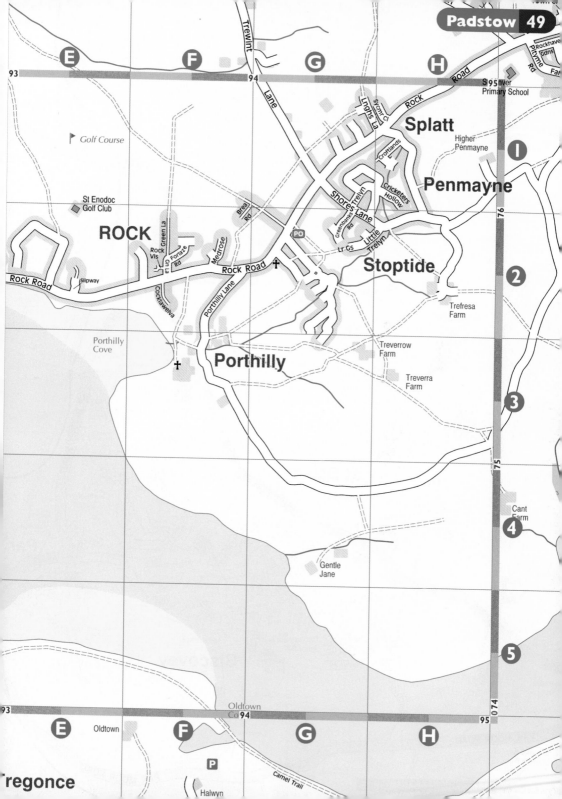

E F G H

93 94 95

Trewint Lane

ROCK Road

River Primary School

Splatt

Lnghs La

Sycmr Cl

Higher Penmayne

I

Golf Course

Croftlands

76

Penmayne

St Enodoc Golf Club

Cricketers Hollow

Shores Lane

Greenbanks Rd

Trelyn

ROCK

Breal Rd

Stoptide

2

Green La

Rock Vls

Ln Forlaze Rd

PO

Lr Gs

Little Trelyn

Rd

Trefresa Farm

Rock Road

Medrose

Rock Road

Porthilly Lane

Cockawelva

Treverrow Farm

Slipway

Treverra Farm

Porthilly Cove

3

75

Porthilly

Cant Farm

4

Gentle Jane

074

5

E F G H

93 94 95

Oldtown Co

Tregonce

Oldtown

P

Camel Trail

Halwyn

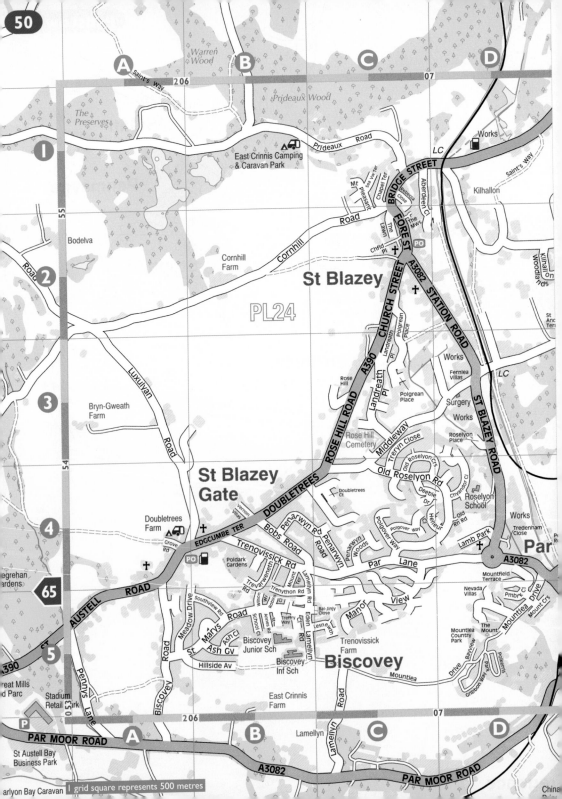

A   B   C   D

Saint's Way   206   07

Warren Wood

Prideaux Wood

The Preserves

I

Works

LC

East Crinnis Camping & Caravan Park

Prideaux   Road

Kilhallon

Bodelva

Saint's Way

Road

55

Cornhill Farm

Cornhill

Road

Mt Pleasant

Sea Vw Ter

Chapel Ter

BRIDGE STREET

Aberdeen St

The MWS

Kilhallon Woodlands

2

FORE ST

Chfld Pl

The Lawn

PO

St Andr Terr

St Blazey

A3082 STATION ROAD

PL24

CHURCH STREET

Landreath Pl

Polgrean Place

LC

A390

Works

Fernlea Villas

Road

Luxulyan

Rose Hill

Landreath

Polgrean Place

Surgery

Works

3

Bryn-Gweath Farm

Rose Hill Cemetery

ROSE HILL ROAD

Middleway

Treryn Close

Roselyon Place

ST BLAZEY ROAD

54

Old Roselyon Rd

Old Roselyon Crs

Deeble Dr

Chyandor Cl

Roselyon School

St Blazey Gate

DOUBLETREES

Doubletrees Ct

Old Rn Rd

Helleur

Works

Tredenham Close

Doubletrees Farm

Vernon Villas

Penarwyn Rd

Polgover Way

Polgover Way

Lamb Park

Par

4

EDGCUMBE TER

Grove Rd

Bobs Road

Penarwyn Road

Penarwyn Woods

A3082

Trenovissick Rd

Poldark Gardens

Par   Lane

Mountfield Terrace

Nevada Villas

Pmbr

Mount Crs

PO

Southview Rd

Trevarwenneth Rd

Trenython Rd

Lamellyn Rd

Eden Rd

Lamellyn Rd

Manor View

Mountlea Country Park

The Mount

Mountlea Drive

65

AUSTELL   ROAD

Meadow Drive

School Rd

Treffry Way

Bal-Jinjy Close

Lesneweth

Trenovissick Farm

Barview Drive

Mountlea Park

Pol...

Negrehan Gardens

St Marys Road

Ash Cl

Ash Gv

Biscovey Junior Sch

Biscovey Inf Sch

Manor

5

A390

Biscovey Road

Pennys Lane

Hillside Av

Biscovey

East Crinnis Farm

Mountlea

China ...

Great Mills Rd Parc

Stadium Retail Park

Lamellyn Road

A3082

P

St Austell Bay Business Park

PAR MOOR ROAD

206

A   B   C   D

Lamellyn

PAR MOOR ROAD

07

arlyon Bay Caravan

1 grid square represents 500 metres

E   F   G   H

Grove Park

A390

Driving Lane

Porcupine Road

Lanescot

Treesmill

I

Saint's Way

55

2

Yogogue Farm

Marsh Villa Gardens

Tywardreath

Trevance Park

End Cl

Glen View

St Spsrs

Bennett Road

Poldrea

St Andrew's Road

Tywardreath Cemetery

Tywardreath Prim Sch

Wood Lane

Swallowfield Close

North St

Nursery

Binnrt St

Mount

Poldrea

Poldrea

3

Southpark Road

Woodland Avenue

St Benedicts Place

Vine Place

Fore St

Church St

Legion Lane

Penstrasse Pl

Polpey Lane

Eastcliffe Road

Vicarage Road

Priory Cl

Anjardyn Pl

St Benedicts Cl

Well St

Trenant Road

54

Par Station

Tehidy

Newhouse

4

Lampetho

Tywardreath Hill

Polmear

Moorland Road

Eastcliffe Road

Dun Mere Cl

Ugor Est Rd

Polmear Parc

PO

PAR GREEN

POLMEAR ROAD

Hill

3082

5

Trewrong Farm

Polmear Hill

P

53

POLMEAR

HILL

Par Sands

A3082

E   F   G   H

Trill Farm

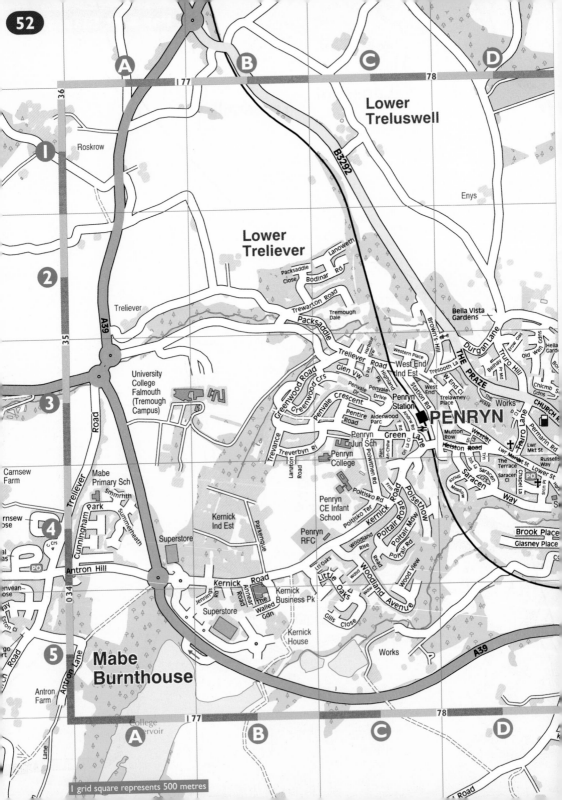

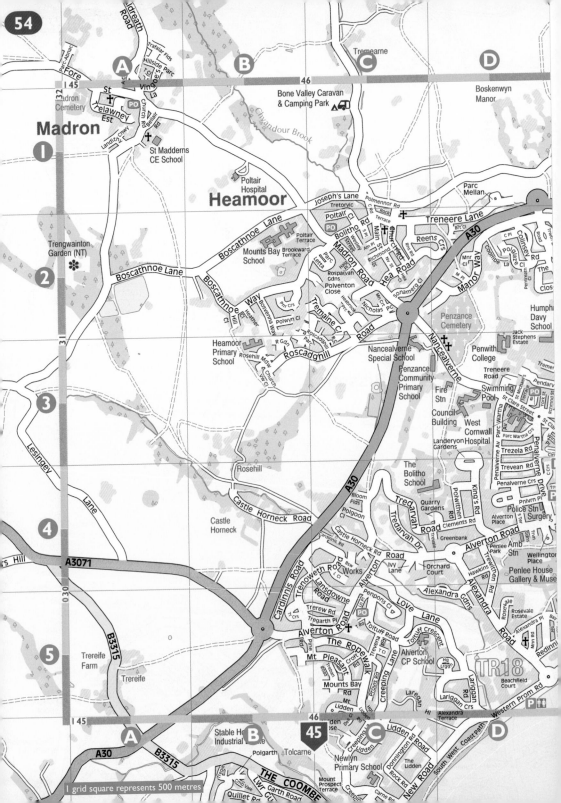

Mount's Bay

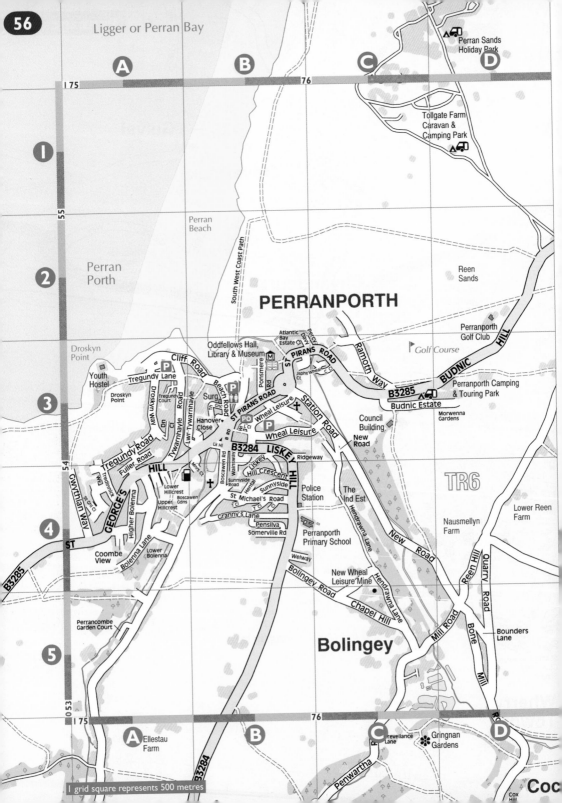

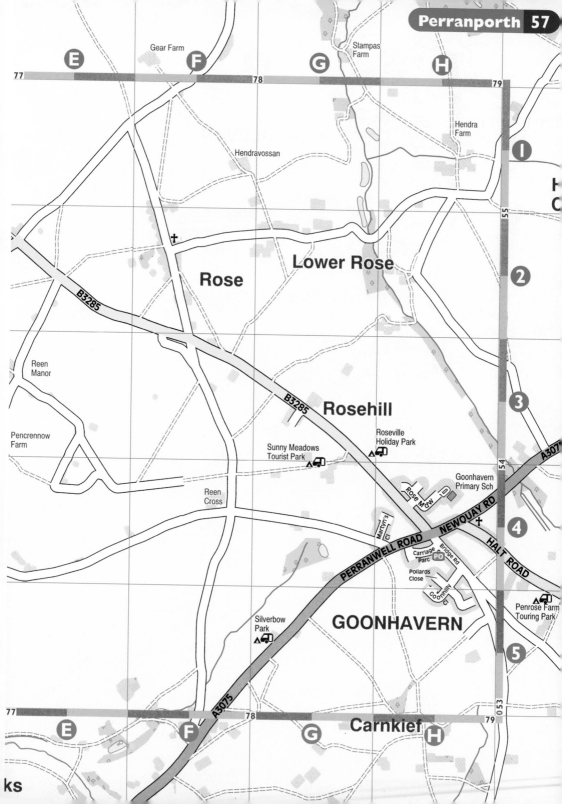

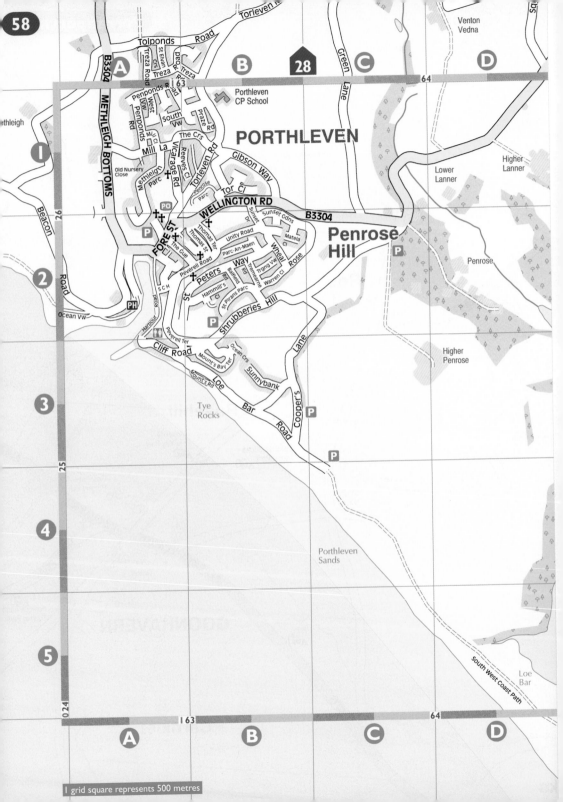

Bulwark Road

Loe Valley

Nansloe
Primary
School

E 65 **F** **29** **G** 66 **H**

An Wy

Boscawen

Casterllis Rd

Higher
Nansloe
Farm

Helston
Community
Hospital

Penventon
Farm

Degibna Lane

I

26

Culdr
Airfiel

Nansloe

2

Nancewidden

A3083

Goonhusband

Higher
Goonhusband

3

Degibna Lane

P

Degibna

†

_Degibna
Wood_

Higher
Pentire

25

Keepers
Cottage

The
Loe

Lower
Goonhusband

4

Pentire
Wood

Tangies

Carminowe
Creek

Little
Nanspean

Carminowe
Wood

5

024

E 65 **F** Nanspean **G** 66 **H** Carminowe

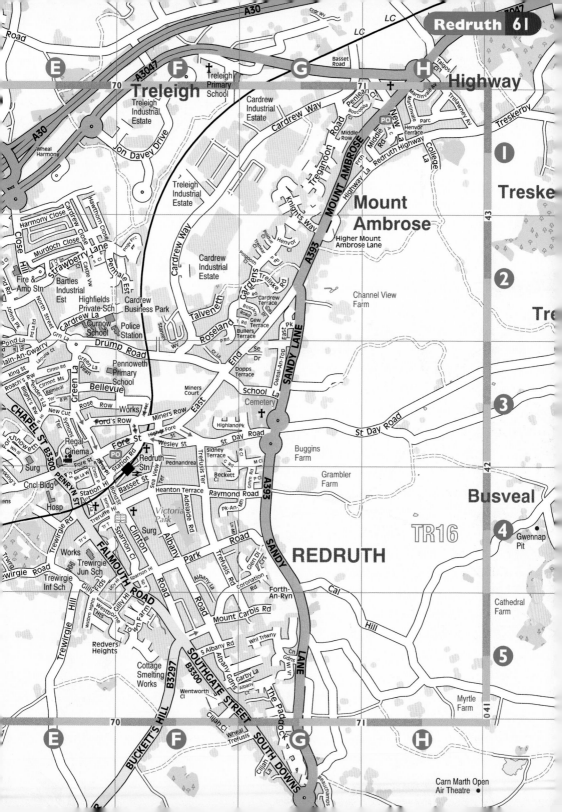

A 1 98 **B** **C** 99 **D**

54

Penisker Farm

Blackpool China Clay Works

1

Hornick Hill

Carne Farm

Carne Hill

2

Trevanion Lane

LC

School Hill

Brookfield Cl

53

Coombe

Road

A3058

Pyramid Cl

WESTBRIDGE RD

Trevanion Rd

St Anne's Rd

Trev Hill

PO

Hembal La

Hembal Cl

The Green

3

Works

Works

Trewoon

Lane

4

Burngullow

Hembal Lane

Bosithow

052

5

Poltarrow

Trethullan

Nanphysick Barton

A 1 98 **B** **C** 99 **D**

Tregandanel

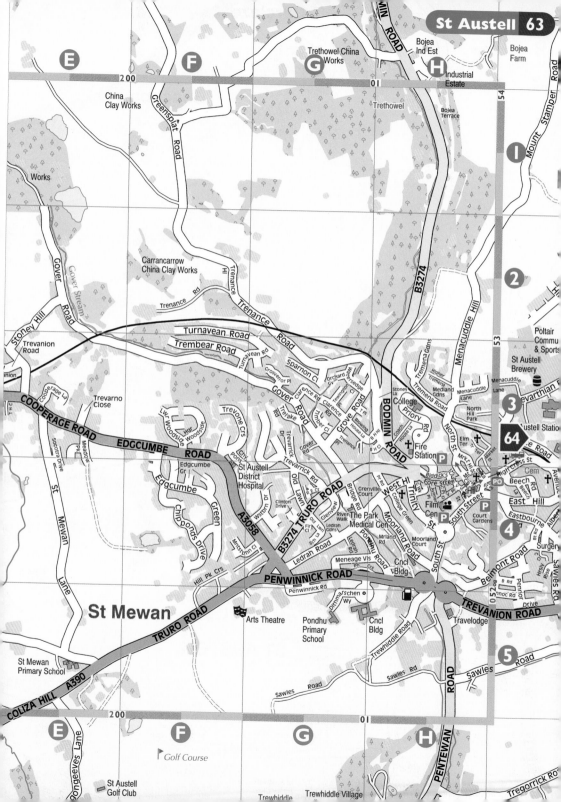

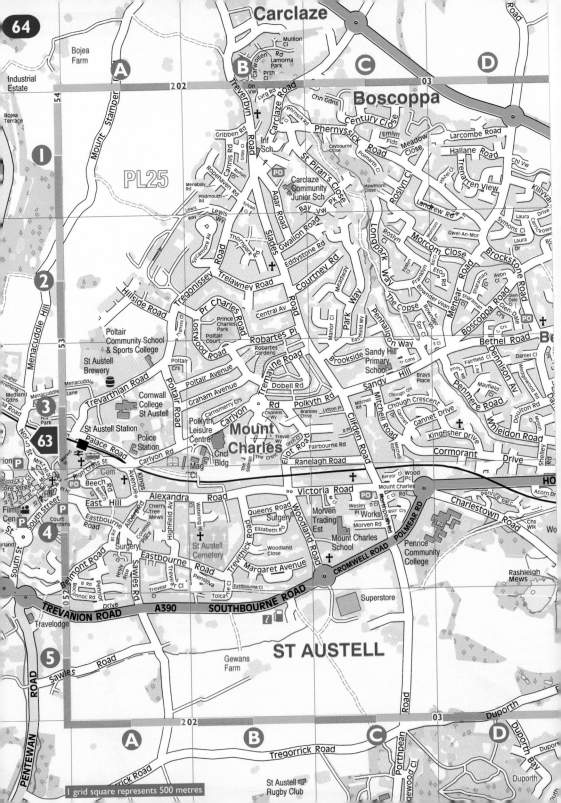

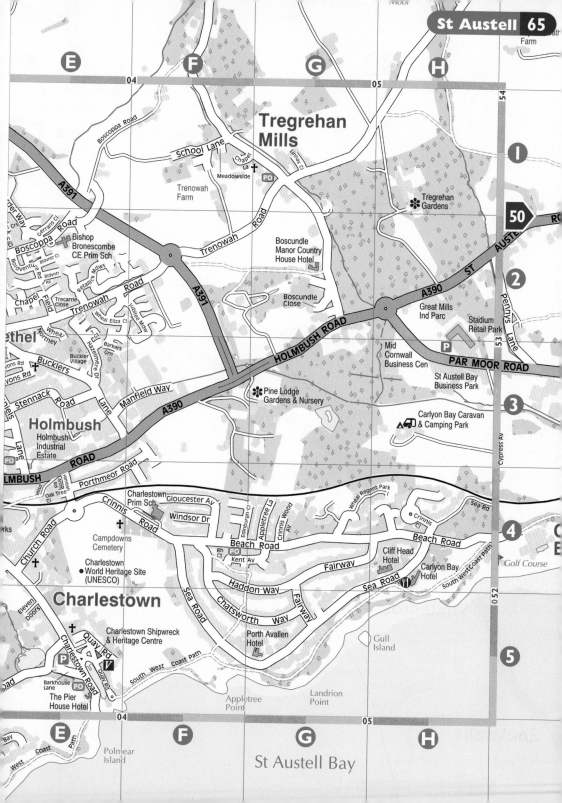

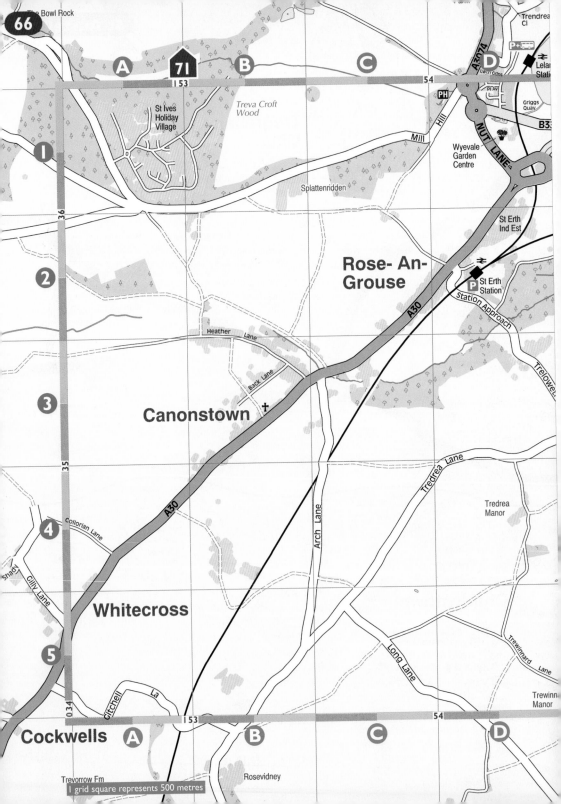

The Bowl Rock

Trendrea Cl

A
71
B
C
D

I 53 54

Lwui Gdns

P +

Lela Stati

Griggs Quay

PH

Pl Av

B3

St Ives Holiday Village

Treva Croft Wood

Mill Hill

NUIT LANE

Wyevale Garden Centre

Splattenridden

St Erth Ind Est

36

Rose- An- Grouse

P St Erth Station

A30

Station Approach

35

Heather Lane

Trelowe

Back Lane

Canonstown

Tredrea Lane

Arch Lane

Tredrea Manor

Collorian Lane

A30

Shady

Cilly Lane

Whitecross

Long Lane

Trewinnard Lane

Trewinn Manor

Gitchell La

0 34

Cockwells
A
B
C
D

I 53 54

Trevorrow Fm

Rosevidney

1 grid square represents 500 metres

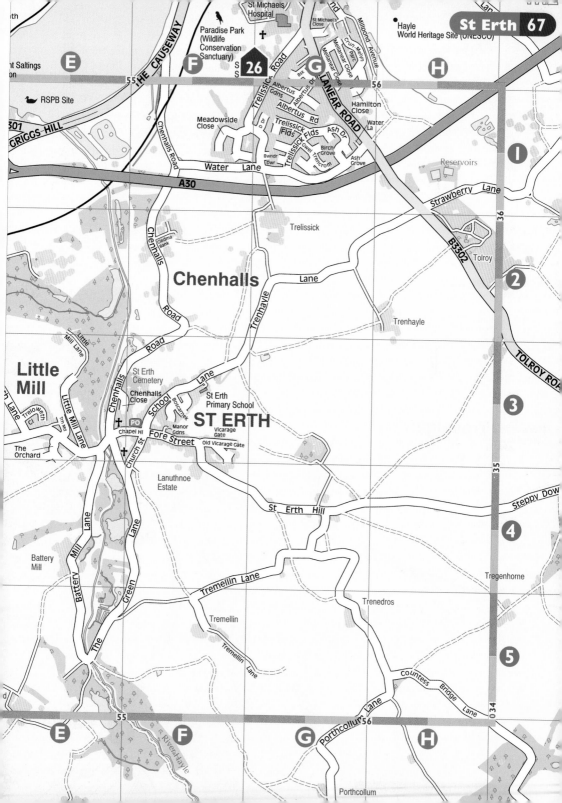

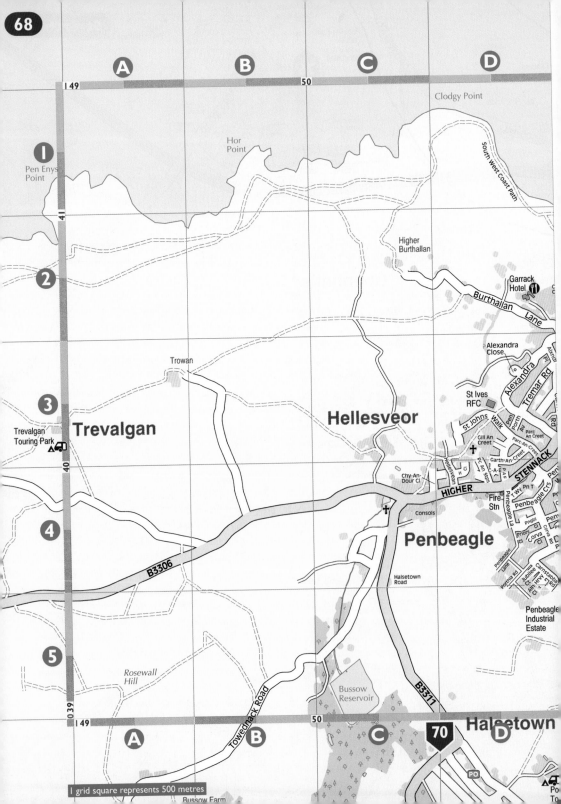

A B C D

149 50

Clodgy Point

I

Pen Enys
Point

Hor
Point

South West Coast Path

41

Higher
Burthallan

2

Garrack
Hotel

Burthallan Lane

Alexandra
Close

Trowan

St Ives
RFC

Alxmbr

Tremar Rd

Alexandra

3

Trevalgan
Touring Park

Trevalgan

Hellesveor

St Johns Walk

Peth
Porth
Av

Parc
An Creet

Parc-An-Creet

Rd

40

Gill An
Creet

Garth-An-Creet

Chy-An-
Dour Cl

Pc An Stps

STENNACK

Hellesvean

C·A·E

P·A·F

T WI Pn T

Pen

HIGHER

Fire
Stn

Penbeagle Crs

Pr

4

B3306

Consols

Penbeagle La

Pnabi

Priors
Cl

Penbeagle
Lane

Pen

Penbeagle

Corva
Cl

Corva Rd

Cl

Jubilee

Carnstabba
Rd

Alt Hrvy

Porthia Rd

Halsetown
Road

Penbeagle
Industrial
Estate

5

Rosewall
Hill

Towednack Road

Bussow
Reservoir

B3311

Halsetown

149 50

A B C 70 D

Bussow Farm

PO

Po
To

The Island or
St Ives Head

Porthmeor
Beach

St Nicholas
Court

Porthgwidden

Penameyne
Court

Norway
Lane

St Ives
Museum

Porthmeor
Square

Wheal
Dream

Tate
St Ives

Sea
View
Place

Baileys
Lane

Carthew
Close

Beach Road

Back
Lane

Westward
Rd

Cemetery

Orange Lane

Carthew Wy

Market
Strand

Holiday
Park

Barbara Hepworth
Mus & Sculpture
Garden

Western Pier

Youth
Hostel

Guildhall

Surgery

FORE ST

Pedn-Olva
Hotel

Treverbyn Road

CHAPEL ST

ST IVES

Trelawney Av

T STNNCK

Police Stn

Cin

B3306

Warren

Park Avenue

PEARCE'S LA

Tregenna Ter

THE TERRACE

St Ives
Station

Porthminster
Beach

The Burrows

Trenwith
Square

Bishop's Road

Albert Road

St Ives
Leisure
Centre

Talland Road

The Eagle

Edward Hain
Hospital

St Ives
Infant
School

St Ives
Junior
School

Hotel

Primrose Va

Coastguard
Station

Porthminster
Point

The Belyars

Chy-an-
Albany
Hotel

Hotel
St Eia

Gwel An
Wheal

TRELYON

Belyars
Court

Tregenna Castle
Gardens

Higher
Burrow
Close

Belyars Lane

Porthia
Close

AVENUE

Tregenna Castle Hotel,
Golf & Country Club

Hain Walk

A3074

Trenwith
Lane

Golf Course

St Ives
School

Higher Tregenna Road

Treloyhan
Park Road

Trelyon

Steeple
Lane

ST IVES ROAD

Wheal
Venture Rd

Wheal
Margery

Kew Vean

St Michael's Way

Steeple
Woods

Fuggoe
Close

Superstore

Pannier

71

Carbis
Bay Ht

CARBIS BAY

Spernen Ci

Beach Road

Menhyr Drive

Mount House La

Valley
Road

Carbis
Bay Station

Wheal
Speed

Boskerris
Cottage

Hotel

Headland Rd

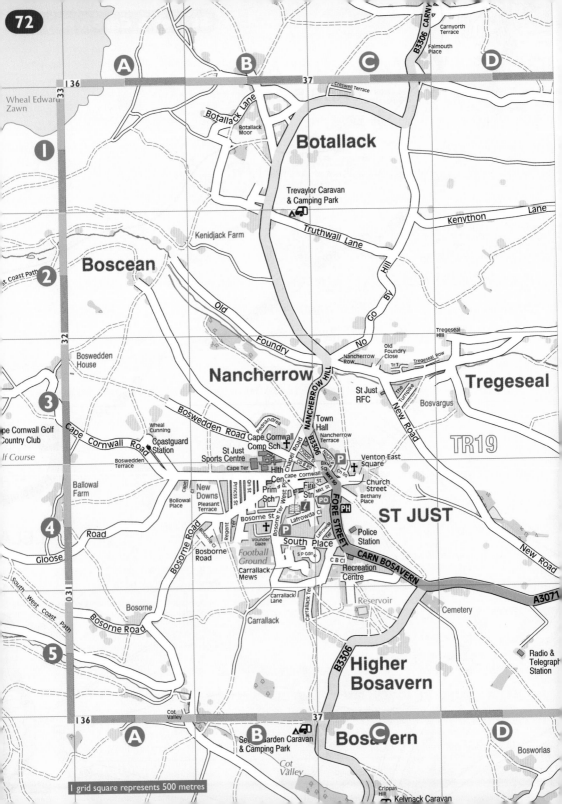

Wheal Edward Zawn

I

St Coast Path

Boscean

2

Botallack Lane

Botallack Moor

Creswell Terrace

Botallack

B3306 CARN

Carnyorth Terrace

Falmouth Place

Trevaylor Caravan & Camping Park

Truthwall Lane

Kenidjack Farm

Kenython Lane

Old Foundry

No Go By Hill

Boswedden House

Nancherrow

Nancherrow Row

Old Foundry Close

Tregeseal Hill

Tregeseal Row

Tr T

Tregeseal

St Just RFC

New Road

Bosvargus

3

Boswedden Road

ape Cornwall Golf Country Club

If Course

Cape Cornwall Road

Wheal Cunning

Coastguard Station

Pednandrea

Cape Cornwall

NANCHERROW HILL

Town Hall

Cape Cornwall Comp Sch

B3306

Nancherrow Terrace

North St

The Turnpike

TR19

Boswedden Terrace

St Just Sports Centre

Cape Ter

Hlth Cen

Prim Sch

Cape Cornwall

Chapel Road

West Pl

Cape Cornwall

CB Cl

Bk Vds

Mkt St

St

Ch Sq

Venton East Square

4

Ballowal Farm

Cape

New Downs

Princss St

Qu St

Bosorne Ter

Fire Stn

PO

Lafrowda

Lafrowda Cl

FORE STREET

PH

Church Street

Bethany Place

ST JUST

New Road

A3071

Bollowal Place

Pleasant Terrace

Regent

Bosorne St

Vounder Glaze

South Place

S P Gdn

CB Cl

Police Station

Road

Gloose

Bosborne Road

Football Ground

Carrallack Mews

CARN BOSAVERN

Recreation Centre

Reservoir

Cemetery

5

Bosorne

Bosorne Road

Carrallack Lane

Carrallack

Carrallack Ter

B3306

Higher Bosavern

Radio & Telegraph Station

South West Coast Path

Cot Valley

A

B

Sea Garden Caravan & Camping Park

Cot Valley

C

Bos∙ern

D

Bosworlas

Crippas Hill

Kelynack Caravan

33

32

31

36

37

I grid square represents 500 metres

E F G H

38 39 40

33

I

Air Cot

St Just Mining District
● World Heritage Site
(UNESCO)

Caynorth
Common

Boslow
Farmhouse

B3318

Truthwall
Common

2

32

3

Wheal
er

Bostraze

Boslow
Farmhouse

Jericho Farm

Lower Bostraze
China Clay Works

A3071

Busvargus and Tregeseal
Common

4

South Bosvargus
Farm

Higher
Botrea

O 31

Works

5

Botrea

38 39 40

E F G H

Crugkern

Roselands
Caravan Park

Leswidden
Farm

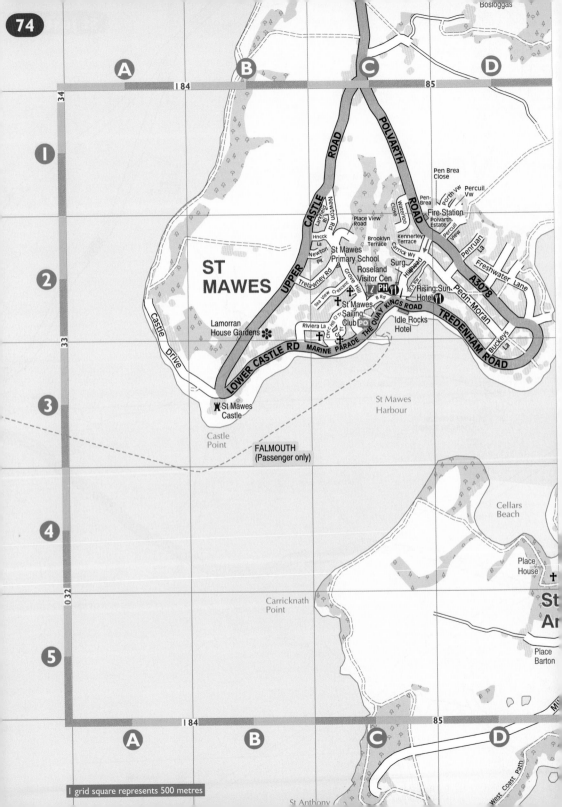

ST MAWES

St Mawes Harbour

Castle Point

FALMOUTH
(Passenger only)

Carricknath
Point

Cellars
Beach

Place
House

Place
Barton

1 grid square represents 500 metres

E   Percu F   Trewince Touring Pa   G   H

Trewince

Treloan Coastal
Farm Holidays

I

Trewince
Manor

Rosteague

Percuil River

Froe

2

South West Coast Path

3

Porth
Farm

Bohortha

4

Killigerran
Head

Porthmellin
Head

thony

Porthbeor
Beach

5

lary Road

E   86   F   G   87   H

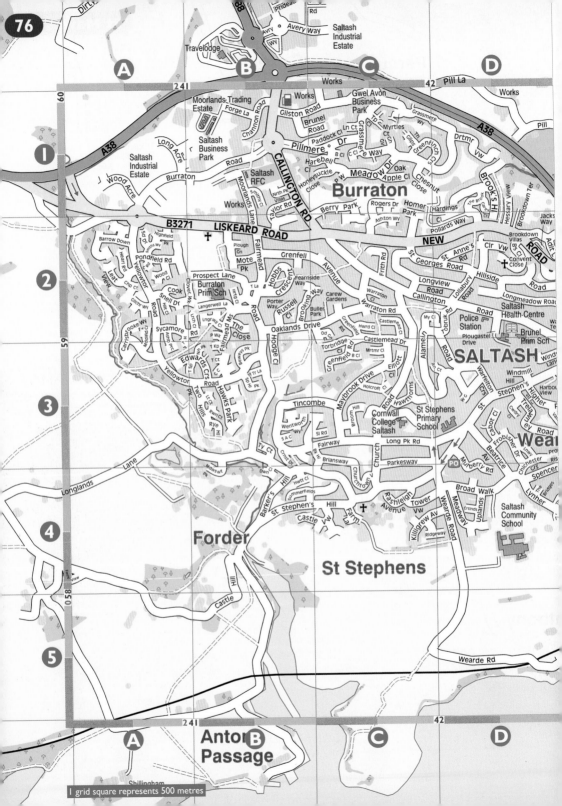

Golf Course

E   F   G   H

43   44   60

Cornwall C
City of Plym

Works

North

River Tamar

I

Saltmill
Creek

Beaumont
Terrace

Salt
Mill

River
View

Moorland
Vw

Lane

Newman
Road

Lr Rd

Rt VW

Clanville
Ter

Lander
Road

Wezd Ter

2

59

B3271

Deer Park

Barn Pk

Hillside Av

Old
Pounds Pk

St Budeaux

South
Pill

Felton
Terrace

Glebe Av

Belle Vue
Road

Home Pk

Ferry
Road

Works

Tavy Rd
Pk
Mc

Pre Pk

Road

Tamar
Bridge

Toll

3

Kg Edward Rd

symons
W u

Fore
Street

Fore
St

Lwr
Alxnd

Silver St

Tamar
St

THE PARKWAY

TAMAR BR

Admiralty
Rd

Normandy

Waverley
Rd

Essa
Rd

PO

Victoria Rd

Albert Rd

View

Normandy

Rd Rd

Normandy Hl

Surgery

Culver
Road

Road

Mary Newman's
Cottage

Mckiz

Birgwr

Waiters
Rd

Tenby Rd

Stanhope Rd

Loftus
Gardens

Ivanhoe Ct

Lyr

St-Barnabas
Hosp

View
Wy

Saltash
Station

Tamar
Terrace

Lghbr
Rd

Stfing Ct

Saltburn
Rd

Stirling
Road

Evelyn

Lower
Road

Port

Vincent
Wy

Albert Rd

Lti Ash Gdns

Pemros
Rd

St Pauls RC
Primary School

Health
Centre

Florence
St

Kathle

de

Gardens

Babis
Close

Babis
Farm

Babis
Farm RW

Coombe

Little
Ash

Vicarage
Gdns

Road

Percy
St

Edith
St

Riverside

Wolseley
Road

Works

Way

4

Victoria Rd

Trelaw

Drive

Lane

Deacon Drive

Deacon
Close

Works

Wolseley Road

PO

Bishop Cornish
CE Primary School

Warburton
Gdns

Sithney

St Budeaux
Victoria Rd Stn

St Budeaux Ferry
Road Station

Wolseley

Fegen Rd

Foulston

Rennie Av

Road

Bull Point

Bull-Point
Primary School

Scott Av

Reynolds
Cv

Haydon
Cv

Barne

Landrake
Cl

Barne Barton
Primary School

Wearde Quay

Esmonde
Gdns

Beatrice
Rd

Barne Cl

Kit Hill Crs

Ln Gdns

Klin Cl

Od Sl Rd

Tr Cl

Ark Ryl Cl

5

Kinterbury
Road

Kinterbury Ter

Berthon
Rd

Bertho
Rd

Police
Stn

Miers Cl

Ms
Ct

Poole Park
Road

Old Farm

Roberts Road

Mantle
Gdns

Barne
Barton

Savage
Road

Poole Park Road

Wilkinson
Road

Road

Dennis
Cl

Kelly

Furse Park

Talbot Gdns

E   F   G   H

43   44

A   205   B   06   C   D   The Sister

I

Willapark

Gullastem

Tintagel
Haven

2   The Island

South West Coast Path

Back Lane   Bossiney
Lane

Tintagel
Castle   Bossiney   Bossiney
House
Hotel

89   Knights
Close   Gavercoombe
Park   PL34   Tintagel
CC

Castle View   Laura   Westground
Way

3   Castle
Heights   Headland Caravan
& Camping Park   The Butts

Tintagel
Head   Atlantic Road   Atlantic Road   Tintagel Toy
Museum   TINTAGEL   BOSSINEY ROAD

Castle Road   Atlantic Way   P

Round's
Lane

Fore Street   Merlins Way   Tren

Church Hill   Vicarage Hill   Old Post
Office (NT)   B3263

Dunder
Hole   South West Coast Path   Works   Trevena
Ct   Danmore
Cl   PO

4   Fosters Lane

MOLESWORTH STREET   Trerammett

088   Treven

Trevillick
Farm   Tintagel
Primary
School

Higher Pe
Point   5

Tregatta

A   205   B   06   C   D

Hole   Tregeath

Saddle Rocks

Trevalga Farm

Trambley Cove

Hevalga

E F G

07 08

90

B3263

Trewethet Gut

I

e Rock

Trewethett Farm

Bossiney Haven

Benoath Cove

Trethevy

2

89

B3263

Halgabron

The Hermitage

St. Nectan's Glen

3

Fenterleigh

West Park Farm

Quarry

4

Trewin

Lane

Trevillett

Works

Trevillett Parc

88

Trenale

Tintagel Heights

Kingsway Farm

5

Downrow

E F G H

07 08

E F G H

43 44 57

Weston Mill Lake

I

Cove Meadow

Looking Glass

Hamoaze

Wilcove

2

56

City of Plymouth
Cornwall County

Maryfield

3

De

Thanckes Lake

Torpoint Community School

The Lawns

Pengelly Hill
Pengelly Pk

Pentire Rd

Woodland Way

Carbeile Junior School

Sennen Cl
Canyon Cl
Avenue

Evenden Court

Gravesend Road

Torpoint Infant Sch
Road

Sydney
Road
Clarence

Adela Rd
Thanckes Dr

Wilts Pk Rd
Surg

Albion Court

Racquets Sports Club

GV Gs

PO

Works

Wesley Court

TORPOINT

Gurney
Trevol Road

Hawthorn Avenue

Chestnut Drive

Sycamore Drive

Maple Av

Sycamore Drive

Beech Drive

Carbeile

Mill Lane

Millhouse Park

Chapeldown Road

Maker Road

Peacock Avenue

Kingsley Av

Cremyll Rd

Hamoaze Road

Sconner Rd
Buller Rd
York Road

Roselare Av

Cn Rd

Roberts Av

Rslr

Lg

Liscawn Ter

Vicarage

North

Moor Vw

Union
Rd

B Rd

Eoyle St

Salamanca St

Wellmoor

St James Rd

Barossa Road

Kmbth Ter

Ferry St

Marine Dr

Arthur Terrace

FORE ST
HARVEY ST

Quarry St

Et Sq

A374

FERRY ST

Fire Station

Police Station

4

55

Carew Wharf Business Centre

5

E F G H

43 44

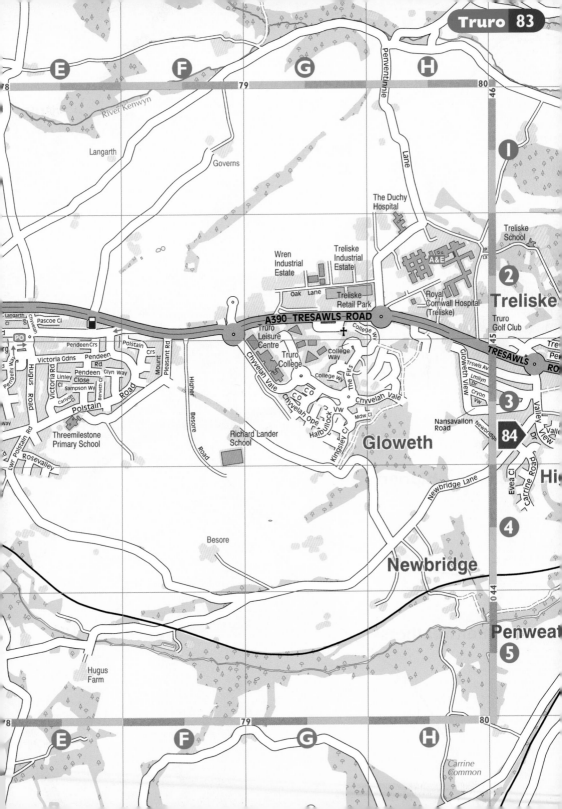

E   F   G   H

79   80

46

I

River Kenwyn

Langarth

Governs

Penventinnie Lane

The Duchy Hospital

Treliske School

2

Wren Industrial Estate

Treliske Industrial Estate

A&E

Treliske

Oak Lane

Treliske Retail Park

Royal Cornwall Hospital (Treliske)

Truro Golf Club

Langarth Rd

Chyvelah

Pascoe Cl

PO

A390 TRESAWLS ROAD

TRESAWLS RO

Pendeen Crs

Poistain

Mount Pleasant Rd

Truro Leisure Centre

College Wy

Gloweth View

Trswls Av

Lmllyn Dr

3

84

Victoria Gdns

Pendeen Rd

Poistain Crs

Truro College

College Way

Cryon Vw

Linley Cl

Pendeen Close

Glyn Way

Chyvelah Vale

College Wy

the Firs

Chyvelah Vale

Pengelly Wy

Hugus Rd

Sampson Wy

Berwin Cl

Canyon

Poistain Road

Higher Besore Road

Chyvelah ope

Co

Co

Mdw Cl

Vw

Nansavallon Road

Newbridge

Evea Cl

Carrine Road

Valley View

Hig

Polstain

Halbullock

Kingsley Cl

4

Lwr Poistain Rd

Threemilestone Primary School

Rosevalley

Richard Lander School

Gloweth

Newbridge Lane

Newbridge

044

Besore

Penweat

5

Hugus Farm

E   F   G   H

79   80

Carrine Common

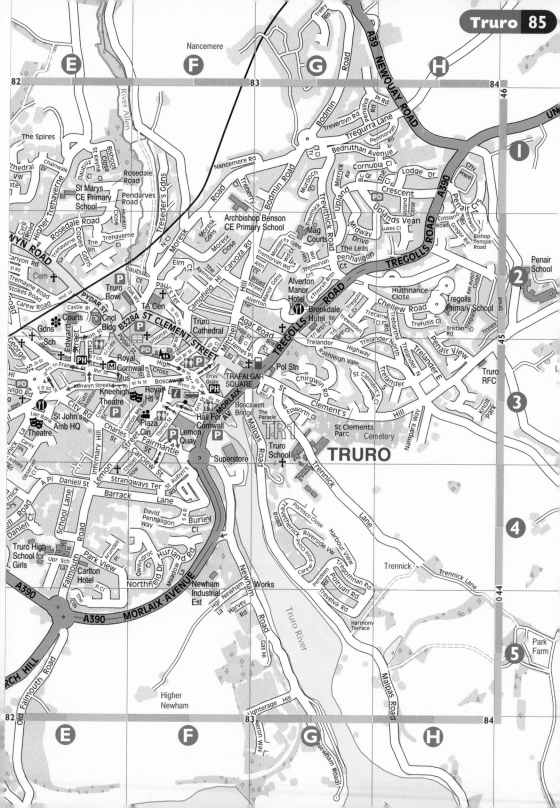

Kelly

E   F   G   H **Three Holes Cross**

I

Little Bodieve Holiday Park

Ball

A39

200   01   73

2

Higher Treworder

Middle Treworder

BODIEVE ROAD

B3314 CONVENA HILL

Cncl Bldg

Ind Est

Palmers Way

Trenant Ind Est

Trevarner

St Endodoc

Fisher Cl

St Matthews Hill

School Walk

St Cadoc Dr

Franklin Cl

Bellatt

Victoria Pk

Trenant Vale

Winwell Fld

Hill Park

Bt Pk

Little

Warner Way

Treguddock

Tregleath

Bridge Park

Foxdown Manor

Foxdown

Marshall Av

Green Hill

Treworder   Lane

Lower Treworder

3

72

Trev Woo

Margaret Cons

Eglos Parc

Broomfield Rd

Branksome Dr

Greenhill Villas

Kel Gdns

West Park

Tower Hill

Higher Cl

Higher Lane

Westpark Rd

Cem

A389

Higher Lane

shayle

Road

Egloshayle Road

ADEBRIDGE

Clapper

4

Garden Centre

Sladesbridge

PL27

River Allen

River Camel

Camel Trail

Lane

Treraven

Pendavey

A389

5

Tredannick

Trevaven Wood

Camel Trail

Derry's Wood

200   01

E   F   G   H

USING THE COUNTY MAP INDEX

Town and village names on the County map (pages 2 to 7) are listed alphabetically. Each town or village name is followed by the page number and the reference to the square in which the town or village is found. Entries followed by *IOS* refer to the Isles of Scilly inset on page 2.

Standard index entries are shown as follows:

Altarnun 5 F2

A

Albaston 5 H3
Altarnun 5 F2
Angarrack 2 C3
Antony 5 H5
Ashton 2 D4

B

Bangors 6 B5
Barkla Shop 3 E1
Barripper 2 D3
Bathpool 5 F3
Bealsmill 5 G3
Bennacott 5 G1
Bissoe 3 F2
Blackwater 3 E2
Blisland 4 D3
Bodinnick 3 E5
Bodmin 4 D4
Bodwen 4 D4
Bohortha 3 F3
Bolingey 3 E1
Bolventor 5 E3
Boscastle 4 D1
Bosoughan 4 B4
Bossiney 4 D1
Boswinger 3 H2
Botallack 2 A3
Botusfleming 5 H4
Boyton 5 G1
Bray Shop 5 G3
Breage 2 D4
Brill 3 E3
Budd's Titson 6 B5
Bude 6 B4
Budge's Shop 5 G4
Budock Water 3 F3
Bugle 4 D4
Burlawn 4 C3

C

Cadgwith 3 E5
Callestick 3 F1
Callington 5 G3
Calstock 5 H3
Camborne 2 D2
Cambrose 3 E2
Camelford 4 D2
Canonstown 2 C3
Canworthy Water 5 F1
Carbis Bay 2 C2
Cardinham 5 E3
Cargreen 5 H4
Carharrack 3 E2
Carkeel 5 H4
Carleen 2 D5
Carn Brea 3 E2
Carnhell Green 2 D3
Carnkie 3 E2
Carnkie 3 E3
Carnon Downs 3 F2
Carthew 3 H1
Cawsand 5 H5
Chacewater 3 E2
Chapel Amble 4 C3
Charlestown 3 H1
Chilsworthy 5 H3
Church Cove 3 E5
Churchtown 4 D2
Chyandour 2 B3
Coad's Green 5 F3
Colan 4 B4
Common Moor 5 F3
Congdon's Shop 5 F3
Connor Downs 2 D2
Constantine 3 E3
Constantine Bay 4 B3
Coppathorne 6 B5
Copperhouse 2 C3
Coverack 3 F5
Coverack Bridges 6 A5
Coxford 6 A5
Crackington Haven 6 A5
Crafthole 5 G4
Crantock 4 A4
Creed 3 G2
Cremyll 5 H5
Crowan 2 D3
Crowlas 2 C3
Crowntown 2 D3

Crows-an-Wra 2 B4
Crumplehorn 5 F5
Cubert 4 A5
Cury 2 D4

D

Darite 5 F3
Davidstow 5 E1
Delabole 4 D2
Devoran 3 F2
Dobwalls 5 F4
Downderry 5 G5
Downgate 5 F3
Downgate 5 G3
Drift 2 B4
Drym 2 D3
Duloe 5 F4
Durgan 3 E4

E

East Taphouse 5 E4
Egloshayle 4 C3
Egloskerry 5 F1

F

Falmouth 3 F3
Feock 3 F2
Fiddlers Green 3 F1
Fivelanes 5 F2
Flexbury 6 B4
Flushing 3 F3
Four Lanes 3 E2
Fowey 5 E5
Foxhole 3 H1
Fraddon 4 B4
Freathy 5 H5
Frogwell 5 G3

G

Garras 3 E4
Gerrans 3 G3
Gluvian 4 C4
Godolphin Cross 2 D3
Golant 5 E5
Golberdon 5 G3
Goldsithney 2 C3
Goonbell 3 E1
Goonhavern 3 F1
Goonvrea 3 E1
Gorran 3 H2
Gorran Haven 3 H2
Grampound 3 G1
Grampound Road 3 G1
Grimscott 6 B4
Gulval 2 B3
Gunnislake 5 H3
Gunwalloe 2 D4
Gweek 3 E4
Gwennap 3 E2
Gwinear 2 D3
Gwithian 2 D2

H

Halsetown 2 C2
Harlyn 4 B3
Harrowbarrow 5 H3
Hatt 5 H4
Hayle 2 C3
Heamoor 2 B3
Helford 3 E4
Helford Passage 3 E4
Helland 4 D3
Hellescott 5 F1
Helston 2 D4
Helstone 4 D2
Henwood 5 F3
Herodsfoot 5 F4
Hessenford 5 G5
Hewas Water 3 H1
Hexworthy 5 G2
High Lanes 2 C3
High Street 3 H1
Higher Town 3 F2
Higher Town 4 C4

Crows-an-Wra

Higher Town *IOS* 2 b1
Holmbush 3 H1
Holywell 4 A4
Hugh Town *IOS* 2 b2

I

Idless 3 F2
Illand 5 F2
Illogan 2 D2
Indian Queens 4 B4

J

Jacobstow 5 E1

K

Kea 3 F2
Kehelland 2 D2
Kelynack 2 A3
Kenwyn 3 F2
Kerris 2 B4
Kestle 3 H2
Kestle Mill 4 B4
Kilkhampton 6 B4
Kingsand 5 H5
Kingston 5 G3
Kuggar 3 E5

L

Ladock 3 G1
Lamorna 2 B4
Lamorran 3 G2
Landrake 5 G4
Landulph 5 H4
Lane 4 B4
Laneast 5 F2
Langore 5 G1
Lanivet 4 D4
Lank 4 D3
Lanlivery 4 D4
Lanner 3 E2
Lanreath 5 E5
Lansallos 5 E5
Lanteglos 4 D2
Lanteglos Highway 5 E5
Latchley 5 H3
Launcells 6 B4
Launceston 5 G2
Lawhitton 5 G2
Leedstown 2 D3
Lelant 2 C3
Lerryn 5 E4
Lesnewth 5 E1
Lewannick 5 F2
Lezant 5 G2
Linkinhorne 5 G3
Liskeard 5 F4
Little Petherick 4 C3
Lizard 3 E5
Lockengate 4 D4
London Apprentice 3 H1
Longdowns 3 E3
Longrock 2 B3
Looe 5 F5
Lostwithiel 5 E4
Luckett 5 G3
Ludgvan 2 C3
Luxulyan 4 D4

M

Mabe Burnthouse 3 E3
Madron 2 B3
Malpas 3 F2
Manaccan 3 E4
Marazanvose 3 F1
Marazion 2 C3
Marhamchurch 6 B5
Marshgate 5 E1
Mawgan 3 E4
Mawgan Porth 4 B4
Mawla 3 E1
Mawnan 3 F4
Mawnan Smith 3 F4
Maxworthy 5 F1
Menheniot 5 F4

Merrymeet 5 F4
Merther 3 F2
Metherell 5 H3
Mevagissey 3 H2
Michaelstow 4 D2
Middle Town *IOS* 2 a2
Middlewood 5 F3
Millbrook 5 H5
Minions 5 F3
Mitchell 3 F1
Mithian 3 E1
Moorswater 5 F4
Morvah 2 B3
Morval 5 F5
Morwenstow 6 B3
Mount 5 E3
Mount Ambrose 3 E2
Mount Hawke 3 E2
Mountjoy 4 B4
Mousehole 2 B4
Muchlarnick 5 F5
Mullion 2 D5
Mullion Cove 2 D5
Mylor 3 F3
Mylor Bridge 3 F3

N

Nanpean 3 G1
Nanstallon 4 D4
New Grimsby *IOS* 2 a1
New Mill 2 B3
New Mills 3 G1
Newbridge 2 B3
Newlyn 2 B4
Newlyn East 3 F1
Newport 5 G2
Newquay 4 A4
Newton Ferrers 5 G4
North Hill 5 F3
North Petherwin 5 F1
North Tamerton 6 C5
Notter 5 H4

O

Old Grimsby *IOS* 2 a1
Old Kea 3 F2
Old Town *IOS* 2 b2
Oldmill 5 G3
Otterham 5 E1

P

Padstow 4 C3
Par 4 D5
Paul 2 B4
Pelynt 5 F5
Pendeen 2 A3
Pendoggett 4 D2
Pengelly 3 E1
Penhallow 3 E1
Penlean 6 B5
Penpoll 5 E5
Penponds 2 D2
Penrose 4 B3
Penryn 3 F3
Pensilva 5 F3
Pentewan 3 H2
Pentire 4 A4
Penwithick 3 H1
Penzance 2 B3
Perranarworthal 3 F2
Perranporth 3 E1
Perranuthnoe 2 C3
Perranwell 3 F2
Perranzabuloe 3 E1
Petherwin Gate 5 F1
Phillack 2 C2
Philleigh 3 F2
Pillaton 5 G3
Polbathic 5 G4
Polgooth 3 H1
Polkerris 4 D5
Polmassick 3 H2
Polperro 5 F5
Poldruan 5 E5
Polyphant 5 F2
Polzeath 4 C2
Ponsanooth 3 E3
Porkellis 3 E3
Port Gaverne 4 C2

Port Isaac	4 C2	St Clether	5 F2
Port Quin	4 C2	St Columb Major	4 B4
Porth	4 B4	St Columb Minor	4 B4
Porth Navas	3 E4	St Columb Road	4 B4
Porthallow	3 F4	St Day	3 E2
Porthallow	5 F5	St Dennis	4 C5
Porthcothan	4 B3	St Dominick	5 H3
Porthcurno	2 A4	St Endellion	4 C2
Porthgwarra	2 A4	St Enoder	3 G1
Porthleven	2 D4	St Erme	3 F1
Porthoustock	3 F4	St Erney	5 G4
Porthpean	3 H1	St Erth	2 C3
Porthtowan	3 E2	St Erth Praze	2 C3
Portloe	3 G2	St Ervan	4 B3
Portmellon	3 H2	St Eval	4 B3
Portreath	2 D2	St Ewe	3 H2
Portscatho	3 G3	St Gennys	6 A5
Portwrinkle	5 G5	St Germans	5 G5
Poughill	6 B4	St Hilary	2 C3
Poundstock	6 B5	St Issey	4 C3
Praa Sands	2 D3	St Ive	5 G4
Praze-an-Beeble	2 D3	St Ives	2 C2
Probus	3 G2	St John	5 H5
Prospidnick	2 D3	St Just	2 A3
		St Just-in-Roseland	3 F3
Q		St Keverne	3 F4
Quethiock	5 G4	St Kew	4 D3
Quintrell Downs	4 B4	St Kew Highway	4 D3
		St Keyne	5 F4
R		St Levan	2 A4
Rame	3 E3	St Mabyn	4 D3
Rame	5 H5	St Martin	3 E4
Redruth	3 E2	St Martin	5 F5
Relubbus	2 C3	St Mawes	3 F3
Rescassa	3 H2	St Mawgan	4 B4
Reskadinnick	2 D2	St Mellion	5 H4
Rezare	5 F3	St Merryn	4 B3
Rilla Mill	5 F3	St Mewan	3 H1
Roche	4 C4	St Michael Caerhays	3 G2
Rock	4 C3	St Michael Penkevil	3 F2
Rose	3 F1	St Minver	4 C2
Rosenannon	4 C4	St Neot	5 E3
Ruan Lanihorne	3 G2	St Pinnock	5 E4
Ruan Major	3 E5	St Stephen	3 G1
Ruan Minor	3 E5	St Stephen's Coombe	3 G1
Rumford	4 B3	St Stephens	5 G2
Rutherbridge	4 D4	St Stephens	5 H4
Ruthvoes	4 C4	St Teath	4 D2
		St Tudy	4 D3
S		St Veep	5 E5
St Agnes	3 E1	St Wenn	4 C4
St Allen	3 F1	Saltash	5 H4
St Ann's Chapel	5 H3	Sancreed	2 B3
St Anthony	3 F4	Sandplace	5 F5
St Austell	3 H1	Scarcewater	3 G1
St Blazey	4 D5	Scorrier	3 E2
St Breock	4 C3	Seaton	5 G5
St Breward	4 D3	Sennen	2 A4
St Buryan	2 B4	Sennen Cove	2 A4
St Cleer	5 F3	Seworgan	3 E3
St Clement	3 F2	Sheviock	5 G5
		Shop	6 B4
		Shortlanesend	3 F2
		Sithney	2 D4
		South Hill	5 G3
		South Petherwin	5 G2
		South Pill	5 H4
		South Tehidy	2 D2
		South Wheatley	5 F1
		Southcott	5 E1

Stenalees	3 H1	Treween	5 F2
Stibb	6 B4	Trewen	5 F2
Sticker	3 H1	Trewint	5 F2
Stithians	3 E3	Trewithian	3 G3
Stoke Climsland	5 G3	Trewoon	3 H1
Stratton	6 B4	Trispen	3 F1
Summercourt	3 G1	Troon	2 D3
Sweets	5 E1	Truro	3 F2
Sweetshouse	4 D4	Tuckingmill	2 D2
		Twelveheads	3 E2
T		Tywardreath	4 D5
Talskiddy	4 B4		
Temple	5 E3	**U**	
Tideford	5 G4	Upton	5 F3
Tintagel	4 D1		
Torpoint	5 H5	**V**	
Towednack	2 B3	Veryan	3 G2
Townshend	2 D3	Victoria	4 C4
Trebarwith	4 D2		
Trebetherick	4 C2	**W**	
Trebullett	5 G2	Wadebridge	4 C3
Treburley	5 G2	Wainhouse Corner	5 F1
Tredaule	5 F2	Warbstow	5 F1
Treen	2 A4	Warleggan	5 E3
Trefrew	4 D2	Washaway	4 D3
Tregadillett	5 G2	Watergate	5 E2
Tregeare	5 F1	Week St Mary	6 B5
Tregole	6 A5	Wendron	2 D3
Tregonetha	4 C4	Werrington	5 G1
Tregony	3 G2	West Pentire	4 A4
Trehan	5 H4	West Taphouse	5 E4
Trekenner	5 G2	West Youlstone	6 B3
Treknow	4 D1	Westdowns	4 D2
Trelights	4 C2	White Cross	3 E4
Trelill	4 D2	Whitemoor	3 H1
Trelow	4 C3	Whitstone	6 B5
Tremail	5 E1	Widegates	5 F4
Tremaine	5 F1	Widemouth Bay	6 B5
Tremar	5 F3	Windmill	4 B3
Trematon	5 H4	Withiel	4 C4
Trenance	4 B3	Woodford	6 B4
Trenance	4 C3		
Trenear	2 D3	**Y**	
Treneglos	5 F1	Yeolmbridge	5 G1
Trequite	4 D2		
Trerulefoot	5 G4	**Z**	
Trescowe	2 C3	Zennor	2 B2
Tresean	4 A4		
Tresillian	3 F2		
Treskinnick Cross	6 B5		
Tresmeer	5 F1		
Tresparrett	5 E1		
Trethevey	4 D1		
Trethewey	2 A4		
Trethurgy	3 H1		
Trevalga	4 D1		
Trevarrian	4 B4		
Treveal	4 A4		
Treveighan	4 D2		
Trevellas Downs	3 E1		
Trevelmond	5 F4		
Treverva	3 E3		
Trevescan	2 A4		
Treviscoe	3 G1		
Trevone	4 B3		
Trewalder	4 D2		
Trewarmett	4 D1		

USING THE TOWNS & VILLAGES INDEX

Town and village names on the Street mapping (pages 10 to 87) are listed alphabetically. Each town or village name is followed by the page number and the reference to the square in which the name is found.

Standard index entries are shown as follows:

Anderton 43 G2

Anderton	43 G2	Bude	12 D3	Crantock	21 F5	Gwealfolds	29 G1
Ball	87 F1	Burraton	76 C1	Cripplesease	70 A5	Halgabron	79 F3
Balnoon	70 B2	Busveal	61 H4	Degibna	59 F3	Halsetown	70 B1
Barne Barton	77 H5	Camborne	14 D3	Devoran	19 F4	Hannafore	35 F4
Beacon	14 D5	Camelford	17 F4	Dinas	48 A4	Hayle	27 E4
Bethel	64 D3	Canonstown	66 A3	Downrow	79 E5	Heamoor	54 B1
Biscovey	50 C5	Carbis Bay	71 F1	Drift	44 B2	Hellesveor	68 C3
Bissom	53 F3	Carn Arthen	15 G3	East Looe	35 F3	Helston	29 H3
Bodieve	86 D1	Carn Brea Village	60 C5	Egloshayle	86 D3	Hendra	16 C4
Bodinnick	24 D1	Carnon Downs	19 E2	Falmouth	23 F2	Higher Bosavern	72 C5
Bodmin	10 D3	Cawsand	43 G5	Flexbury	12 C2	Higher Condurrow	15 F5
Bohortha	75 F4	Chapel	31 E4	Forder	76 B4	Highertown	84 A4
Bolingey	56 C5	Chapel	47 G5	Fowey	24 B2	High Lanes	27 F4
Boscean	72 A2	Charlestown	65 E5	Freathy	42 A1	Holmbush	65 E3
Boscoppa	64 C1	Chenhalls	67 F2	Gloweth	83 G3	Hugus	82 D5
Bosleake	15 H3	Church Town	60 D5	Goldsithney	39 G3	Joppa	27 G5
Boslowick	22 B4	Chyandour	55 F2	Goonhavern	57 G5	Kenwyn	84 D1
Bossiney	78 C3	Chycoose	19 H4	Goonhusband	59 H3	Kerley Downs	82 A5
Botallack	72 B1	Clapper	87 F4	Green Bottom	82 B2	Kerris	44 C5
Brea	15 F3	Cooksland	11 E1	Greenwith Common	18 A2	Kestle	40 C2
Brunnion	70 B5	Copperhouse	27 F3	Gulval	55 H1	Kingsand	43 G4

Lamellion 32 D4
Lanescot 51 F1
Launceston 30 D3
Lelant 26 A4
Liskeard 33 E2
Little Mill 67 E3
Longstone 71 E2
Looe 35 F4
Looe Mills 32 A2
Lostwithiel 36 D4
Lower Rose 57 G2
Lower Treliever 52 B2
Lower Treluswell 52 C1
Lynstone 12 B5
Mabe Burnthouse 52 A5
Marazion 38 B3
Maryfield 81 E3
Mevagissey 41 F2
Millbrook 43 F2
Millendreath 35 G1
Mongleath 22 A2
Moorswater 32 B3
Mount Ambrose 61 G1
Mount Charles 64 B3
Nancherrow 72 B3
Newbridge 83 H4
Newlyn 45 G2
New Mill 84 B1
Newport 31 F2
Newquay 46 B2
Padstow 48 C4
Par 50 D4
Paul 45 G5
Penbeagle 68 C4
Pengegon 15 F4
Penhallick 15 H3

Penmayne 49 H1
Penponds 14 A5
Penrose Hill 58 C2
Penryn 52 C3
Pentire 21 F2
Penweathers 84 A5
Penzance 55 F3
Perranporth 56 B2
Perranuthnoe 39 F5
Perranwell 18 A4
Perranwell Station 18 C3
Perran Wharf 18 C5
Phillack 27 F2
Piece 15 H4
Plaidy 35 G1
Plain-an-Gwarry 60 D3
Plain-an-Gwarry 39 E2
Polmear 51 F4
Polmorla 86 B4
Polruan 24 D3
Pont 25 H1
Pool 15 H1
Porth 47 F1
Porthilly 49 F3
Porthleven 58 B1
Portlooe 34 C4
Portmellon 41 G5
Redmoor 36 B1
Redruth 61 G4
Riverside 77 G4
Rock 49 E2
Rose 57 F2
Rose-an-Grouse 66 C2
Rosehill 57 G5
Rosewarne 14 C2
Rosudgeon 39 H5

St Anthony 74 D5
St Austell 64 B5
St Blazey 50 B2
St Blazey Gate 50 B4
St Breock 86 A4
St Budeaux 77 H3
St Columb Minor 47 H2
St Erth 67 F3
St Gluvias 53 E2
St Hilary 59 H2
St Ives 69 G3
St Just 72 C4
St Mawes 74 B2
St Mewan 63 E5
St Stephens 76 C4
St Stephens 30 D1
St Thomas 30 E2
Saltash 76 D3
Shutta 35 E1
Sithney 28 A1
Sithney Common 28 C2
Sladesbridge 87 H5
South Pill 77 E2
Splatt 49 H1
Stoptide 49 G2
Stratton 13 G2
Threemilestone 82 B3
Tintagel 78 C3
Tolgus Mount 60 C2
Tolskithy 60 B3
Tomperrow 82 C4
Torpoint 81 F4
The Towans 26 D1
Tredannick 87 H5
Tredavoe 45 E2
Treesmill 51 G1

Trefrew 17 F2
Tregatta 78 C5
Tregeseal 72 D3
Tregoodwell 17 G4
Tregrehan Mills 39 F2
Tregurtha Downs 51 F1
Treleigh 84 A2
Treliske 79 E5
Tenale 79 E5
Tenance 46 A4
Trenant Girt 86 D3
Trencreek 47 E4
Trencrom 70 D5
Treneague 86 C5
Trethevy 79 G2
Trevalgan 68 A3
Trevanson 86 A2
Trevarrack 55 C1
Treven 78 C5
Trevia 16 D4
Trevillett 79 G4
Trewartha 70 D3
Trewen 16 B5
Trewoon 62 C3
Truro 85 G3
Tuckingmill 15 E2
Tywardreath 51 F7
Ventonleague 27 H2
Wadebridge 86 D4
Wearde 76 D3
West Looe 35 E3
West Pentire 20 C4
Wherry Town 55 E5
Whitecross 66 A5
Whiterock 86 B3
Wilcove 81 E1

USING THE STREET INDEX

Street names are listed alphabetically. Each street name is followed by its postal town or area locality, the Postcode District, the page number, and the reference to the square in which the name is found.

Standard index entries are shown as follows:

Abbey HI *STIVES* TR26 .... **26** A5

Street names and selected addresses not shown on the map due to scale restrictions are shown in the index with an asterisk:

Academy Pl *STIVES* TR26 * **69** F2

GENERAL ABBREVIATIONS

ACC	ACCESS	E	EAST	LDG	LODGE	R	RIVER
ALY	ALLEY	EMB	EMBANKMENT	LGT	LIGHT	RBT	ROUNDABOUT
AP	APPROACH	EMBY	EMBASSY	LK	LOCK	RD	ROAD
AR	ARCADE	ESP	ESPLANADE	LKS	LAKES	RDG	RIDGE
ASS	ASSOCIATION	EST	ESTATE	LNDG	LANDING	REP	REPUBLIC
AV	AVENUE	EX	EXCHANGE	LTL	LITTLE	RES	RESERVOIR
BCH	BEACH	EXPY	EXPRESSWAY	LWR	LOWER	RFC	RUGBY FOOTBALL CLUB
BLDS	BUILDINGS	EXT	EXTENSION	MAG	MAGISTRATES'	RI	RISE
BND	BEND	F/O	FLYOVER	MAN	MANSIONS	RP	RAMP
BNK	BANK	FC	FOOTBALL CLUB	MD	MEAD	RW	ROW
BR	BRIDGE	FK	FORK	MDW	MEADOWS	S	SOUTH
BRK	BROOK	FLD	FIELD	MEM	MEMORIAL	SCH	SCHOOL
BTM	BOTTOM	FLDS	FIELDS	MI	MILL	SE	SOUTH EAST
BUS	BUSINESS	FLS	FALLS	MKT	MARKET	SER	SERVICE AREA
BVD	BOULEVARD	FM	FARM	MKTS	MARKETS	SH	SHORE
BY	BYPASS	FT	FORT	ML	MALL	SHOP	SHOPPING
CATH	CATHEDRAL	FTS	FLATS	MNR	MANOR	SKWY	SKYWAY
CEM	CEMETERY	FWY	FREEWAY	MS	MEWS	SMT	SUMMIT
CEN	CENTRE	FY	FERRY	MSN	MISSION	SOC	SOCIETY
CFT	CROFT	GA	GATE	MT	MOUNT	SP	SPUR
CH	CHURCH	GAL	GALLERY	MTN	MOUNTAIN	SPR	SPRING
CHA	CHASE	GDN	GARDEN	MTS	MOUNTAINS	SQ	SQUARE
CHYD	CHURCHYARD	GDNS	GARDENS	MUS	MUSEUM	ST	STREET
CIR	CIRCLE	GLD	GLADE	MWY	MOTORWAY	STN	STATION
CIRC	CIRCUS	GLN	GLEN	N	NORTH	STR	STREAM
CL	CLOSE	GN	GREEN	NE	NORTH EAST	STRD	STRAND
CLFS	CLIFFS	GND	GROUND	NW	NORTH WEST	SW	SOUTH WEST
CMP	CAMP	GRA	GRANGE	O/P	OVERPASS	TDG	TRADING
CNR	CORNER	GRG	GARAGE	OFF	OFFICE	TER	TERRACE
CO	COUNTY	GT	GREAT	ORCH	ORCHARD	THWY	THROUGHWAY
COLL	COLLEGE	GTWY	GATEWAY	OV	OVAL	TNL	TUNNEL
COM	COMMON	GV	GROVE	PAL	PALACE	TOLL	TOLLWAY
COMM	COMMISSION	HGR	HIGHER	PAS	PASSAGE	TPK	TURNPIKE
CON	CONVENT	HL	HILL	PAV	PAVILION	TR	TRACK
COT	COTTAGE	HLS	HILLS	PDE	PARADE	TRL	TRAIL
COTS	COTTAGES	HO	HOUSE	PH	PUBLIC HOUSE	TWR	TOWER
CP	CAPE	HOL	HOLLOW	PK	PARK	U/P	UNDERPASS
CPS	COPSE	HOSP	HOSPITAL	PKWY	PARKWAY	UNI	UNIVERSITY
CR	CREEK	HRB	HARBOUR	PL	PLACE	UPR	UPPER
CREM	CREMATORIUM	HTH	HEATH	PLN	PLAIN	V	VALE
CRS	CRESCENT	HTS	HEIGHTS	PLNS	PLAINS	VA	VALLEY
CSWY	CAUSEWAY	HVN	HAVEN	PLZ	PLAZA	VIAD	VIADUCT
CT	COURT	HWY	HIGHWAY	POL	POLICE STATION	VIL	VILLA
CTRL	CENTRAL	IMP	IMPERIAL	PR	PRINCE	VIS	VISTA
CTS	COURTS	IN	INLET	PREC	PRECINCT	VLG	VILLAGE
CTYD	COURTYARD	IND EST	INDUSTRIAL ESTATE	PREP	PREPARATORY	VLS	VILLAS
CUTT	CUTTINGS	INF	INFIRMARY	PRIM	PRIMARY	VW	VIEW
CV	COVE	INFO	INFORMATION	PROM	PROMENADE	W	WEST
CYN	CANYON	INT	INTERCHANGE	PRS	PRINCESS	WD	WOOD
DEPT	DEPARTMENT	IS	ISLAND	PRT	PORT	WHF	WHARF
DL	DALE	JCT	JUNCTION	PT	POINT	WK	WALK
DM	DAM	JTY	JETTY	PTH	PATH	WKS	WALKS
DR	DRIVE	KG	KING	PZ	PIAZZA	WLS	WELLS
DRO	DROVE	KNL	KNOLL	QD	QUADRANT	WY	WAY
DRY	DRIVEWAY	L	LAKE	QU	QUEEN	YD	YARD
DWGS	DWELLINGS	LA	LANE	QY	QUAY	YHA	YOUTH HOSTEL

POSTCODE TOWNS AND AREA ABBREVIATIONS

BUDE................Bude	LANDS................Lands End	PAR................Par/St Blazey	RTRUNW........Rural Truro north & west
BODM................Bodmin	LAUN................Launceston	PENRYN................Penryn	RTRUS................Rural Truro south
BOSC................Boscastle	LISK................Liskeard	PENZ................Penzance	SALT................Saltash
CAMBORNE................Camborne	LIZ................Lizard	PERRAN................Perranporth	STAUS................St Austell
CAMEL................Camelford	LOOE................Looe	PLY................Plymouth	STIVES................St Ives
DELAB................Delabole	LOST................Lostwithiel	PLYNW................Plymouth northwest	TINT................Tintagel
FAL................Falmouth	MARAZ................Marazion	RBODM................Rural Bodmin	TOR................Torpoint
FOW................Fowey	MBRK/KGSD................Millbrook/	RED................Redruth	TRU................Truro
HAYLE................Hayle	Kingsand	RNEWQ................Rural Newquay	WADE................Wadebridge
HELS................Helston	MEVA................Mevagissey	RPENZ................Rural Penzance	
KEY/HAM/PCR................Keyham/	NEWQ................Newquay	RTRUE/STMW................Rural Truro east/	
Ham/Pennycross	PADS................Padstow	St Mawes	

Index - streets

A

Abbey Hl *STIVES* TR26	26 A5
Abbey Ms *BODM* PL31	10 B3
NEWQ TR7 *	46 B4
Abbey St *PENZ* TR18	55 E4
Abbots Cl *BODM* PL31	11 E3
Aberdeen Cl *PAR* PL24	50 C1
Acacia Rd *FAL* TR11	22 B1
Academy Pl *STIVES* TR26 *	69 F2
Academy Ter *STIVES* TR26 *	69 F2
Acland Cl *BUDE* EX23	12 C1
Acland Gdns *NEWQ* TR7	46 A3
Acorn Dr *STAUS* PL25	64 D4
Adams Cl *TOR* PL11	80 D4
Adams Crs *TOR* PL11	80 D4
Addington North *LISK* PL14 *	33 F2
Addington South *LISK* PL14 *	33 F2
Addison Ter *LOST* PL22	37 F4
Adelaide Rd *RED* TR15	61 F4
Adelaide St *CAMBORNE* TR14	14 D3
PENZ TR18	55 E3
Adelaide Ter *TRU* TR1 *	85 F3
Adela Rd *FAL* TR11	81 F4
Adit La *PENZ* TR18	45 C3
SALT PL12	76 D2
Admirals Quay *FAL* TR11 *	22 C1
Admiralty Rd *PLYNW* PL5	77 G3
Agar Ct *TRU* TR1	85 F2
Agar Crs *RED* TR15	60 A4
Agar Mdw *RTRUS* TR3	19 F2
Agar Rd *NEWQ* TR7	46 B4
STAUS PL25	64 D4
TRU TR1	85 F2
Agar Ter *BODM* PL31	10 C2
Agar Wy *RED* TR15	15 H1
Agnes Cl *BUDE* EX23	12 D4
Alamein Cl *SALT* PL12	76 C3
Alamein Rd *SALT* PL12	76 C3
Alan Harvey Cl *STIVES* TR26	68 D5
Alan Rd *PADS* PL28	48 B4
Albany Cl *RED* TR15	61 G5
Albany Gdns *RED* TR15	61 G5
Albany La *RED* TR15	61 F4
Albany Pl *FAL* TR11	22 C3
Albany Rd *FAL* TR11	22 C3
NEWQ TR7	46 C3
RED TR15	61 F4
TRU TR1	84 C3
Albany Ter *STIVES* TR26 *	69 F4
Albert Pl *CAMBORNE* TR14	14 D3
STIVES TR26 *	69 F3
TRU TR1	85 E4
Albert Rd *SALT* PL12	77 E3
STAUS PL25	64 A4
STIVES TR26	69 F3
Albert St *CAMBORNE* TR14	14 D3
PENZ TR18	55 E3
Albert Ter *LOST* PL22 *	37 F4
PENZ TR18	55 E3
STIVES TR26 *	69 F3
Albertus Dr *HAYLE* TR27	67 G1
Albertus Gdns *HAYLE* TR27	26 D5
Albertus Rd *HAYLE* TR27	67 G1
Albion Ct *TOR* PL11	81 G4
Albion Rd *HELS* TR13	29 F5
TOR PL11	81 G4
Alderwood Parc	
PENRYN TR10	52 C3
Alexandra Cl *STIVES* TR26	68 D3
Alexandra Ct *NEWQ* TR7	47 F1
Alexandra Gdns *PENZ* TR18	54 C5
Alexandra Pl *PENZ* TR18	54 D4
STIVES TR26	68 D3
Alexandra Rd *BODM* PL31	10 A2
NEWQ TR7	47 F1
PENZ TR18	54 C5
STAUS PL25	64 A4
STIVES TR26	68 D3
Alexandra Rw *STIVES* TR26 *	69 E2
Alexandra Sq *SALT* PL12	77 F3
Alexandra Ter *LAUN* PL15	31 F4
PENZ TR18	54 C5
STIVES TR26	69 E2
TRU TR1 *	84 D3
Alford Cl *BUDE* EX23	12 D3
Alldritt Cl *NEWQ* TR7	47 G2
Allen V *LISK* PL14	32 D3
Alma Pl *NEWQ* TR7	46 A3
PADS PL28 *	48 B3
PENZ TR18	54 C2
RED TR15	61 E3
Alma Rd *TRU* TR1	84 B3
Alma Ter *PENZ* TR18	55 E3
STIVES TR26 *	69 F3
Almshouse Hl *HELS* TR13	29 F4
Alphington *PENZ* TR18 *	54 D4
Alverne Blds *PENZ* TR18 *	54 D4
Alverton Ct *TRU* TR1	85 F2
Alverton Gdns *TRU* TR1	85 F2
Alverton Pl *PENZ* TR18	54 D4
Alverton Rd *PENZ* TR18	54 B5
Alverton St *PENZ* TR18	55 E4
Alverton Ter *PENZ* TR18 *	54 D4
TRU TR1	85 F2
Alwyn Cl *NEWQ* TR7	47 H3
Amal An Avon *HAYLE* TR27	27 G1
Ambrose Ct *RED* TR15	61 H1
Anderton Quay	
MBRK/KGSD PL10 *	43 G1
Anderton Ri *MBRK/KGSD* PL10 *	43 G1
Andrewartha Rd	
PENRYN TR10	52 C3
Aneray Rd *CAMBORNE* TR14	14 C2
Angel Hl *LAUN* PL15	31 F3
Angel Pl *HELS* TR13 *	29 F4
An Gof Gdns *BODM* PL31	10 B3
Anjardyn Pl *PAR* PL24	51 E3
Annear Rd *PENRYN* TR10	52 B5
Anson Wy *HELS* TR13	29 H5
Anthony Rd *NEWQ* TR7	46 A5
Antoine Ct *PENZ* TR18	45 G2
Antoine Ter *PENZ* TR18	45 G2
Anvil Rd *TOR* PL11	81 F3
Anvil Rd *CAMEL* PL32	17 F4
Appletree La *STAUS* PL25	65 G4
The Arcade *PENZ* TR18 *	55 E4
RTRUE/STMW TR2 *	74 C2
Arch Hl *TRU* TR1	84 D5
Arena Crs *STAUS* PL25	64 D3
Armada Rd *MBRK/KGSD* PL10	43 H5
Armchair Cnr *BODM* PL31 *	10 B2
Art Gallery Ter *PENZ* TR18 *	45 G1
Arthur Ter *TOR* PL11	81 H5
Arundell Gdns *FAL* TR11	53 F5
Arundell Pl *TRU* TR1	85 E4
Arundel Ter *BUDE* EX23	12 B4
Arundel Wy *NEWQ* TR7	47 E2
Arwenack Av *FAL* TR11	23 E3
Arwenack St *FAL* TR11	22 D2
Arworthal Mdw *RTRUS* TR3	18 B4
Arwyn Pl *FAL* TR11 *	23 E3
Ashburgh Parc *SALT* PL12	76 A2
Ashbury Cl *LISK* PL14	33 G1
Ash Cl *PAR* PL24	50 B5
Ash Dr *HAYLE* TR27	67 G1
Ashfield Gdns *FAL* TR11	53 F5
Ashfield Rd *FAL* TR11	53 F5
Ash Gv *HAYLE* TR27	67 G1
PAR PL24	50 B5
Ashley Rd *TRU* TR1	85 E3
Ash Park Ter *LISK* PL14	33 E3
Ashton Ct *NEWQ* TR7 *	46 D2
Ashton Ms *SALT* PL12 *	76 C2
Ashton Wy *SALT* PL12	76 C2
Athelstan Pk *BODM* PL31	11 E4
Atlantic Bay Est *PERRAN* TR6	56 B2
Atlantic Cl *CAMBORNE* TR14	14 D4
Atlantic Rd *NEWQ* TR7	21 H3
TINT PL34	78 C3
Atlantic Ter *CAMBORNE* TR14	14 D4
STIVES TR26 *	69 F2
Atlantic Wy *TINT* PL34	78 B3
Audierne *PENRYN* TR10 *	52 D4
Avenue Rd *FAL* TR11	23 E3
The Avenue *TRU* TR1	85 F2
Avery Ter *LOST* PL22 *	37 F4
Avon Cl *STAUS* PL25	64 D2
Avondale Rd *TRU* TR1	84 D3
Avrack Cl *LANDS* TR19	44 B2
Aylmer Pl *STAUS* PL25	63 H4
Aylmer Sq *STAUS* PL25	63 H4
Ayr *STIVES* TR26 *	69 E2
Ayr La *STIVES* TR26 *	69 F2
Ayr Ter *STIVES* TR26 *	69 E2

B

Babis Farm Cl *SALT* PL12	77 E4
Babis Farm Rw *SALT* PL12	77 E3
Babis La *SALT* PL12	77 E4
Back Hl *SALT* PL12	76 D4
Back La *HAYLE* TR27	66 B3
MARAZ TR17	38 D3
STIVES TR26	69 F2
TINT PL34	78 D2
Back La West *RED* TR15	61 E4
Back Quay *TRU* TR1	85 F3
Back Rd East *STIVES* TR26	69 G1
Back Rd West *STIVES* TR26	69 F2
Back St *STIVES* TR26	69 F2
Bagbury Rd *BUDE* EX23	12 C5
Baileys La *STIVES* TR26	69 F2
Balfield Rd *HELS* TR13	58 B2
Bal-Jinjy Cl *PAR* PL24	50 C5
Ball Pk *SALT* PL12	76 C4
Balmoral Rd *RED* TR15	61 E3
Balmoral Ter *RED* TR15	61 E3
Bangors Rd *LAUN* PL15	30 C5
Bank Pl *FAL* TR11	22 D2
Bank Sq *LANDS* TR19	72 C4
Bank St *NEWQ* TR7	46 A3
Bank Ter *NEWQ* TR7	46 A3
Baptist Hl *HAYLE* TR27	27 G1
Barbican Cl *HELS* TR13	29 H1
LOOE PL13	35 F5
Barbican Ct *LOOE* PL13	35 F1
Barbican Hl *LOOE* PL13	35 F1
Barbican La *PENZ* TR18	54 D5
Barbican Rd *LOOE* PL13	35 F5
Barkers Gn *STAUS* PL25	65 E3
Barker's Hl *SALT* PL12	76 B4
Barkhouse La *STAUS* PL25	65 E5
Barlandhu *PENZ* TR18	45 G2
Bar La *FAL* TR11	23 F3
Barlanwick *PENZ* TR18 *	54 B5
Barlowena *CAMBORNE* TR14	14 C5
Barnaloft *STIVES* TR26 *	69 F2
Barncoose La *RED* TR15	60 B4
Barncoose Ter *RED* TR15	60 B4
Barne Cl *PLYNW* PL5	77 H5
Barne Rd *PLYNW* PL5	77 H5
Barnfield Gdns *PENZ* TR18	55 G2
Barnfield Pk *BUDE* EX23	13 F3
Barnfield Ter *LISK* PL14	33 F3
Barn La *BODM* PL31	10 B3
Barn Meadow Pk *LOOE* PL13	34 D3
Barnoon Hl *STIVES* TR26	69 F2
Barnoon Ter *STIVES* TR26 *	69 F2
Barn Pk *LOST* PL22	37 G3
SALT PL12	77 E2
Barn Park La *BODM* PL31	11 E3
Barn St *LISK* PL14	33 F3
Barons Meadow *BODM* PL31	11 E2
Barossa Rd *TOR* PL11	81 G5
Barrack La *TRU* TR1	85 E4
Barras Cross *LISK* PL14	33 F2
Barras Pl *LISK* PL14	33 F2
Barras St *LISK* PL14	33 F3
Barrepta Cl *STIVES* TR26	71 F2
Barrie Crs *BODM* PL31	10 C3
Bar Rd *FAL* TR11	23 E3
Barrow Down *LISK* PL14	76 A2
Barrowfield Vw *NEWQ* TR7	46 D2
Barry's La *PADS* PL28	48 B3
Bar Ter *FAL* TR11 *	23 E3
Bartles Rw *CAMBORNE* TR14	15 F1
Bartlett Av *BUDE* EX23	12 D3
Barton Cl *BODM* PL31 *	10 C2
HELS TR13	29 H2
PENZ TR18	54 D2
Barton Meadow *TRU* TR1	84 C2
Barview La *HAYLE* TR27	27 E5
Barwis Hl *PENZ* TR18	55 E3
Barwis Ter *PENZ* TR18 *	55 E3
Basset Pl *FAL* TR11 *	22 C1
Basset Rd *CAMBORNE* TR14	14 C4

Abb - Bel

Basset St *CAMBORNE* TR14	14 C4
FAL TR11	22 C1
RED TR15	61 F4
Battery La *FOW* PL23	24 C4
Battery Mill La *HAYLE* TR27	67 E5
Battery Pk *FOW* PL23	24 C4
Battery Rd *PENZ* TR18	55 F5
Battery Ter *MEVA* PL26	41 H3
Bawden Rd *BODM* PL31	10 A4
Baydown *LOOE* PL13	35 F1
Baynards Ct *TRU* TR1 *	85 F3
The Bay *LOOE* PL13	35 F3
Baytree Hl *LISK* PL14	33 F3
Bayview *PAR* PL24	50 D5
Bay View Crs *FAL* TR11	23 F3
Bayview Dr *LOOE* PL13	35 F2
Bay View Pk *STAUS* PL25	64 B1
Bay View Ter *HAYLE* TR27	27 E3
NEWQ TR7	46 B4
PENZ TR18	54 D5
Beachfield Av *NEWQ* TR7	46 A3
Beachfield Ct *PENZ* TR18	54 D5
Beach La *PERRAN* TR6 *	56 B3
Beach Pde *NEWQ* TR7 *	46 A3
Beach Rd *MEVA* PL26	41 H2
NEWQ TR7	46 A3
PERRAN TR6	56 B3
RNEWQ TR8	21 E4
STAUS PL25	65 F4
STIVES TR26	71 F1
Beach View Cl *NEWQ* TR7	47 F3
Beach Wk *NEWQ* TR7	47 E2
Beacon Cl *FAL* TR11	22 C1
STAUS PL25	64 D2
Beacon Crs *FAL* TR11 *	22 C1
Beacon Flds *CAMBORNE* TR14	14 D4
Beacon Hl *BODM* PL31	10 C3
Beacon Hill Ms *BODM* PL31 *	10 C2
Beacon Lanes *BODM* PL31	10 C3
Beacon Parc *HELS* TR13	29 G3
Beacon Rd *BODM* PL31	10 C3
FAL TR11	22 C1
MARAZ TR17	38 B3
NEWQ TR7	46 A2
Beaconsfield Ter *BODM* PL31 *	10 B2
Beacon St *FAL* TR11	22 C1
Beacon Ter *CAMBORNE* TR14	14 D5
FAL TR11 *	22 C1
HELS TR13	29 G3
The Beacon *FAL* TR11	22 C1
Beacon View Pk *RTRUNW* TR4	60 A1
Beatrice Av *SALT* PL12	76 D3
Beatrice Gdns *SALT* PL12 *	76 D4
Beatrice Rd *BODM* PL31	11 F5
Beatrice Ter *HAYLE* TR27	27 G2
Beattie Rd *PLYNW* PL5	77 G5
Beaufort Pl *PENZ* TR18	45 G1
Beaumont Ter *SALT* PL12	77 E1
Beckett Cl *RED* TR15	61 F4
Bede Haven Cl *BUDE* EX23	12 C4
Bederkesa Ct *BODM* PL31 *	10 C3
Bedford Pl *STIVES* TR26 *	69 F3
Bedford Rd *STIVES* TR26	69 F3
Bedruthan Av *TRU* TR1	85 G3
Beech Av *LISK* PL14	33 E3
Beech Cl *FAL* TR11	22 B1
TOR PL11	81 F4
Beech Dr *BODM* PL31	10 A3
Beech La *STAUS* PL25	64 A4
Beech Rd *FAL* TR11	22 B1
STAUS PL25	65 E3
Beech Ter *LOOE* PL13	35 E3
Beechwood Dr *CAMEL* PL32	17 F3
Beechwood Gdns *TRU* TR1	85 G1
Behenna Dr *TRU* TR1	84 B3
Bekelege Dr *CAMBORNE* TR14	15 E5
Belgrave Ter *LISK* PL14 *	33 G1
Belgravia St *PENZ* TR18	55 E4
Belhay *PENRYN* TR10	52 D3
Bellair Rd *RPENZ* TR20	54 A1
Bellair Ter *STIVES* TR26 *	69 F2
Bellatt *WADE* PL27	87 E2
Bellatt Pk *WADE* PL27	87 E2
Bella Vista Gdns *PENRYN* TR10	52 D2
Bellers Rd *STIVES* TR26	69 F4
Bellever Parc *CAMBORNE* TR14	15 E4

Belle Vue BUDE EX23.....12 B2
  PENZ TR18.....45 G3
Bellevue RED TR15.....61 G3
Belle Vue Av BUDE EX23.....12 B2
Belle Vue La BUDE EX23.....12 B2
Belle Vue Pl SALT PL12.....77 E2
Bellevue Sq TOR PL11.....81 G5
Belle Vue Ter
  CAMBORNE TR14 *.....15 F1
  PENZ TR18.....55 E3
Bellevue Ter RTRUS TR3 *.....18 B3
Bell La BODM PL31.....10 D2
Bells Ct FAL TR11 *.....22 D2
Belmont Pl NEWQ TR7.....46 A2
Belmont Rd FAL TR11.....22 C3
  STIVES TR26 *.....69 E2
Belmont Ter FAL TR11.....22 C3
  HELS TR13.....29 G3
  STAUS PL25.....64 A4
Belmont St PAR PL24.....51 G3
Belmont Ter RTRUS TR3.....19 E4
  STIVES TR26 *.....69 F4
Belyars Ct STIVES TR26.....69 F4
Belyars La STIVES TR26.....69 F4
The Belyars STIVES TR26.....69 F4
Benallack Ct TRU TR1.....85 G3
Bencoolen Rd BUDE EX23.....12 B3
Bennets La SALT PL12.....77 E2
Benson Gdns TRU TR1.....85 E3
Benson Rd TRU TR1.....84 D2
Bentley Dr BUDE EX23.....13 F3
Beraton Ct BODM PL31 *.....10 C2
Berkeley Cl BUDE EX23.....13 F3
Berkeley Cots FAL TR11.....22 C2
Berkeley Hl FAL TR11.....22 C2
Berkeley Ms FAL TR11.....22 C2
Berkeley Pth FAL TR11.....22 C2
Berkley V FAL TR11.....22 C2
Berries Av BUDE EX23.....12 C4
Berries Mt BUDE EX23.....12 C4
Berrycoombe Hl BODM PL31.....10 B2
Berrycoombe Rd BODM PL31.....10 C2
Berrycoombe V BODM PL31.....10 A2
Berry La BODM PL31.....10 B2
Berryman Crs FAL TR11.....22 B3
Berry Pk SALT PL12.....76 C1
Berry Rd NEWQ TR7.....46 B3
Berry Towers BODM PL31.....10 C2
Berthon Rd PLYNW PL5.....77 G5
Berveth Cl RTRUS TR3.....83 E3
Bess Park Rd WADE PL27.....87 E2
Bethan Dr WADE PL27.....86 B3
Bethany Homes
  CAMBORNE TR14.....14 B4
Bethany Pl LANDS TR19.....72 C4
Bethel Rd STAUS PL25.....64 D3
Bethesda Hl STIVES TR26 *.....69 F2
Bethesda Pl STIVES TR26.....69 F2
Beverley Crs HAYLE TR27.....27 G2
Beweys Pk SALT PL12.....76 B3
Bezant Pl RTRUE TR2.....21 G3
Bickern Rd TOR PL11.....81 G4
Bickford Rd LAUN PL15.....31 E1
Biddick's Ct STAUS PL25.....63 H4
Billings Dr NEWQ TR7.....47 E4
Binhamy Cl BUDE EX23.....12 D4
Binhamy Rd BUDE EX23.....13 E4
Birch Gv HAYLE TR27.....67 G1
Birkdale Cl SALT PL12 *.....76 B3
Biscombe Gdns SALT PL12.....77 F2
Bishops Cl SALT PL12.....76 D2
  TRU TR1.....85 E1
Bishop's Rd STIVES TR26.....69 F3
Bishop Temple Rd TRU TR1.....85 H2
Bissoe Rd RTRUS TR3.....19 E1
Bissom Rd PENRYN TR10.....53 F3
Blackberry Wy TRU TR1.....85 H2
Blackbird Crs LAUN PL15.....31 H5
Black Rd HAYLE TR27.....27 F2
Blackwell Rd BUDE EX23.....12 D4
Blairgowrie Rd PLYNW PL5.....77 H4
Blakes Pk LISK PL14 *.....33 G1
Blanchminster Rd BUDE EX23.....12 C3
Bligh Crs HELS TR13.....29 G4
Blight's Rw RED TR15.....61 G3
Blindhole La LAUN PL15.....31 F3
Bloom Flds PENZ TR18.....54 C4
Blowing House Cl
  STAUS PL25.....63 G3
Blowinghouse Hl RED TR15.....60 C4
Blowing House Hl
  STAUS PL25.....63 H3
Blowing House La
  STAUS PL25.....63 G3
Bluebell Cl SALT PL12.....76 D3
Bluebell Wy LAUN PL15.....31 H5
Boase St PENZ TR18.....45 E3
Bobs Rd PAR PL24.....50 B4
Boconnoc Rd STAUS PL25.....64 A4
Bodgara Wy LISK PL14.....33 F2
Bodieve Rd WADE PL27.....87 E1
Bodinar Rd PENRYN TR10.....52 B2
Bodiniel Rd BODM PL31.....10 B1
Bodiniel Vw BODM PL31.....10 A2
Bodinnick Hts FOW PL23.....25 E1
Bodmin Hl LOST PL22.....37 E3
Bodmin Rd TRU TR1.....85 G1
Bodrigan Rd LOOE PL13.....35 F2
Bodriggy Ct HAYLE TR27.....27 F3
Bodriggy Crs HAYLE TR27.....27 F3
Bodriggy St HAYLE TR27.....27 F3

Bodriggy Vls HAYLE TR27.....27 F3
Bodrugan Hl MEVA PL26.....41 G5
Bodvean Ct NEWQ TR7 *.....21 H3
Bohelland Ri PENRYN TR10.....53 E3
Bohelland Rd PENRYN TR10.....53 E3
Bohelland Wy PENRYN TR10.....52 D3
Bohelia Rd
  RTRUE/STMW TR2.....74 C2
Bohill PENRYN TR10.....53 E4
Boiler Works Rd
  CAMBORNE TR14.....14 D1
Bojea Ter STAUS PL25.....63 H1
Boldventure Av STAUS PL25.....65 E2
Boldventure Cl STAUS PL25.....65 E2
Boldventure Rd STAUS PL25.....65 E2
Bolenna La PERRAN TR6.....56 A4
Bolingey Rd PERRAN TR6.....56 B4
Bolitho Rd PENZ TR18.....54 C2
Bollowal Pl LANDS TR19.....72 A4
Bolowthas Wy NEWQ TR7.....47 F2
Boltern Rd MARAZ TR17.....39 E3
Bon Cot Rd PENZ TR18.....45 G2
Bond St RED TR15.....61 E4
Bone Mill Rd PERRAN TR6.....56 D5
Bonson Ct LOOE PL13.....35 E2
Bonython Rd NEWQ TR7.....47 E2
Bonython Ter LISK PL14.....33 F4
Borlase Cl HELS TR13.....29 F4
Borough Pk TOR PL11.....80 D3
Boscarne Crs STAUS PL25.....64 C4
Boscarnek HAYLE TR27.....67 F3
Boscarn Rd RED TR15.....61 G2
Boscathnoe La RPENZ TR20.....54 A1
Boscathnoe Wy PENZ TR18.....54 B2
Boscawen Br TRU TR1.....85 F3
Boscawen Gdns PERRAN TR6.....56 A4
Boscawen Rd FAL TR11.....22 D5
  HELS TR13.....29 H5
  PERRAN TR6.....56 B3
Boscawen St TRU TR1.....85 F3
Boscoppa Cl RED TR15.....61 G1
Boscoppa Rd STAUS PL25.....64 D3
Boscundle Av FAL TR11.....22 B5
Boscundle Cl STAUS PL25.....65 G2
Boscundle Rw SALT PL12 *.....77 F3
Bosinney Rd STAUS PL25.....64 A4
Boskennal Dr HAYLE TR27.....26 D5
Boskennel Dr HAYLE TR27.....26 D5
Boskenza Ct STIVES TR26.....71 F3
Boskerris Crs STIVES TR26.....71 F1
Boskerris Rd STIVES TR26.....71 F2
Boskerris Ms STIVES TR26.....71 F2
Boskerris Rd STIVES TR26.....71 F1
Bosleake Rw RED TR15.....15 E3
Bosloggas Ms FAL TR11.....23 E3
Boslowick Cl FAL TR11.....22 A3
Boslowick Rd FAL TR11.....22 A4
Bosmeor Cl FAL TR11.....22 A4
Bosmeor Pk FAL TR11.....60 A4
Bosmeor Rd FAL TR11.....22 A4
Bosnoweth HELS TR13.....29 H4
Bosorne Cl LANDS TR19.....72 B4
Bosorne Rd LANDS TR19.....72 B4
Bosorne St LANDS TR19.....72 B4
Bosorne Ter LANDS TR19.....72 B4
Bossiney La TINT PL34.....78 D3
Bossiney Rd TINT PL34.....78 D4
Bostennack Pl STIVES TR26 *.....69 E3
Bostennack Ter
  STIVES TR26.....69 E3
Bosuen Rd NEWQ TR7.....46 D2
Bosvean Gdns TRU TR1.....84 D2
Bosvenna Vw BODM PL31.....10 D4
Bosvenna Vw PENZ TR18.....54 B2
Bosvigo La TRU TR1.....84 D3
Bosvigo Rd TRU TR1.....84 D3
Bosweddan Rd LANDS TR19.....72 A3
Bosweddan Ter LANDS TR19.....72 A3
Boswergy PENZ TR18.....54 C4
Botallack La LANDS TR19.....72 B1
Botallack Moor LANDS TR19.....72 B1
Bothwicks Rd NEWQ TR7.....46 B3
Boundary Cl PENZ TR18.....45 G3
Bounders La PERRAN TR6.....56 D5
Boundervean La
  CAMBORNE TR14.....14 A4
The Bound MBRK/KGSD PL10.....43 H5
Bounsall's La LAUN PL15.....31 F4
Boveway Dr LISK PL14.....33 H3
Bowden BUDE EX23 *.....13 F3
Bowdens Rw RED TR15.....60 D4
Bowjey Ct PENZ TR18 *.....45 G3
Bowjey Hi PENZ TR18 *.....45 G3
Bowjey Ter PENZ TR18 *.....45 G3
Bowles Rd FAL TR11.....15 H5
Bowling Gn STIVES TR26 *.....69 F2
Bowling Green Ct HAYLE TR27.....27 E4
Bowling Green Ter
  STIVES TR26.....69 F2
Bowder Dowr HAYLE TR27.....67 G1
Bowder Vean STAUS PL25.....64 C3
Boxwell Pk BODM PL31.....11 E3
Boyd Av PADS PL28.....48 A3
Bracken Cl BODM PL31.....10 D3
Bracken Ter NEWQ TR7.....46 B4
Brackwell Pl WADE PL27.....86 C2
Bradley Rd NEWQ TR7.....46 B4
Brake La MBRK/KGSD PL10.....42 C1
Bramble Cl NEWQ TR7.....46 D5
Bramble Hl BUDE EX23.....12 C3
The Brambles LOST PL22.....37 G4

Bramley Cl STAUS PL25.....64 B3
Bramley Pk BODM PL31.....11 E2
Branksome Dr WADE PL27.....87 F3
Branwell La PENZ TR18.....55 G2
Brays Pl STAUS PL25.....64 C3
Brea Arch CAMBORNE TR14.....15 F3
Bread St PENZ TR18.....55 E4
Breakwater Rd BUDE EX23.....12 A3
Brea Rd WADE PL27.....49 F2
Breaside CAMBORNE TR14.....15 F3
Brecke Hts WADE PL27.....86 B2
Brewers Rd TRU TR1.....85 H1
Brewery Hl STIVES TR26.....26 B4
Brewery La HELS TR13.....29 F3
Briansway SALT PL12.....76 B2
Briar Rd BUDE EX23.....12 C4
Briarwood LISK PL14.....33 G3
Bridge Cl NEWQ TR7.....46 D5
Bridgend LOOE PL13 *.....35 E2
Bridge Rd RTRUNW TR4.....57 H4
  STAUS PL25.....76 D4
The Bridges SALT PL12.....76 D4
Bridge St BUDE EX23.....13 F3
  PAR PL24.....50 C1
Bridge Vw WADE PL27.....86 D2
Brighton Ter PENZ TR18 *.....55 E5
Brisbane Ter LISK PL14.....33 E3
Britons Hl PENZ TR18.....55 F3
Brixton Ter RED TR15.....29 G3
Broadclose Hl BUDE EX23.....12 C3
Broad Pk LAUN PL15.....31 E2
Broad St LAUN PL15.....31 E2
  PADS PL28.....48 B3
  PENRYN TR10.....53 E4
  TRU TR1.....85 F2
Broad Wk HELS TR13.....29 H5
  SALT PL12.....76 D4
Brocks La MBRK/KGSD PL10.....45 E3
Brockstone Rd STAUS PL25.....64 D2
Bronescombe Cl
  PENRYN TR10.....53 E4
Brook Cl HELS TR13.....29 F3
Brookdown Ter SALT PL12.....76 D2
Brookdown Vls SALT PL12.....76 D2
Brook Dr BUDE EX23.....12 C1
Brooking Wy SALT PL12.....76 B2
Brooklyn Ter
  RTRUE/STMW TR2.....74 C2
  PENRYN TR10.....22 C2
Brook Rd FAL TR11.....22 B3
Brook's Hl SALT PL12 *.....76 D1
Brookside STAUS PL25.....64 C3
Brookside Cl LAUN PL15.....31 E1
Brook St FAL TR11.....22 C2
The Brook SALT PL12.....76 D1
Brookward Ter PENZ TR18.....54 B2
Brookway HAYLE TR27.....27 F2
Broomfield Dr BODM PL31.....10 A4
Broomfield Rd WADE PL27.....87 E3
Broom Hl SALT PL12.....76 C3
Broomhill La BUDE EX23.....13 E1
Browning Dr BODM PL31.....10 B4
Brownlow Pl BODM PL31 *.....10 C2
Browns Hl FOW PL23.....24 C2
Brown's Hl PENRYN TR10.....52 C2
Brunel Quays LOST PL22.....37 G4
Brunel Vw SALT PL12 *.....77 F2
Brush End STIVES TR26.....26 A4
Buckeys La RTRUE/STMW TR2.....74 D3
Buckinghams Ter
  .....82 B2
Bucklers La STAUS PL25.....65 E3
Buckler Village STAUS PL25.....65 E3
Budnic Est PERRAN TR6.....56 B3
Budnic Hl PERRAN TR6.....56 D3
Budnick Est PERRAN TR6 *.....56 C3
Budock Pl FAL TR11.....22 D2
Budock Ter FAL TR11.....22 D2
Bullan's La STIVES TR26.....69 E2
Bullans Ter STIVES TR26.....69 E2
Bulleid Wy BUDE EX23.....12 C4
Buller Pk LISK PL14.....33 G3
  SALT PL12.....76 B2
Buller Rd TOR PL11.....81 G4
Bullers Ter RED TR15.....61 F2
Buller St LOOE PL13.....35 E2
Bull Hl FOW PL23 *.....24 C2
Bullock La HELS TR13.....29 F4
Bullock Market Ter
  PENZ TR18.....55 E3
Bulwark Rd HELS TR13.....29 G3
Bunkers Hl STIVES TR26.....69 E2
Burden Cl BODM PL31.....10 B4
Bureau Pl WADE PL27.....86 D2
Buriton Rw PENZ TR18.....54 D4
Burley Cl TRU TR1.....85 H2
Burnards La BODM PL31 *.....10 C2
Burnett Cl SALT PL12.....77 E2
Burnthouse La HAYLE TR27.....27 F5
Burn Vw BUDE EX23.....12 B2
Burraton Rd SALT PL12.....76 A1
Burrow Rd STIVES TR26.....69 F2
The Burrows STIVES TR26.....69 E3
Burthallan La STIVES TR26.....68 D2
Bush La LAUN PL15.....31 G4
Buttercup Meadow
  LAUN PL15.....31 H5
Butts Pk LOST PL22.....37 G4

The Butts TINT PL34.....78 D3

C

Cabot Cl SALT PL12.....76 D3
Cades Parc HELS TR13.....29 G3
Cadogan Cl CAMBORNE TR14.....14 C5
Cadogan Rd CAMBORNE TR14.....14 C5
Caldwells Rd PENZ TR18.....55 E3
Calenick St TRU TR1.....85 E3
Cal Hi RTRUNW TR4.....61 G4
Callington Rd LISK PL14.....33 G1
  SALT PL12.....76 B1
Calshot Cl NEWQ TR7.....47 H2
Camaret Dr STIVES TR26.....69 F4
Cambeltown Wy FAL TR11.....23 E3
Cambridge Pl FAL TR11.....22 C3
Camel Cl PADS PL28.....48 B4
Camel Ct BODM PL31.....10 B1
Camel Trail PADS PL28.....48 C5
  WADE PL27.....86 C2
Cameron Cl BUDE EX23.....12 B1
Campfield Hl TRU TR1.....85 F2
Campian Cl SALT PL12.....76 C1
Camulias Wy NEWQ TR7.....21 E3
Canfield Pl RED TR15.....60 F3
Canfield Ter RED TR15.....60 F3
Cannis Rd STAUS PL25.....64 B1
Cannon Hl LISK PL14.....33 F3
Cannons Pl HELS TR13.....29 H2
Cannon Ter LISK PL14.....33 F3
Canons Pl HELS TR13.....29 H2
Canyke Rd BODM PL31.....11 F5
Cape Boswedden Rd
  LANDS TR19.....72 B4
Cape Cl LANDS TR19.....72 A4
Cape Cornwall St LANDS TR19.....72 B4
Cape Ter LANDS TR19.....72 B4
Captain's Wk FAL TR11.....22 C3
Caradon Dr LISK PL14.....33 E2
Caradon Hts LISK PL14.....33 G1
Caravan Pk MARAZ TR17.....38 C2
Carbeile La TOR PL11.....81 F4
Carbes La LOST PL22.....37 F4
Carbis Ct RED TR15.....60 D3
Carboth La LAUN PL15.....31 E4
Carclaze Rd STAUS PL25.....64 B1
Carclew Av NEWQ TR7.....46 D3
Carclew St RTRUS TR3.....19 F3
Carclew Ter RTRUS TR3.....19 E3
  TRU TR1 *.....85 F4
Cardell Rd BODM PL31.....10 C2
Cardell Wy NEWQ TR7.....46 D4
Cardinnis Gn LISK PL14.....33 G2
Cardinnis Rd PENZ TR18.....54 C4
Cardrew La RED TR15.....61 E1
Cardrew Dr RED TR15.....61 G2
Cardrew La RED TR15.....61 E2
Cardrew Ter RED TR15.....61 F2
Cardrew Wy RED TR15.....61 F2
Carew Gdns SALT PL12.....76 C2
Carew-Pole Cl TRU TR1.....85 G4
Carew Rd TRU TR1.....85 E2
Carew Ter TOR PL11.....81 G5
Carey Ct SALT PL12.....76 D2
Carey Pk HELS TR13.....29 F2
  STIVES TR26.....69 E3
Carlyon Ct RTRUS TR3.....83 E3
Carlyon Rd STAUS PL25.....64 A3
  TOR PL11 *.....81 E3
  TRU TR1 *.....85 H4
Carmen Sq PENZ TR18 *.....54 D2
Carminowe Crs PENZ TR18.....54 C4
Carminow Wy NEWQ TR7.....46 D2
Carmython Ct NEWQ TR7.....46 D2
Carnarthen Moor RED TR15.....15 H3
Carnarthen Rd
  CAMBORNE TR14.....14 D3
Carnarthen St
  CAMBORNE TR14.....14 D4
Carn Av CAMBORNE TR14.....15 E4
Carn Bosavern LANDS TR19.....72 C4
Carn Bosavern Cl LANDS TR19.....72 C4
Carn Brea Av RED TR15.....15 H1
Carn Brea La RED TR15.....15 H1
Carncrows St STIVES TR26.....69 G2
Carne Hi STAUS PL25.....62 C2
Carnellis Rd STIVES TR26.....68 D3
Carne Rd PENZ TR18.....45 G1
Carnes Blds PENZ TR18 *.....55 E3
Carneton Cl RNEWQ TR8.....21 E5
Carne View Cl CAMBORNE TR14.....15 F1
Carnglaze Cl LISK PL14.....33 H2
Carn Gwavas Ter PENZ TR18.....45 H3
Carninney La STIVES TR26.....71 E2
Carnon Crs RTRUS TR3.....19 E4
Carnon Ter RTRUS TR3.....19 E4
Carnoustie Dr SALT PL12.....76 B3
Carn Rock PENRYN TR10.....53 E4
Carnsew Meadow HAYLE TR27.....26 C5
Carnsew Rd HAYLE TR27.....26 C5
Carnsmerry Crs STAUS PL25.....64 B3
Carnstabba Rd STIVES TR26.....68 D4
The Carn PENZ TR18 *.....45 G3
Caroline Cl HAYLE TR27.....27 G2
Caroline Rw HAYLE TR27.....27 G2
Carpenter Cl BODM PL31.....10 C2
Carpenter St BODM PL31.....10 C2

Carpmael Av RNEWQ TR8 * 47 E5
Carrack Dhu STIVES TR26 * 69 F2
Carrack Dhu Est STIVES TR26 * .. 69 E2
Carrack Gladden STIVES TR26 .... 71 F1
Carrallack La LANDS TR19 .... 72 B5
Carrallack Ms LANDS TR19 .... 72 B5
Carriage Parc RTRUNW TR4 .... 57 H4
Carrickowel Crs STAUS PL25 ..... 65 E2
Carrick Rd FAL TR11 .... 22 A4
Carrick Wy RTRUE/STMW TR2 ...... 74 C2
Carrine Rd TRU TR1 .... 84 A4
Carrisbrooke Wy SALT PL12 ...... 76 A3
Carnrown Gdns RED TR15 .... 61 C5
Carter CI NEWQ TR7 .... 46 D4
Carteret Rd BUDE EX23 .... 12 C3
Carthew CI PL14 .... 33 C3
  STIVES TR26 .... 69 E2
Carthew Ct STIVES TR26 .... 68 D2
Carthew Ter STIVES TR26 .... 69 E2
Carthew Wy STIVES TR26 .... 69 E2
Carvoza Rd TRU TR1 .... 85 F2
Carwin Ri HAYLE TR27 .... 27 C2
Castel Wary CI HELS TR13 .... 29 F4
Casterills Rd HELS TR13 .... 29 H5
Castle Canyke Rd BODM PL31 ..... 11 E4
Castle CI FAL TR11 .... 23 C3
Castle Ct SALT PL12 .... 76 B3
Castle Dr BODM PL31 .... 11 E2
  FAL TR11 .... 23 C3
  RTRUE/STMW TR2 .... 74 A2
Castle Dyke LAUN PL15 .... 31 F3
Castle Gdns LISK PL14 .... 33 F2
Castle Gn HELS TR13 .... 29 F4
Castle Hts TINT PL34 .... 78 B3
Castle HI LISK PL14 * 33 F2
  LOST PL22 .... 37 F5
  SALT PL12 .... 76 B5
Castle Hill Ct BODM PL31 * 10 D2
Castle Hill Gdns BODM PL31 ..... 11 E2
Castle Horneck La PENZ TR18 * .. 54 C4
Castle Horneck Rd
  RPENZ TR20 .... 54 B4
Castle La LISK PL14 .... 33 F2
Castlemead CI SALT PL12 .... 76 C2
Castlemead Dr SALT PL12 .... 76 C2
Castle Mdw LAUN PL15 .... 30 D5
Castle Ri TRU TR1 .... 85 E2
Castle Rd PENZ TR18 .... 55 C4
  TINT PL34 .... 78 B3
Castle St BODM PL31 .... 10 D2
  LAUN PL15 .... 31 F3
  LISK PL14 .... 33 F2
  LOOE PL13 .... 35 F3
  TRU TR1 .... 85 E3
Castle Vw LISK PL14 .... 33 F2
  LOST PL22 .... 37 H5
  SALT PL12 .... 76 B3
  TINT PL34 .... 78 B3
Castle View CI RED TR15 .... 61 G2
Caswarth Dr PADS PL28 .... 48 B3
Catchfrench CI LISK PL14 .... 33 H2
Cathedral La TRU TR1 * 85 F3
Cathedral Vw TRU TR1 .... 84 D1
Catherine CI BUDE EX23 .... 12 C4
  PERRAN TR6 .... 56 C3
Catherine's HI LAUN PL15 .... 31 G3
Caunter Rd LISK PL14 .... 33 G2
Causewayhead PENZ TR18 .... 55 E3
The Causeway FAL TR11 .... 22 B2
  HAYLE TR27 .... 67 F1
Causley CI LAUN PL15 .... 31 F2
Cedar CI TOR PL11 .... 81 E5
Cedar Dr TOR PL11 .... 81 E5
Cedar Gv BUDE EX23 .... 12 C1
The Cedars TRU TR1 .... 85 E5
Celia Hts BODM PL31 .... 11 E4
Centenary Row Middle
  CAMBORNE TR14 * 14 D3
Centenary Rw West
  CAMBORNE TR14 .... 14 D4
Centenary St CAMBORNE TR14 ..... 14 D4
Central Av STAUS PL25 .... 64 B2
Central Sq NEWQ TR7 .... 46 A3
Central St NEWQ TR7 * 46 A3
Century CI HELS TR13 .... 29 H1
  STAUS PL25 .... 64 C1
Century Ct NEWQ TR7 .... 47 F2
Ceres Ct BUDE EX23 .... 12 C4
Chainwalk Dr TRU TR1 .... 85 E1
Chalacombe Gdns
  PENRYN TR10 .... 52 B3
Challenger Quay FAL TR11 * 23 E3
Champion's Ct HELS TR13 .... 29 F3
Champions Yd PENZ TR18 * 55 E4
Chancery La PENZ TR18 * 55 E4
Chandlers Wk STAUS PL25 .... 64 A4
Chandos PI STAUS PL25 .... 63 H4
Channel Vw FOW PL23 * 24 C2
  STAUS PL25 .... 64 D1
  STIVES TR26 .... 69 E5
Channel View Ter RED TR15 * 61 F4
Channon Rd SALT PL12 .... 76 B1
Chantry La LOOE PL13 .... 35 G2
Chapel CI CAMBORNE TR14 .... 15 E2
Chapeldown Rd TOR PL11 * 81 F5
Chapel End STAUS PL25 * 65 G2
Chapel Gnd LOOE PL13 * 35 G2
Chapel HI CAMBORNE TR14 .... 15 F3
  HAYLE TR27 .... 67 E3
  LAUN PL15 .... 31 E4

NEWQ TR7 .... 46 A3
PERRAN TR6 .... 56 C5
RED TR15 .... 15 H1
TRU TR1 .... 84 D3
Chapel La BODM PL31 .... 10 C2
  FOW PL23 .... 24 D4
  HAYLE TR27 .... 27 F3
  PENRYN TR10 .... 52 D4
  STAUS PL25 .... 65 F1
  WADE PL27 .... 86 C3
Chapel Pk LAUN PL15 .... 30 D4
Chapel Park Ter LAUN PL15 ...... 31 E4
Chapel Point La MEVA PL26 ...... 41 H5
Chapel Rd CAMBORNE TR14 .... 15 F2
  LANDS TR19 .... 72 B4
  PAR PL24 .... 51 E4
  PENZ TR18 .... 54 C1
  SALT PL12 .... 76 A2
Chapel Rw RED TR15 * 61 E3
Chapel Sq MEVA PL26 .... 41 G3
Chapel St CAMBORNE TR14 .... 14 C4
  CAMEL PL32 .... 17 E4
  LANDS TR19 .... 72 B3
  MARAZ TR17 .... 38 B3
  MEVA PL26 .... 41 G3
  PENZ TR18 .... 55 E3
  RED TR15 .... 61 E3
  STIVES TR26 .... 69 F5
Chapel Ter HAYLE TR27 .... 26 D4
  HELS TR13 * 29 F4
  PAR PL24 .... 51 E4
  RED TR15 .... 60 C1
  RTRUE/STMW TR2 .... 74 C2
  RTRUS 19 F4
Chapman Ct SALT PL12 .... 76 A2
Chapmans Wy STAUS PL25 .... 64 B3
Chard Ter FAL TR11 * 22 C3
Chariot Rd RED TR15 .... 60 A4
Charles Av FAL TR11 .... 22 A4
Charles Bassett CI HELS TR13 ... 29 H4
Charles CI STAUS PL25 .... 64 C4
Charles St PENZ TR18 .... 45 G1
  TRU TR1 .... 85 F2
Charlestown Rd STAUS PL25 ...... 64 D4
Charter CI HELS TR13 .... 29 F5
  PENRYN TR10 .... 53 E4
Charter Dr PENRYN TR10 .... 53 E4
Charter Wy LISK PL14 .... 33 H5
Chatsworth Wy STAUS PL25 .... 65 F5
Chellew Rd TRU TR1 .... 85 H2
Cheltenham PI NEWQ TR7 .... 46 A3
Chenhalls CI HAYLE TR27 .... 67 F3
Chenhalls Rd HAYLE TR27 .... 67 E3
Chenoweth CI
  CAMBORNE TR14 .... 14 B2
Cherrill Gdns BUDE EX23 .... 12 C1
Cherry Gdns PENZ TR18 * 55 F3
Cherry Tree CI BODM PL31 .... 10 B3
Cherry Tree Ms STAUS PL25 ...... 64 A4
Chesnut CI SALT PL12 .... 76 A2
Chester CI NEWQ TR7 .... 46 D5
Chester Rd NEWQ TR7 .... 46 D5
Chesterton PI NEWQ TR7 .... 46 D2
Chestnut CI FAL TR11 .... 22 B1
  TOR PL11 .... 81 E4
Chestnut Gv BODM PL31 .... 10 A3
Cheviot Rd NEWQ TR7 .... 46 B5
Chichester Crs NEWQ TR7 .... 46 C5
Chili Rd RED TR15 .... 60 A4
Chings Aly LISK PL14 * 31 F3
Chings Ct LAUN PL15 * 31 F3
Chipponds Dr STAUS PL25 .... 63 F4
Chirgwin Ct PENZ TR18 * 55 E4
Chirgwin Rd TRU TR1 .... 85 F3
Chisholme CI STAUS PL25 .... 64 A4
Chough CI LAUN PL15 .... 31 H5
Chough Crs STAUS PL25 .... 64 C5
Choughs CI CAMBORNE TR14 .... 14 A2
Christian Wy NEWQ TR7 .... 47 F2
Church Av FOW PL23 * 24 C2
Church End LOOE PL13 .... 35 F3
Churchfield PI PAR PL24 .... 50 C2
Church Hl HELS TR13 .... 29 F3
Church La G LISK PL14 .... 33 F3
Church HI HELS TR13 .... 29 F3
  PENRYN TR10 .... 53 E3
  RTRUE/STMW TR2 .... 74 C2
  TINT PL34 .... 78 B4
Churchill Wk SALT PL12 * 76 D4
Churchlands LOOE PL13 .... 35 F1
Church La BODM PL31 .... 10 D2
  BUDE EX23 .... 12 B3
  CAMBORNE TR14 .... 14 C3
  HELS TR13 .... 29 F3
  LOST PL22 .... 37 F4
  MEVA PL26 .... 41 G2
  NEWQ TR7 .... 47 G2
  PADS PL28 .... 48 B3
  RED TR15 .... 60 D5
  STIVES TR26 .... 26 B4
Church Lea LAUN PL15 .... 30 D2
Church Pk BODM PL31 .... 10 D5
Church Park Ms WADE PL27 .... 86 C4
Church Pth BUDE EX23 .... 12 A3
Church PI LISK PL14 .... 33 F3
  STIVES TR26 .... 69 F2
Church Rd CAMBORNE TR14 .... 14 A3
  PENRYN TR10 .... 52 B1
  RPENZ TR20 .... 54 A1

RTRUS TR3 .... 18 B5
SALT PL12 .... 76 C4
STAUS PL25 .... 65 E4
STIVES TR26 .... 26 B4
Church Side FOW PL23 * 24 C2
Church Sq BODM PL31 * 10 D2
  LANDS TR19 .... 72 C1
Church Stile LAUN PL15 * 31 F3
Church St CAMBORNE TR14 .... 14 C4
  FAL TR11 .... 22 D2
  HAYLE TR27 .... 67 F4
  HELS TR13 .... 29 F3
  LANDS TR19 .... 72 C4
  LAUN PL15 .... 31 F3
  LISK PL14 .... 33 F2
  LOOE PL13 .... 35 F3
  MEVA PL26 .... 41 G2
  NEWQ TR7 .... 47 G3
  PADS PL28 .... 48 A3
  PAR PL24 .... 50 C3
  PENZ TR18 .... 45 G3
  STAUS PL25 .... 63 H4
Church St North LISK PL14 ...... 33 F3
Church St South LISK PL14 ...... 33 F3
Church Ter RTRUS TR3 .... 19 E4
Churchtown HAYLE TR27 .... 27 E2
Churchtown V SALT PL12 .... 76 C4
Church Vw CI STIVES TR26 * 54 B3
Church View Rd
  CAMBORNE TR14 .... 15 E2
Church Wk RED TR15 * 60 D1
Church Wy FAL TR11 .... 22 A3
Churchway MARAZ TR17 .... 38 D3
  RPENZ TR20 .... 54 A1
Chy An Chy STIVES TR26 * 69 E2
Chyandaunce CI PENZ TR18 .... 55 F1
Chyandaunce Ter PENZ TR18 * 55 F1
Chyandor CI PAR PL24 .... 50 D4
Chyandour RED TR15 .... 60 D4
Chyandour Cliff PENZ TR18 ...... 55 F3
Chy-an-Dour CI STIVES TR26 ..... 68 C4
Chyandour Coombe
  PENZ TR18 .... 55 F2
Chyandour La PENZ TR18 .... 55 F3
Chyandour PI PENZ TR18 .... 55 F3
Chyandour Sq PENZ TR18 * 55 F2
Chyandour Ter PENZ TR18 * 55 F2
Chy An Dowr HAYLE TR27 .... 27 E3
Chy Cober HAYLE TR27 .... 27 E2
Chycoose Parc RTRUS TR3 .... 19 H5
Chycornick Ter PENZ TR18 * 55 F1
Chygothow HELS TR13 * 29 G5
Chy Hwel TRU TR1 .... 85 H1
Chy Kensa CI HAYLE TR27 .... 27 E4
Chylan Crs NEWQ TR7 .... 47 G3
Chy Nampara FAL TR11 * 22 C2
Chynance Dr NEWQ TR7 .... 46 A4
Chynoon Gdns STAUS PL25 .... 64 C1
Chynoweth Gdns PENZ TR18 .... 55 F1
Chy Pons STAUS PL25 .... 63 F3
Chypon Ter PENZ TR18 * 45 G2
Chypraze Ct CAMBORNE TR14 ...... 14 A3
Chytroose CI HELS TR13 .... 29 H1
Chyvelah Ope TRU TR1 .... 83 G3
Chyvelah Rd RTRUNW TR4 .... 82 D3
Chyvelah V TRU TR1 .... 83 G3
Chyvellas CI PENZ TR18 .... 45 F3
Chyverton CI NEWQ TR7 .... 46 C4
Chyvogue Meadow RTRUS TR3 ...... 18 B4
Chywoone Av FAL TR11 .... 45 G3
Chywoone Crs PENZ TR18 .... 45 G3
Chywoone HI PENZ TR18 .... 45 G3
Chywoone Rd PENZ TR18 .... 45 G3
Chywoon Gdns RED TR15 .... 60 A3
City Rd TRU TR1 .... 85 G3
Claremont Av RED TR15 .... 61 E3
Claremont Ms RED TR15 .... 61 E3
Claremont Rd RED TR15 .... 61 E3
Claremont Ter FAL TR11 .... 22 C1
  TRU TR1 .... 85 E2
Clarence PI PENZ TR18 .... 54 C1
Clarence Rd STAUS PL25 .... 63 G3
  TOR PL11 .... 81 F4
Clarence St PENZ TR18 .... 55 E4
Clarence Ter PENZ TR18 * 55 F3
  WADE PL27 .... 86 C3
Clare Ter FAL TR11 .... 22 D2
Claybourne CI STAUS PL25 .... 64 C1
Clear Vw SALT PL12 .... 76 D2
Clease Mdw CAMEL PL32 .... 17 E5
Clease Rd CAMEL PL32 .... 17 E5
Cleaverfield Ms LAUN PL15 ...... 31 F2
The Cleaves LAUN PL15 .... 31 F2
The Cleave MBRK/KGSD PL10 ...... 43 H4
Cleavewell WADE PL27 .... 86 D4
Cledma Bank HAYLE TR27 .... 67 F2
Clegg Av TOR PL11 .... 80 D4
Clemens Av NEWQ TR7 * 46 A5
Clemens CI NEWQ TR7 .... 47 E4
Clemens Rd PENZ TR18 .... 54 D4
Clemo Rd LISK PL14 .... 33 H1
Cleswith TRU TR1 * 84 B2
Clevedon Rd NEWQ TR7 .... 46 A4
Cleveland Av LOOE PL13 .... 35 F2
The Clies HELS TR13 * 29 G4
Clifden CI NEWQ TR7 .... 46 B4
Clifden Rd STAUS PL25 .... 64 B1
Clifden Ter BODM PL31 * 10 C2
  LOST PL22 .... 37 F4
Cliff End Pk WADE PL27 .... 87 E2

Cliff La MBRK/KGSD PL10 .... 42 B2
Cliff Park Ter WADE PL27 * 86 D3
Cliff Ri FOW PL23 .... 24 D4
Cliff Rd FAL TR11 .... 23 E4
  HELS TR13 .... 58 A3
  LANDS TR19 .... 45 H4
  MEVA PL26 .... 41 H3
  NEWQ TR7 .... 46 B3
  PERRAN TR6 .... 56 A3
Cliff St MEVA PL26 .... 41 H2
Cliff View CI CAMBORNE TR14 .... 14 D2
Cliff View Ter CAMBORNE TR14 ... 14 D2
Clifton Crs FAL TR11 .... 22 C2
Clifton Gdns TRU TR1 * 84 D3
Clifton HI PENZ TR18 .... 45 G2
Clifton PI FAL TR11 .... 22 C2
Clifton Ter FAL TR11 .... 22 C2
  HAYLE TR27 .... 26 D3
  LISK PL14 .... 32 D3
  PENZ TR18 * 45 G2
Clijah CI RED TR15 .... 61 F5
Clinton CI BUDE EX23 .... 12 C3
Clinton Dr STAUS PL25 .... 63 G4
Clinton Pas RED TR15 .... 61 E4
Clinton Rd RED TR15 .... 61 F4
Clodgey La HELS TR13 .... 29 G5
Clodgey Wy HELS TR13 .... 29 H5
Clodgy Vw STIVES TR26 .... 69 E5
Close HI RED TR15 .... 61 E2
The Close CAMEL PL32 .... 17 F4
  PENZ TR18 .... 54 D2
  SALT PL12 .... 76 B2
  TRU TR1 .... 85 H1
Clos Trevithick
  CAMBORNE TR14 * 14 D4
Clover Wk SALT PL12 .... 76 A2
Coachmans Ar LOOE PL13 * 35 E2
Coach House La STAUS PL25 ...... 63 H3
Coach La RED TR15 .... 60 D4
Coastguard Crs PENZ TR18 .... 55 F3
Coastguard Station MI
  MEVA PL26 .... 41 H3
Coast Vw BUDE EX23 .... 13 E3
Cobbs Well FOW PL23 * 24 C2
Cobbs Well HI FOW PL23 * 24 C2
Cocklawelva WADE PL27 .... 49 F2
Codiford Crs CAMBORNE TR14 ..... 14 D2
Coffa Bridge CI LOST PL22 ...... 37 G4
Coffeelake Meadow LOST PL22 .... 37 G4
Coinagehall PI PENZ TR18 * 55 F5
Coinagehall St HELS TR13 .... 29 F4
Coldrose Ct TRU TR1 .... 84 D3
Coldstyle Rd LISK PL14 .... 33 F1
Colebrook Rd RED TR15 .... 60 D3
Colenso PI STAUS PL25 .... 64 A4
Colinsey PI PENZ TR18 .... 54 D2
Colinsey Rd PENZ TR18 .... 54 D2
College Gn BODM PL31 .... 10 D5
  STAUS PL25 .... 63 H4
College HI PENRYN TR10 .... 52 D4
College La BODM PL31 .... 10 D5
College Ope PENRYN TR10 .... 53 E4
College Rd CAMEL PL32 .... 17 E4
College St CAMBORNE TR14 .... 14 B3
College Wy TRU TR1 .... 83 G3
Collygree Parc RPENZ TR20 ...... 39 G2
Col-Moor CI HAYLE TR27 .... 27 G2
Colvreath Rd NEWQ TR7 .... 46 C3
Colworth Av FAL TR11 .... 22 B3
Colwyn Rd TOR PL11 .... 81 F4
Commercial Rd HAYLE TR27 .... 27 E3
  PENRYN TR10 .... 53 E3
Commercial Sq
  CAMBORNE TR14 * 14 C3
Commercial St
  CAMBORNE TR14 .... 14 C3
Commercial Ter PADS PL28 * 48 A3
Commissioners Rd WADE PL27 ..... 86 C2
Comprigney CI TRU TR1 .... 84 D2
Comprigney HI TRU TR1 .... 84 D2
Condurrow Rd
  CAMBORNE TR14 .... 15 F5
Connoc CI LISK PL14 .... 33 G3
Consols STIVES TR26 .... 68 C4
Convent CI SALT PL12 .... 76 D2
Conway CI FAL TR11 .... 22 A2
Cook Ct SALT PL12 .... 76 A2
Cooksland La BODM PL31 .... 11 F1
Cooksland Rd BODM PL31 .... 11 F3
Coombe La PENZ TR18 .... 54 D2
Coombe Pk MBRK/KGSD PL10 .... 43 H4
  PENZ TR18 .... 55 E3
  SALT PL12 .... 77 E3
The Coombe PENZ TR18 .... 55 E2
Coombe Rd PENZ TR18 .... 55 E2
  SALT PL12 .... 77 E4
Coombe V PENZ TR18 .... 45 F1
Coombe Vw PERRAN TR6 .... 56 A4
Cooperage La STAUS PL25 .... 63 G3
Cooperage Rd STAUS PL25 .... 63 G3
Cooper's La HELS TR13 .... 58 B3
Coosebean La RTRUNW TR4 .... 84 C2
Copes Gdns TRU TR1 .... 85 E2
Copper HI HAYLE TR27 .... 27 F3
Copper Ter HAYLE TR27 .... 27 E3
The Copse STAUS PL25 .... 64 C2
Cormoran Ct MARAZ TR17 .... 38 C3
Cormorant Dr STAUS PL25 .... 64 D3

Corner Gdns *BUDE* EX23 ....13 F3
Cornflower Crs *LAUN* PL15 ....31 H5
Cornhill Rd *PAR* PL24 ....50 B2
Cornish Crs *TRU* TR1 ....84 B2
Cornubia Cl *HAYLE* TR27 ....27 E4
   TRU TR1 ....85 G1
Cornwall County *PENRYN* TR10 ...52 D3
Cornwall Ter *PENZ* TR18 ....55 E5
   TRU TR1 * 85 E2
Coronation Av
   CAMBORNE TR14 ....14 A3
Coronation Pl *HELS* TR13 ....29 C5
Coronation Rd *HAYLE* TR27 ....27 F4
   RED TR15 ....61 F4
Coronation Ter *TRU* TR1 * 84 D3
Coronation Wy *NEWQ* TR7 ....47 F2
Corporation Rd *BODM* PL31 ....31 F4
Corva Cl *STIVES* TR26 ....68 D4
Corva Rd *STIVES* TR26 ....68 D4
Cot Hl *BUDE* EX23 ....13 G2
Cotsland Rd *TRU* TR1 ....85 H2
Cott Rd *LOST* PL22 ....37 G4
Cot Va *LANDS* TR19 ....72 A5
Couchwell La *LOST* PL22 ....37 F4
Coulsons Blds *PENZ* TR18 * 55 E5
Coulsons Pl *PENZ* TR18 ....55 E5
Coulsons Ter *PENZ* TR18 * 55 E5
Countess Bridge La
   HAYLE TR27 ....67 H5
Count House La *STIVES* TR26 ....71 E1
Court Cocking *STIVES* TR26 * 69 F2
Courtenay La *LOOE* PL13 ....35 F2
Court Gdns *STAUS* PL25 ....63 H4
Courtlands *SALT* PL12 ....76 D4
Courtlands Crs *STAUS* PL25 ....65 G4
Courtney Cl *LOOE* PL13 ....35 G2
Courtney Rd *LISK* PL14 ....33 C2
   STAUS PL25 ....64 B2
   TRU TR1 ....84 D2
The Courtyard *TRU* TR1 * 84 C3
Cove Hl *RTRUS* TR3 ....18 A5
Cove Meadow *TOR* PL11 ....81 F2
Cowdray Cl *SALT* PL12 ....76 D3
Cowdray Ter *SALT* PL12 * 76 D3
Cow Lard La *LAUN* PL15 ....30 D5
Cowling Rd *RTRUS* TR3 ....19 F1
Crabbtree Cl *LISK* PL14 ....33 E3
Crabtree La *RBODM* PL30 ....10 B5
Cranberry Rd *CAMBORNE* TR14 ...14 A4
Crane Rd *CAMBORNE* TR14 ....14 B4
Cranfield Rd *CAMBORNE* TR14 .....14 A4
Crantock St *NEWQ* TR7 ....21 H2
Creathorne Rd *BUDE* EX23 ....12 C1
Creeping La *PENZ* TR18 ....54 C5
Crembling Well *RED* TR15 ....60 B4
Cremyll Rd *TOR* PL11 ....81 G5
Crescent Cl *HAYLE* TR27 ....84 D3
Crescent Gdns *TRU* TR1 ....84 D3
Crescent Ri *TRU* TR1 ....84 D3
Crescent Rd *TRU* TR1 ....84 D3
The Crescent *BUDE* EX23 ....12 B3
   CAMBORNE TR14 ....14 C4
   HELS TR13 ....58 A1
   LISK PL14 ....33 F2
   LOOE PL13 ....35 E5
   NEWQ TR7 ....46 A4
   STAUS PL25 ....64 B3
   STIVES TR26 ....71 F3
   TRU TR1 ....84 D3
Creswell Ter *BODM* PL31 * 10 C2
Cribbage Ter *BODM* PL31 * 10 C2
Cricketers Hollow *WADE* PL27 .....49 H1
Crinnick's Hl *BODM* PL31 ....10 D3
Crinnis Cl *STAUS* PL25 ....65 H4
Crinnis Rd *STAUS* PL25 ....65 E4
Crinnis Wood Av *STAUS* PL25 ......65 G4
Crockwell St *BODM* PL31 ....10 D2
Croftlands *WADE* PL27 ....49 H1
Croft Rd *PENZ* TR18 ....54 C5
Crofty Cl *RED* TR15 ....15 H1
Cromwell Rd *STAUS* PL25 ....64 C4
Crooklets Cl *BUDE* EX23 ....12 A1
Crooklets Rd *BUDE* EX23 ....12 A1
Cross Cl *NEWQ* TR7 ....47 F2
Cross La *BODM* PL31 ....10 D2
   STAUS PL25 ....63 H4
Cross Lanes *LAUN* PL15 ....31 F1
Cross Park Ter *MEVA* PL26 ....41 G2
Cross St *CAMBORNE* TR14 ....14 C4
   HAYLE TR27 ....27 E3
   HELS TR13 ....29 F3
   PADS PL28 ....48 B3
   PENZ TR18 ....55 E4
   RED TR15 ....61 E4
   WADE PL27 ....86 C2
Crosswalla Flds *HELS* TR13 ....22 B4
Crossways *FAL* TR11 ....22 B4
Crown Cl *NEWQ* TR7 ....46 D5
Crows-an-Eglos *STIVES* TR26 ....68 D4
Crun-Melyn Parc *HAYLE* TR27 .....26 D5
Cryon Vw *TRU* TR1 ....83 H3
Culverland Pk *LISK* PL14 ....33 F1
Culver Rd *SALT* PL12 ....77 E3
The Culvery *WADE* PL27 ....86 C4
Cunnack Cl *HELS* TR13 ....58 B2
Cunningham Pk *PENRYN* TR10 ....52 A4
Cunningham Wy *SALT* PL12 * 76 C3
Curlew Cl *NEWQ* TR7 ....21 G3
Curnows Rd *STIVES* TR26 ....69 F4
Custom House Ct *PENZ* TR18 * 55 F4
Custom House Hl *FOW* PL23 ....24 D4

Custom House La *PENZ* TR18 ....55 E4
Cuth Avallon *TRU* TR1 ....85 E3
Cyril Rd *TRU* TR1 ....85 E2

D

Daglands Hl *FOW* PL23 ....24 C2
Daglands Rd *FOW* PL23 ....24 C3
Dale Cl *NEWQ* TR7 ....46 D5
Dale Rd *NEWQ* TR7 ....46 A2
Dane Rd *NEWQ* TR7 ....46 A2
Daniel Cl *STAUS* PL25 ....64 D3
Daniel Ct *TRU* TR1 ....85 E4
Daniell Rd *TRU* TR1 ....84 D4
Daniell St *TRU* TR1 ....85 E4
Daniel Pl *PENZ* TR18 ....55 E5
Daniels La *STAUS* PL25 ....64 D3
Danmore Cl *TINT* PL34 ....78 C4
Dark La *CAMEL* PL32 ....17 E4
   LISK PL14 ....33 G2
   LOST PL22 ....37 F5
Darloe La *LOOE* PL13 ....35 E3
Dartmoor Vw *SALT* PL12 ....76 D1
Daubuz Cl *TRU* TR1 ....85 E1
Daubuz Ct *TRU* TR1 ....85 E2
Davey's Cl *FAL* TR11 ....22 A5
David Penhaligon Wy *TRU* TR1 ...85 F4
Davy Cl *TOR* PL11 ....81 E4
Dawe Crs *BODM* PL31 ....10 B4
Dawes La *LOOE* PL13 ....35 F4
   MBRK/KGSD PL10 ....43 F1
Dawn Rd *LISK* PL14 ....33 H4
Daw's Meadow *CAMEL* PL32 ....17 G4
Deacon Cl *SALT* PL12 ....77 E4
Deacon Dr *SALT* PL12 ....77 E4
Dean Hl *LISK* PL14 ....33 E2
Dean Rd *LISK* PL14 * 33 E2
Dean St *LISK* PL14 ....33 E2
Dean Ter *LISK* PL14 ....33 E2
Deeble Cl *RTRUS* TR3 ....82 D3
Deeble Dr *PAR* PL24 ....50 C4
Deer Pk *NEWQ* TR7 ....46 A3
   SALT PL12 ....77 E2
Degibna La *LIZ* TR12 ....59 F3
Delavue Camel PL32 ....17 E5
Dell Cl *PENZ* TR18 ....45 G1
Dennis Av *PADS* PL28 ....48 B4
Dennison Av *STAUS* PL25 ....64 D3
Dennison Rd *BODM* PL31 ....10 C2
Dennis Rd *LISK* PL14 ....33 G2
   PADS PL28 ....48 B3
De Pass Gdns *FAL* TR11 ....23 E4
De Pass Rd *FAL* TR11 ....23 E3
Dereham Ter *TRU* TR1 * 84 D3
Derowen Dr *HAYLE* TR27 ....67 G3
Devonport Hl
   MBRK/KGSD PL10 ....43 H4
Devonshire Ter *TRU* TR1 * 85 E4
Devoran La *RTRUS* TR3 ....19 E4
Diana Cl *FAL* TR11 ....22 A3
Diddies La *BUDE* EX23 ....13 H3
Diddies Rd *BUDE* EX23 ....13 G3
The Digey *STIVES* TR26 ....69 F2
Dithmarsche Wy *STAUS* PL25 .....63 G5
Dobbs La *TRU* TR1 ....84 C3
Dobell Rd *STAUS* PL25 ....64 B3
Dockacre Rd *LAUN* PL15 ....31 F3
Dockey *LAUN* PL15 ....31 F4
Dock La *PENZ* TR18 ....55 F4
The Docks *FAL* TR11 ....23 F2
Doctor's La *LISK* PL14 ....33 F2
Dodbrook *MBRK/KGSD* PL10 ....43 F2
Dola La *RPENZ* TR20 ....39 H5
Dolcoath Av *CAMBORNE* TR14 ....14 D2
Dolcoath Cl *CAMBORNE* TR14 .....15 E2
Dolcoath Rd *CAMBORNE* TR14 ....14 D3
Donierts Cl *LISK* PL14 ....33 E3
Donkey La *MBRK/KGSD* PL10 ......42 D3
Donnington Rd *PENZ* TR18 ....45 G1
Dopps Ter *RED* TR15 ....61 F3
Doubletrees Cl *PAR* PL24 ....50 B4
Doubletrees Ct *PAR* PL24 ....50 B4
Doulton Rd *STAUS* PL25 ....64 D3
Dove St *STIVES* TR26 ....69 F3
Down Cl *SALT* PL12 ....77 E3
Downside Cl *NEWQ* TR7 ....46 D5
Downs La *LAUN* PL15 ....31 F3
Downs Lane Pk *LOOE* PL13 ....34 D3
Downs Rd *LOOE* PL13 ....35 E2
The Downs *LOOE* PL13 ....35 E5
Downstream Cl *PADS* PL28 ....48 A3
Downs Vw *BUDE* EX23 ....12 B1
   LOOE PL13 ....35 E3
Dracaena Av *FAL* TR11 ....53 G5
   HAYLE TR27 ....27 F3
Dracaena Cs *HAYLE* TR27 ....27 F3
Dracaena Pl *FAL* TR11 ....22 B2
Dracaena Vw *FAL* TR11 ....22 B2
Drakefield Dr *SALT* PL12 ....77 E2
Drake Rd *PADS* PL28 ....48 A3
Draycott Ter *STIVES* TR26 * 69 F4
Drift Cl *LANDS* TR19 ....44 B2
Drillfield La *STIVES* TR26 ....69 F3
The Drive *HELS* TR13 ....29 H2
Driving La *PAR* PL24 ....51 E1
Droskyn Cl *PERRAN* TR6 ....56 A3
Droskyn Point *PERRAN* TR6 ....56 A3
Droskyn Wy *PERRAN* TR6 ....56 A3

Druckham Pl *LAUN* PL15 ....31 F4
Druckham Ter *LAUN* PL15 * 31 G4
Druids Ldg *RED* TR15 * 60 A5
Druid's Rd *RED* TR15 ....60 A5
Duchy Av *NEWQ* TR7 ....47 F2
Duchy Cl *LAUN* PL15 ....31 F2
   STAUS PL25 ....63 H4
Dudman Rd *TRU* TR1 ....84 B3
Dudnance La *RED* TR15 ....30 D1
Duke St *LISK* PL14 ....37 F4
   LOST PL22 ....37 F4
   PADS PL28 ....48 B3
   PENZ TR18 * 45 G2
   STAUS PL25 ....63 H4
Duke's Wy *NEWQ* TR7 ....46 A4
Duke Ter *LAUN* PL15 ....30 D1
Duncannon Dr *FAL* TR11 ....22 B2
Dungarth Gn *LISK* PL14 ....33 G2
Dungarth Rd *LISK* PL14 ....33 G2
Dunheved Flds *LAUN* PL15 ....31 E4
Dunheved Rd *LAUN* PL15 ....31 E4
   SALT PL12 ....76 D4
Dun Mere Cl *PAR* PL24 ....51 E4
Dunstan Cl *PENRYN* TR10 ....52 C3
Dunstanville Ter *FAL* TR11 * 22 C1
Dunvegan Rd *PENRYN* TR10 ....52 C3
Dunveth Rd *WADE* PL27 ....86 B3
Durgan La *PENRYN* TR10 ....52 D3
Durston Rd *BUDE* EX23 ....12 C1
Dutson Rd *LAUN* PL15 ....31 F2
Dutson Ter *LAUN* PL15 ....31 F2
Dynas-la Rd *STIVES* TR26 ....69 F4

E

The Earl's Dr *MBRK/KGSD* PL10 ..43 H5
Earls Ri *NEWQ* TR7 ....47 E4
Eastbourne Cl *STAUS* PL25 ....64 B4
Eastbourne Rd *STAUS* PL25 ....64 A4
East Charles St
   CAMBORNE TR14 ....14 C4
East Cliff *LOOE* PL13 ....35 F3
Eastcliffe Rd *PAR* PL24 ....50 A4
East Cliff La *MARAZ* TR17 ....38 C5
East Cl *HELS* TR13 ....29 H2
   RED TR15 ....61 F5
Eastern Av *LISK* PL14 ....33 G2
Eastern Gn *PENZ* TR18 ....55 F2
Eastern Green Park One
   PENZ TR18 * 55 G2
Eastern Green Park Three
   PENZ TR18 * 55 G2
Eastern Green Park Two
   PENZ TR18 * 55 G2
Eastern La *CAMBORNE* TR14 ....14 C4
East Fairholme Rd *BUDE* EX23 ....12 D1
Eastfield Wy *STAUS* PL25 ....64 C3
East Hl *CAMBORNE* TR14 ....15 F1
   STAUS PL25 ....63 H4
Eastland Cl *TRU* TR1 * 85 H3
East Pool Pk *RED* TR15 ....60 A4
East Quay *HAYLE* TR27 ....26 D5
   MEVA PL26 ....41 H5
East Ri *FAL* TR11 ....22 B3
East St *FOW* PL23 ....24 D4
   NEWQ TR7 ....46 B4
East Ter *HAYLE* TR27 ....26 D3
   PENZ TR18 * 55 F3
East Whf *MEVA* PL26 ....41 H3
Eastwood Rd *PENRYN* TR10 ....53 E4
Ebenezer Pl *PENZ* TR18 * 45 G3
Eddystone Pl *WADE* PL27 ....86 C3
Eddystone Ri *LISK* PL14 ....33 G1
Eddystone Rd *STAUS* PL25 ....64 B3
   WADE PL27 ....86 C2
Eddystone Ter *WADE* PL27 * 86 C3
Eden Cl *PAR* PL24 ....50 B5
Eden Gdns *PENZ* TR18 * 45 G3
Eden Ter *PENZ* TR18 * 45 G3
Edgcumbe Av *NEWQ* TR7 ....46 C3
Edgcumbe Gn *STAUS* PL25 ....63 F3
Edgcumbe Gn *STAUS* PL25 ....63 E5
Edgcumbe Ter *PAR* PL24 ....50 B4
Edgecombe Rd *LOST* PL22 ....36 D5
Edinburgh Cl *STAUS* PL25 ....65 F4
Edmund Rd *RED* TR15 ....60 D2
Ednovean La *RPENZ* TR20 ....39 G5
Edwards Crs *SALT* PL12 ....76 A3
Edwards Rd *RTRUS* TR3 ....19 E4
Edward St *CAMBORNE* TR14 ....15 E2
   TRU TR1 ....85 E3
Edymeade Ct *LAUN* PL15 ....31 F4
Edymeade Gdn *LAUN* PL15 ....31 F4
Efford Down Pk *BUDE* EX23 ....12 A3
Egerton Rd *PADS* PL28 ....48 C4
Egloshayle Rd *HAYLE* TR27 ....27 G4
   WADE PL27 ....86 D3
Eglos Parc *WADE* PL27 ....87 E3
Elderfield Cl *PAR* PL24 ....51 G2
Eleven Doors *STAUS* PL25 ....65 E5
Eliot Cl *NEWQ* TR7 ....46 C3
Eliot Gdns *NEWQ* TR7 ....46 C3
Eliot Rd *STAUS* PL25 ....64 C3
   TRU TR1 ....85 E2
Elizabeth Cl *BODM* PL31 ....10 C3

RTRUS TR3 ....82 D3
Elizabeth Rd *BUDE* EX23 ....12 D3
   STAUS PL25 ....64 B4
Eliza Seller Ct *LISK* PL14 * 33 F3
Elliot Sq *TOR* PL11 ....81 G4
Elliott Cl *SALT* PL12 ....76 C3
Ellis Cl *HAYLE* TR27 ....27 E4
Ellis Wy *HAYLE* TR27 ....27 E4
Elm Cl *NEWQ* TR7 ....46 C5
   RED TR15 ....60 A4
Elm Ct *TRU* TR1 ....85 F2
Elm Dr *BUDE* EX23 ....12 D3
Elm Lea *BUDE* EX23 * 12 D3
Elm Meadow Dr *LOOE* PL13 ....35 F2
Elms Close Ter *PENZ* TR18 ....45 G2
Elmsleigh Rd *WADE* PL27 ....86 C2
Elm Ter *MEVA* PL26 * 41 G3
   RED TR15 ....61 E2
   STAUS PL25 ....63 H3
Elm Tree Rd *LOOE* PL13 ....35 F2
Elowen Cl *FAL* TR11 ....22 A4
Elwell Rd *SALT* PL12 ....77 E3
Emlyn Flds *STAUS* PL25 ....64 C1
Empress Av *PENZ* TR18 ....23 E4
Emslie Rd *FAL* TR11 ....23 E4
Endsleigh Ter *LISK* PL14 ....33 E2
Ennor's Rd *NEWQ* TR7 ....46 A4
Enys Cl *STIVES* TR26 ....71 F2
   TRU TR1 ....84 D3
Enys Quay *TRU* TR1 ....85 F3
Enys Redenek
   CAMBORNE TR14 ....14 D1
Enys Rd *CAMBORNE* TR14 ....14 C3
   TRU TR1 ....84 D2
Epworth Cl *TRU* TR1 ....85 G3
Ergue-Gaberic Wy *BUDE* EX23 ....12 B3
Erisey Ter *TRU* TR1 ....22 D2
Erow Glas *STAUS* PL25 ....52 D3
Esmeralda Gdns *PLYNW* PL5 ......77 G5
Esmonde Rd *HELS* TR13 ....29 H5
Esperanza Ct *FAL* TR11 ....53 C5
Esplanade *FOW* PL23 ....24 C3
Esplanade Rd *NEWQ* TR7 ....21 F3
Essa Rd *SALT* PL12 ....77 E3
Estuary Vw *NEWQ* TR7 ....46 A4
   STAUS PL25 ....26 A5
Eton Rd *STAUS* PL25 ....64 D2
Euny Cl *RED* TR15 ....60 D4
Eureka V *PERRAN* TR6 * 56 B3
Evea Cl *TRU* TR1 ....84 A4
Evely Ct *LISK* PL14 ....33 G1
Evenden Ct *TOR* PL11 ....81 F4
Exeter St *LAUN* PL15 ....31 F3

F

Fairbourne Rd *STAUS* PL25 ....64 B3
Fairfield Cl *STAUS* PL25 ....64 D3
   STIVES TR26 ....26 B4
Fairfield Pl *NEWQ* TR7 ....21 G3
Fairfield Rd *BUDE* EX23 ....12 C3
   FAL TR11 ....22 A5
Fairfields *LOOE* PL13 ....35 F1
Fairmantle St *TRU* TR1 ....85 F3
Fairmarsh *PENRYN* TR10 ....52 C4
Fairmead Ms *SALT* PL12 ....76 B3
Fairmead Rd *SALT* PL12 ....76 B2
Fairpark Rd *LISK* PL14 ....33 E3
   WADE PL27 ....86 C3
Fairview *BODM* PL31 ....10 A3
Fairview Pl *FAL* TR11 * 22 D2
Fairview Ter *NEWQ* TR7 ....46 B3
Fairway *SALT* PL12 ....76 C3
   STAUS PL25 ....64 C3
Falcon Ter *BUDE* EX23 ....12 B3
Falmouth Rd *FAL* TR11 ....29 H2
   HELS TR13 ....29 H2
   PENRYN TR10 ....52 C4
   RED TR15 ....61 E4
   TRU TR1 ....85 E5
Farfield Pl *NEWQ* TR7 * 21 G3
Farmers Meadow *PENZ* TR18 * ...45 G2
Farm La *SALT* PL12 ....76 C4
Farrar Cl *HAYLE* TR27 ....27 G1
Faugan La *PENZ* TR18 ....45 F3
Faugan Rd *PENZ* TR18 ....45 F3
Faulkener Cl *FAL* TR11 ....22 A2
Fearnside Wy *SALT* PL12 ....76 B2
Fegen Rd *PLYNW* PL5 ....77 G4
Feliskirk La *MARAZ* TR17 ....38 B2
Felixstowe Av *NEWQ* TR7 ....47 G2
Fenten Pk *SALT* PL12 ....77 E2
Fentonluna Gdns *PADS* PL28 * 48 B2
Fentonluna La *PADS* PL28 ....48 A3
Fenwick Rd *FAL* TR11 ....22 D4
Ferndale Rd *FAL* TR11 ....23 E4
Ferndale Ter *LISK* PL14 ....33 E2
Fernside Rd *CAMBORNE* TR14 .....14 A5
Fernside Rd *CAMBORNE* TR14 .....14 A5
Ferris Town *TRU* TR1 ....85 E3
Ferris Wy *FOW* PL23 ....25 E4
Ferry La *TOR* PL11 ....80 D2
Ferry St *TOR* PL11 ....81 H4

Festival Gdns TRU TR1 * 85 F2
Finn V C Est BODM PL31 * 10 C2
Fir Cl HELS TR13 .....29 F2
  STAUS PL25 .....63 G4
The Firs TRU TR1 .....83 G3
Fisgard Wy TOR PL11 .....80 C4
Fisher Cl WADE PL27 .....87 E2
Fish Strand Hl FAL TR11 .....22 D2
Fish Strand Quay FAL TR11 .....22 D2
Fish St STIVES TR26 .....69 F2
Fistral Cl TOR PL11 .....81 E3
Fistral Crs NEWQ TR7 .....21 E3
Fitzsimmons Cl HELS TR13 .....29 G4
Five Fields La FAL TR11 .....22 C1
Five Wells La HELS TR13 .....29 F4
Flamank Pk BODM PL31 .....10 B3
Flaxmoor Ter BODM PL31 * 10 C2
Flexbury Av BUDE EX23 .....12 B1
Flexbury Ms BUDE EX23 .....12 C1
Flexbury Park Ms BUDE EX23 * 12 C1
Flexbury Park Rd BUDE EX23 .....12 C2
Flora Pl WADE PL27 .....86 D2
Florence Pl FAL TR11 .....22 D3
  PENZ TR18 * 45 E1
Florence Ter FAL TR11 .....22 D3
Forbes Cl HELS TR13 .....45 F3
Forbes Rd PENZ TR18 .....45 F3
Forder Hl MBRK/KGSD PL10 .....43 G5
Forder La MBRK/KGSD PL10 .....43 G5
Ford's Rw RED TR15 .....61 G3
Fore St BODM PL31 .....10 C2
  BUDE EX23 .....13 G3
  CAMBORNE TR14 .....14 A5
  CAMEL PL32 .....17 F4
  FOW PL23 .....24 D4
  HAYLE TR27 .....67 F3
  LANDS TR19 .....72 C4
  LISK PL14 .....33 F3
  LOOE PL13 .....35 G2
  LOST PL22 .....37 F4
  MARAZ TR17 .....38 C3
  MBRK/KGSD PL10 .....43 F1
  MEVA PL26 .....41 G3
  NEWQ TR7 .....46 B3
  PAR PL24 .....50 C2
  PENZ TR18 .....45 E1
  RED TR15 .....15 G1
  RED TR15 .....61 E3
  SALT PL12 .....77 E3
  STAUS PL25 .....63 H4
  STIVES TR26 .....26 A5
  STIVES TR26 .....69 F2
  TINT PL34 .....78 C3
  TOR PL11 .....81 E4
Forge La SALT PL12 .....76 B1
The Forge RTRUS TR3 .....19 G1
Forlaze Rd WADE PL27 .....49 F2
Forreglos Dr MARAZ TR17 .....38 D2
Fortescue Pl LOST PL22 .....37 G3
Forth An Hellier BODM PL31 .....11 F2
Forth-an-Praze RED TR15 .....60 A4
Forth-an-Ryn RED TR15 .....61 G4
Forth An Streth HAYLE TR27 .....27 G2
Forth An Tewennow HAYLE TR27 .....27 F1
Forth-an-Tre HAYLE TR27 .....27 G2
Forth An Ula HAYLE TR27 .....27 F2
Forth An Vre CAMBORNE TR14 .....15 F3
Forth Coth RTRUS TR3 .....19 G2
Forth Dall RTRUNW TR4 .....60 A1
Forth Kegyn RED TR15 .....15 G2
Forthnoweth RED TR15 .....61 E3
Forth Noweth RTRUS TR3 .....19 F1
Forth Scol RED TR15 .....60 A3
Forthvean CAMBORNE TR14 .....14 C5
Forthveor RED TR15 .....61 G1
The Fort MBRK/KGSD PL10 .....43 F1
Foster Dr BODM PL31 .....10 A4
Foster Pl PENZ TR18 * 55 E4
Fosters La TINT PL34 .....78 C4
Fosters Wy BUDE EX23 .....12 D2
Foulston Av PLYNW PL5 .....77 H4
Foulston Wy BODM PL31 .....10 A3
Foundry Cl WADE PL27 * 86 C3
Foundry Gdns LAUN PL15 * 31 E3
Foundry Hl HAYLE TR27 .....26 D5
Foundry La HAYLE TR27 .....26 D4
  PENZ TR18 .....45 G2
Foundry Rd CAMBORNE TR14 .....14 D3
Foundry Rw RED TR15 * 61 G3
Foundry Sq HAYLE TR27 .....26 D4
Foundry St WADE PL27 .....86 C3
Foundry Ter WADE PL27 * 86 C3
Fountain Ct PENZ TR18 * 54 D3
Foxdown Rd WADE PL27 .....87 E3
Foxdown Mnr WADE PL27 .....87 E3
Foxes Fld PENZ TR18 .....55 G2
Foxglove Cl LAUN PL15 .....31 H5
Foxglove Wy SALT PL12 * 76 A2
Fox's La FAL TR11 .....22 D3
Foxstanton Dr PENRYN TR10 .....53 E4
Fox's Yd PENRYN TR10 * 53 E4
Fradgan Pl PENZ TR18 .....45 G2
The Fradgan PENZ TR18 .....45 G2
Frances St TRU TR1 .....85 E3
Frankland Cl FAL TR11 .....22 B3
Franklin Cl WADE PL27 .....87 E2
Franklyn Cl STAUS PL25 .....64 C2
Frazer Rd NEWQ TR7 * 46 A5
Freeman Collins Dr FAL TR11 .....22 B2
Freshbrook Cl PENZ TR18 .....55 G2

Freshwater La RTRUE/STMW TR2 .....74 D2
Frith Rd SALT PL12 .....76 C3
Frobisher Dr SALT PL12 .....76 D3
Frobisher Ter FAL TR11 * 22 C1
Frobisher Wy TOR PL11 .....80 C4
Frost Ct FAL TR11 .....22 A1
Fuggoe Cft STIVES TR26 .....71 E1
Fuggoe La STIVES TR26 .....71 E1
Fuller Rd PERRAN TR6 .....56 A4
Furniss Cl TRU TR1 * 85 F3
Furry Wy HELS TR13 .....29 F4
Furzedown Ter LOOE PL13 * 35 E2
Furze Hl BODM PL31 .....10 D2
Furze Pk FOW PL23 .....24 D4

G

Gabriel St STIVES TR26 * 69 F3
Gallacher Wy SALT PL12 .....76 A2
Galland Rd TRU TR1 .....84 B2
Gallant's Dr FOW PL23 .....24 B3
Galleon Ct NEWQ TR7 * 46 A5
Gander La HELS TR13 * 29 F2
Gannel Rd NEWQ TR7 .....46 A5
Gannet Dr STAUS PL25 .....64 C3
Garby La RED TR15 .....61 F5
Garcia Ter LAUN PL15 .....31 C5
Garden Meadow FAL TR11 .....22 A3
Garland Pl CAMBORNE TR14 .....14 C2
  PENRYN TR10 * 52 D3
Garrett St MBRK/KGSD PL10 .....43 H5
Garth-an-Creet STIVES TR26 .....68 D4
Garth Marhas CAMBORNE TR14 .....14 B3
Garth Rd PENZ TR18 .....45 F1
Gas Hl TRU TR1 .....85 G5
Gas La RED TR15 .....61 F5
Gas St CAMBORNE TR14 .....14 C3
Gavercoombe Pk TINT PL34 .....78 C4
Gay's Hl HELS TR13 .....29 H5
Gears La RPENZ TR20 .....39 F2
Gendalls Wy LAUN PL15 .....31 E1
George Fox Cl LAUN PL15 .....30 D5
George St TRU TR1 .....84 D3
Gerrans Cl STAUS PL25 .....65 E2
Gew Ter RED TR15 .....61 F5
The Gew MARAZ TR17 .....38 B3
Gibraltar Ter RTRUE/STMW TR2 .....74 C2
Gibralter Sq BUDE EX23 .....13 G3
Gibson Wy HELS TR13 .....58 B1
Gig La RTRUS TR3 .....19 G2
Gilbert Rd BODM PL31 .....11 F3
Gill An Creet STIVES TR26 .....68 D3
Gilley La MEVA PL26 .....40 C2
Gills Cl PENRYN TR10 .....52 C5
Gilly Flds RED TR15 .....61 H5
Gilly Hl RED TR15 .....61 F5
Gilston Rd SALT PL12 .....76 B1
Gipsy La HELS TR13 .....28 C2
  LISK PL14 .....32 D3
Gladstone Rd RBODM PL30 .....10 B5
Gladstone Ter RED TR15 * 61 E3
Gladwell Gdns BUDE EX23 * 13 G3
Glamis Rd NEWQ TR7 .....46 D3
Glanville Ter SALT PL12 .....77 E2
Glasney Pl PENRYN TR10 .....52 D4
Glasney Rd FAL TR11 .....22 C1
Glasney Ter PENRYN TR10 .....53 E4
Glebe Av SALT PL12 .....76 B3
Glebelands LOOE PL13 .....35 F1
Glebe Nw HAYLE TR27 .....27 F2
The Glebe CAMBORNE TR14 .....14 B3
Glencoe Ter WADE PL27 * 86 D3
Glencross Ct LISK PL14 .....33 F2
Glen-Dale Cl STAUS PL25 .....64 D2
Glen-Dale Crs RED TR15 .....61 G4
Glen-Dale Crs STAUS PL25 .....64 D2
Glen Leigh RED TR15 * 60 D2
Glenmore Ter LISK PL14 * 33 G2
Glen Rd WADE PL27 .....86 C3
Glenthorne Rd RTRUS TR3 .....82 D3
Glenvale RED TR15 .....60 B4
Glenview STAUS PL25 .....63 G4
Glen Vw PAR PL24 .....51 G3
  PENRYN TR10 * 52 C3
  WADE PL27 .....86 C4
Glenway PENZ TR18 * 45 G3
Globe Yd STAUS PL25 * 63 H4
Gloucester Av STAUS PL25 .....65 F4
Gloucester Crs PENZ TR18 .....45 F3
Gloucester Pl PENZ TR18 .....45 F2
Gloucester Rd PENZ TR18 .....45 G3
Gloweth Vw TRU TR1 .....83 H3
The Gluyas FAL TR11 .....22 A5
Glyn Av HELS TR13 * 29 F4
Glynn Av HELS TR13 .....29 G5
Glynn Ms LOST PL22 * 37 F4
Glynn Rd LISK PL14 .....32 D3
  PADS PL28 .....48 B3
Glyn Wy RTRUS TR3 .....83 E3
Goad Av TOR PL11 .....80 D4
Goad Cl TOR PL11 .....81 E4
Godolphin Av MARAZ TR17 .....38 B3
Godolphin Cl MARAZ TR17 .....38 B2
Godolphin Dr MARAZ TR17 .....38 B3
Godolphin Pl MARAZ TR17 .....38 B3
Godolphin Rd FAL TR11 .....22 B1
  HELS TR13 .....29 G3

Godolphin Ter MARAZ TR17 .....38 B2
Godolphin Wy NEWQ TR7 .....47 E2
Godrevy Cl STIVES TR26 .....71 F1
Godrevy Ter STIVES TR26 .....71 E2
Goldenbank Pk FAL TR11 .....22 A5
Goldfinch Gv SALT PL12 .....76 C1
Goldsworthy Wy WADE PL27 .....86 C3
Golf House Rd BUDE EX23 .....12 B2
Golf Ter NEWQ TR7 .....21 H2
Gonvena Hl WADE PL27 .....86 D2
Goonhilly Cl RTRUNW TR4 .....57 H5
Goonrea LOOE PL13 .....34 D2
Goonvrea Cl NEWQ TR7 .....46 C5
Goonwartha Cl LOOE PL13 .....34 D3
Goonwartha Rd LOOE PL13 .....34 D3
Gordon Ct SALT PL12 * 76 C3
Gorse Cl NEWQ TR7 .....46 D5
The Gounce PERRAN TR6 .....56 A3
Gover La NEWQ TR7 .....46 A3
Gover Rd STAUS PL25 .....63 E2
Graham Av STAUS PL25 .....64 B3
Graham Rd RED TR15 .....61 F3
Grange Rd HELS TR13 .....29 F4
Grannys Gn BODM PL31 .....10 D3
Granny's La PERRAN TR6 .....56 B4
Grant's Ct STAUS PL25 .....63 H4
Grant's Wk STAUS PL25 .....63 H4
Granville Ter BUDE EX23 .....12 B3
Grassmere Wy SALT PL12 .....76 C1
Gravesend Rd TOR PL11 .....81 G4
Gravesend Gdns TOR PL11 .....81 G4
Gray Crs PLYNW PL5 .....77 H5
Greenbank FOW PL23 .....24 D4
  PENZ TR18 .....54 D4
Greenbank Crs NEWQ TR7 .....47 F1
Greenbank La LISK PL14 .....33 F2
Greenbank Rd LISK PL14 .....33 F2
  RTRUS TR3 .....19 E4
Greenbanks Rd WADE PL27 .....49 G2
Green Cl TRU TR1 .....84 D4
Green Crs HELS TR13 .....29 H2
Greenfield Rd SALT PL12 .....76 C3
Greenfinch Crs SALT PL12 .....76 C1
Green Hl WADE PL27 .....87 F3
Greenhills CAMEL PL32 .....17 E3
Greenhill Vls WADE PL27 .....87 F3
Greenland MBRK/KGSD PL10 .....43 G5
Green La BODM PL31 .....10 D5
  FOW PL23 .....24 C1
  HELS TR13 .....28 B5
  MARAZ TR17 .....38 A2
  PENRYN TR10 .....52 C3
  RED TR15 .....61 G5
  RNEWQ TR8 .....21 E4
  STIVES TR26 .....26 B3
  TRU TR1 .....84 D4
  WADE PL27 .....49 F2
Green Lane Cl PENRYN TR10 .....52 C3
Green Lane Hl PENZ TR18 .....55 F1
The Green La HAYLE TR27 .....67 E5
Green Lane Vean RED TR15 .....61 E3
Green Lane West MARAZ TR17 .....38 D3
Green Market PENZ TR18 * 55 E4
The Greenmarket PENZ TR18 .....55 E4
Green Mdw CAMEL PL32 .....17 E4
Green Parc Rd HAYLE TR27 .....27 E4
Green Pk MBRK/KGSD PL10 .....43 H4
Greensplat Rd STAUS PL25 .....63 F1
Green St PENZ TR18 .....55 F5
  TRU TR1 .....85 E3
The Green MBRK/KGSD PL10 .....43 H4
  SALT PL12 * 76 B3
  STAUS PL25 .....62 D5
Greenwith Cl TRU TR1 .....84 D4
Greenwith Hl RTRUS TR3 .....18 A3
Greenwith Rd RTRUS TR3 .....18 A3
Greenwood Crs PENRYN TR10 .....52 D3
Greenwood Rd PENRYN TR10 .....52 B3
Gregor Rd TRU TR1 .....85 H2
Grenfell Av SALT PL12 .....76 B2
Grenfell Gdns SALT PL12 * 76 B2
Grenifer Rd RED TR15 .....60 A3
Grenina La RTRUS TR3 .....18 C1
Grenna La RTRUS TR3 .....18 C1
Grenville Ct STAUS PL25 .....63 E4
Grenville Crs FAL TR11 .....22 B1
Grenville Mdw LOST PL22 .....37 H4
Grenville Rd FAL TR11 .....22 B1
  HELS TR13 .....29 H4
  LOST PL22 .....37 G4
  PADS PL28 .....48 A3
  TRU TR1 .....84 D2
Gresham Cl NEWQ TR7 .....46 C5
Gribben Cl STAUS PL25 .....64 B1
Gribben Rd STAUS PL25 .....64 B1
Gribbin Wy PAR PL24 * 50 D5
Gribbon Wy PAR PL24 .....50 D5
Griggs Hl HAYLE TR27 .....67 E1
Griggs Quay HAYLE TR27 .....66 D1
Grosvenor Av NEWQ TR7 .....46 B3
Grosvenor Pl STAUS PL25 .....63 G3
Grove Dr LISK PL14 .....32 C3
Grovehill Crs FAL TR11 .....23 E3
Grovehill Dr FAL TR11 .....22 D3
Grove Pk TOR PL11 .....80 D4
Grove Park Ct LISK PL14 .....33 E4
Grove Park Ter LISK PL14 .....33 E4
Grove Pl FAL TR11 .....22 B5
  PADS PL28 .....48 B3
Grove Rd PAR PL24 .....50 A4

  STAUS PL25 .....63 G3
Grylls Parc HELS TR13 .....29 F3
The Gue HELS TR13 .....58 A2
Guildford Rd HAYLE TR27 .....27 G2
Guildhall La LOST PL22 .....37 F4
Guineaport Parc WADE PL27 .....86 D3
Guineaport Rd WADE PL27 .....86 D3
Gulval Cross PENZ TR18 * 55 F1
Gurney Cl BUDE EX23 .....12 C1
  TOR PL11 .....81 E4
Gurney's La CAMBORNE TR14 .....14 C4
Gurnick Est PENZ TR18 .....45 F2
Gurnick Rd PENZ TR18 .....45 F3
Gustavus Rd CAMBORNE TR14 .....14 C3
Gustory Rd RNEWQ TR8 .....21 E5
Gwallon La MARAZ TR17 .....38 D1
Gwallon Rd STAUS PL25 .....63 F3
Gwarnick Rd TRU TR1 .....84 D3
Gwarth An Drae HELS TR13 .....29 F1
Gwarth An Dre HAYLE TR27 .....27 G1
Gwavas Est PENZ TR18 * 45 C3
Gwavas La LANDS TR19 .....45 C4
Gwavas Quay PENZ TR18 .....45 C2
Gwavas Rd PENZ TR18 .....45 C3
Gwavas St PENZ TR18 .....55 E3
Gweal-an-Top RED TR15 .....61 G3
Gwealdues HELS TR13 .....29 H2
Gweal Folds HELS TR13 .....29 G2
Gwealfolds Rd HELS TR13 .....29 G2
Gweal Gollas HAYLE TR27 .....27 G1
Gwealhellis Warren HELS TR13 .....29 G2
Gweal Pawl RED TR15 .....60 D4
Gweal Wartha HELS TR13 .....29 F1
Gwedhnnek PENZ TR18 .....55 F2
Gwel-an-Mor STAUS PL25 .....64 D2
Gwelanmor Cl STIVES TR26 .....71 F1
Gwelanmor Rd STIVES TR26 .....71 F1
Gwel An Nans Cl LISK PL14 .....33 E3
Gwel-an-Skol CAMBORNE TR14 .....14 D1
Gwel An Wheal STIVES TR26 .....69 E4
Gwel An Wheal Crs STIVES TR26 .....69 E4
Gwelavon Cl WADE PL27 .....87 E3
Gwel Lewern PENZ TR18 .....55 G2
Gwelmeneth HELS TR13 .....29 F5
Gwel Mengleth WADE PL27 .....87 E2
Gwelmor CAMBORNE TR14 .....14 D4
Gwel-Tek HAYLE TR27 .....67 G1
Gwel Trencrom HAYLE TR27 .....67 G1
Gwendroc Cl TRU TR1 .....85 F4
Gwendrona Cl HELS TR13 .....29 H1
Gwendrona Wy HELS TR13 .....29 H1
Gwithian Cl TOR PL11 .....81 E3
Gyllyng St SAL TR11 .....22 D2
Gyllyngvase Hl FAL TR11 .....22 D4
Gyllyngvase Rd FAL TR11 .....23 E4
Gyllyngvase Ter FAL TR11 .....23 E4

H

Haddon Wy STAUS PL25 .....65 F4
Haig Pl PENZ TR18 .....54 C2
Hain Wk STIVES TR26 .....69 G4
Halbullock Vw TRU TR1 .....83 G3
Halgavor La BODM PL31 .....10 D5
Halgavor Rd BODM PL31 .....10 D5
Halgavor Vw BODM PL31 .....11 E5
Hallane Rd STAUS PL25 .....64 D1
Hallett Cl SALT PL12 .....76 A2
Hallett Wy BUDE EX23 .....12 D1
Halsetown Rd STIVES TR26 .....68 C4
Halt Rd RTRUNW TR4 .....57 H4
Halwyn Cl RTRUS TR3 .....19 F2
Halwyn Hl RNEWQ TR8 .....21 F5
Halwyn Pl TRU TR1 .....84 D5
Halwyn Rd RNEWQ TR8 .....21 F5
Halwyn Ter TRU TR1 .....84 D4
Hamilton Cl HAYLE TR27 .....67 G1
Hammill's Cl HELS TR13 .....58 B2
Hamoaze Rd TOR PL11 .....81 G5
Hampton Cl NEWQ TR7 .....46 B4
Hancock La RTRUE/STMW TR2 .....74 C2
Hannafore La LOOE PL13 .....35 E3
Hannafore Rd LOOE PL13 .....35 E3
Hanover Cl PERRAN TR6 .....56 B3
Hanover Ct CAMBORNE TR14 .....14 D2
  PENZ TR18 .....55 E4
Hanson Dr FOW PL23 .....24 B3
Hanson Rd LISK PL14 .....33 G2
Harbour Rd HELS TR13 .....58 A2
  WADE PL27 .....86 C2
Harbour Ter FAL TR11 .....22 D1
Harbour Vw FOW PL23 * 24 C2
  HAYLE TR27 .....26 D4
  PENRYN TR10 .....52 C3
  SALT PL12 .....76 D3
  TRU TR1 .....85 G4
Harbour View Crs PENZ TR18 .....55 F3
Harbour Village PENRYN TR10 .....53 E4
Harcourt Cl TRU TR1 .....84 D3
Hardings Cl SALT PL12 .....76 C1
Harebell Cl SALT PL12 .....76 B1
Harbour Rd FAL TR11 .....58 A2
Harefield Crs CAMBORNE TR14 .....14 C2
Harleigh Rd BODM PL31 .....10 D4
Harleigh Ter BODM PL31 .....10 D4
Harmer Cl BODM PL31 .....10 C1
Harmony Cl RED TR15 .....61 E2
Harmony Ter TRU TR1 .....85 G5
Harriet Pl FAL TR11 * 22 C1

Harrison Gdns RED TR15 ...... 60 A3
Harrison Ter TRU TR1 * 84 D3
Harrys Ct STIVES TR26 ...... 69 F2
Hartland Ter BUDE EX23 ...... 12 B2
Harvey Rd TRU TR1 ...... 85 F5
Harveys Towans HAYLE TR27 ... 26 C2
Harvey St TOR PL11 ...... 81 G4
Harvey's Wy HAYLE TR27 ...... 27 E4
Hat La MBRK/KGSD PL10 ...... 43 G4
Haven Ct HAYLE TR27 ...... 26 D4
Hawke Cl NEWQ TR7 ...... 21 H2
Hawke Rd HELS TR13 ...... 29 H5
Hawkins Dr NEWQ TR7 ...... 46 B4
Hawkins Rd NEWQ TR7 ...... 46 B5
  PADS PL28 ......
  PENZ TR18 ...... 54 D4
Hawkins Wy FAL TR11 ...... 22 C2
Hawks Pk SALT PL12 ...... 76 B3
Hawks Point STIVES TR26 ...... 71 G1
Hawthorn Av BUDE EX23 ...... 12 C4
  TOR PL11 ...... 81 E4
Hawthorn Cl BUDE EX23 ...... 12 C4
  RED TR15 ......
  STAUS PL25 ...... 64 C1
Hawthorne Cl CAMEL TR32 ... 17 F4
Hawthorns SALT PL12 ...... 76 C3
Hawthorn Wy RTRUS TR3. ...... 82 D3
Haydon Gv PLYNW PL5 ...... 77 H4
Hay La LOOE PL13 ...... 35 G2
Hayle Ter HAYLE TR27 ...... 26 D3
Hayman Wy FAL TR11 ...... 22 A1
Hayne Corfe Gdns TRU TR1 ... 84 C3
Hazel Cl STAUS PL25 ...... 64 D1
Hazelmead LISK PL14 ...... 33 E3
Hazelmere Av STAUS PL25 * ... 65 E3
Hazelmere Dr STAUS PL25 ... 65 E3
Heabrook Parc PENZ TR18 ... 54 C2
Hea Cl PENZ TR18 ...... 54 C2
Hea Cnr PENZ TR18 * 54 C2
Headland Cl STIVES TR26 ... 71 G1
Headland Rd NEWQ TR7 ...... 21 H1
  STIVES TR26 ...... 71 G1
Headleigh Rd NEWQ TR7 ...... 46 B4
Heanton Ter RED TR15 ...... 61 F4
Hearl Rd SALT PL12 ...... 76 A2
Heather Cl PENZ TR18 ...... 54 B2
Heather La HAYLE TR27 ...... 66 B2
Heathlands Rd LISK PL14 ... 33 F3
The Hedgerows SALT PL12 ... 76 A3
Heica Dr STIVES TR26 ...... 71 E1
Helland Gdns PENRYN TR10 ... 52 D3
Hellescoth Wy HELS TR13 ... 29 H1
Hellesvean STIVES TR26 ...... 68 D4
Hellesvean Cl STIVES TR26 ... 68 D4
Helleur Cl PAR PL24 ...... 50 C4
Hellis Wartha HELS TR13. ... 29 H4
Helman Tor W BODM PL31 ... 10 D5
Helnoweth Gdns RPENZ TR20... 55 F1
Helston Rd PENRYN TR10 ... 52 D3
Hembal Cl STAUS PL25 ...... 62 D3
Hembal La STAUS PL25 ...... 62 D4
Hendra Barton TRU TR1 ...... 84 D2
Hendra Cl TRU TR1 * 85 E2
Hendra Gdns LAUN PL15 ... 31 E4
Hendra La TRU TR1 ...... 85 E2
Hendra Pk LAUN PL15 ...... 31 E4
  LISK PL14 ...... 33 H1
Hendra Rd TRU TR1 ...... 84 D2
Hendras Parc STIVES TR26 ... 71 F1
Hendra V LAUN PL15 ...... 31 E4
Hendra Vean STIVES TR26 ... 71 G2
  TRU TR1 ...... 84 D2
Hendrawna la PERRAN TR6... 56 C4
Henfor Cl MARAZ TR17 ...... 38 C4
Henfordh Gra LISK PL14. ...... 32 D2
Henford Ter MARAZ TR17 ... 38 D3
Henliston Dr HELS TR13 ... 29 G5
Henscol V LISK PL14. ...... 32 D2
Henshorn Ct HELS TR13 * ... 29 G2
Hental PERRAN TR6 ...... 56 B4
Henver Rd NEWQ TR7 ...... 46 D5
Henvor Cl RED TR15 ...... 61 G2
Henvor Ter RED TR15 ...... 61 H1
Henwood Crs NEWQ TR7 ... 47 G2
Heritage Cl SALT PL12 ...... 76 B2
Hermes Cl HELS TR13 ...... 29 G5
Hermes Rd HELS TR13 ...... 29 G5
Herring Cl LISK PL14 ...... 33 G1
Herring Rd LISK PL14 ...... 33 G1
Hessary Vw SALT PL12 ...... 76 B4
Hewitt Cl SALT PL12 ...... 76 B4
Hibernia Rd HELS TR13 ...... 29 C1
Hichens La FAL TR11 * 22 C1
Hicks Ct STIVES TR26 * 69 F2
Highburrow Ct RED TR15 ... 15 H1
Highburrow La RED TR15 ... 15 H1
High Cross TRU TR1 ...... 85 F3
High Cross St STAUS PL25 ... 64 A4
Higher Anderton Rd
  MBRK/KGSD PL10 ...... 43 G1
Higher Beech Ter LOOE PL13... 35 G2
Higher Besore Rd RTRUS TR3.. 83 F3
Higher Bolenna PERRAN TR6... 56 A4
Higher Bore St BODM PL31 ... 10 B2
Higher Boskerris STIVES TR26.. 71 E2
Higher Bridge Pk HAYLE PL27.. 87 E3
Higher Broad La RED TR15 ... 60 A3
Higher Burrow Cl STIVES TR26.. 69 E4

Higher Chapel St LOOE PL13 ... 35 F3
Higher Church St HAYLE TR27... 27 F3
Higher Cleaverfield
  LAUN PL15 * 31 F2
Higher Cl WADE PL27 ...... 87 F4
Higher Cross La CAMEL TR32... 17 G4
Higher Enys Rd
  CAMBORNE TR14 ...... 14 C2
Higher Fernleigh Rd
  WADE PL27 ...... 86 D4
Higher Fore St MARAZ TR17 ... 38 C3
  RED TR15 ...... 61 F3
Higher Green St PENZ TR18 ... 45 G3
Higher Gwavas Rd PENZ TR18.. 45 G3
Higher La WADE PL27 ...... 87 F3
Higher Lariggan PENZ TR18... 54 D5
Higher Lavorrick MEVA PL26... 41 G1
Higher Lidden Rd PENZ TR18... 54 C5
Higher Lux St LISK PL14 ...... 33 F2
Higher Market St LOOE PL13 ... 35 F3
  PENRYN TR10 ...... 52 D4
Higher Mount Ambrose La
  RED TR15 ...... 61 G2
Higher Newham La TRU TR1... 85 F5
Higher Pengegon
  CAMBORNE TR14 ...... 15 E4
Higher Penponds Rd
  CAMBORNE TR14 ...... 14 A5
Higher Peverell Rd PENZ TR18.. 55 E2
Higher Port Vw SALT PL12. ... 76 D3
Higher Redannick TRU TR1 ... 84 D4
Higher Rw MBRK/KGSD PL10 *.. 43 H4
Higher St Clements Hl
  TRU TR1 * 85 H3
Higher Silver Hl HELS TR13 *... 29 G3
Higher Stennack STIVES TR26.. 68 D4
Higher Tower Rd NEWQ TR7 ... 21 H3
Hightown TRU TR1 ...... 84 B3
Higher Tregorran RED TR15... 15 H2
Higher Tregenna Rd
  STIVES TR26 ...... 69 F5
Higher Trehaverne TRU TR1... 85 E2
Higher Tremena STAUS PL25... 63 H3
Higher Trevithick HAYLE TR27.. 27 F4
Higher Trewidden Rd
  STIVES TR26 ...... 69 E4
Higherwell Cl NEWQ TR7 ...... 46 D5
Higher Well La HELS TR13 ... 29 G3
Higher Well Pk MEVA PL26 ... 41 G4
Higher Whf BUDE EX23 ...... 12 B4
Higher Whiterock WADE PL27.. 86 C3
Higher Woodside STAUS PL25.. 63 F3
Highfield Av STAUS PL25 ...... 64 A2
Highfield Pk SALT PL12 ...... 76 A2
Highfield Rd LAUN PL15 ...... 30 D5
Highfield Rd CAMEL PL32 ...... 17 E5
  FAL TR11 ...... 22 B2
Highfields PENZ TR18 * 45 G2
Highland Pk PENRYN TR10 ... 52 C3
  RED TR15 ...... 61 F3
High Lanes HAYLE TR27 ...... 27 F4
High St CAMEL TR32 ...... 17 E5
  FAL TR11 ...... 22 D1
  LAUN PL15 ...... 31 F3
  PADS PL28 ...... 48 A3
  PENZ TR18 ...... 55 E4
  STIVES TR26 ...... 69 F2
Highway La RED TR15 ...... 61 G1
Hilgrove Rd NEWQ TR7 ...... 46 D5
Hill Cl PENZ TR18 ...... 54 B2
Hillcrest HELS TR13 ...... 29 G3
Hillcrest Av TRU TR1 ...... 84 C2
Hillcrest Rd HAYLE TR27 ...... 27 F3
Hill Hay Cl FOW PL23. ...... 24 A2
Hill Head FAL TR11 ...... 53 E5
Hillhead BUDE EX23 * 13 F3
  RTRUE/STMW TR2. ...... 74 C2
Hillhead Gdns CAMEL PL32... 17 F4
The Hillocks LOOE PL13 * ... 35 F2
Hill Pk LAUN PL15 ...... 31 G3
  WADE PL27 ...... 87 E2
Hill Park Crs STAUS PL25 ...... 63 F5
Hill Rd WADE PL27 ...... 86 D3
Hillside NEWQ TR7 * 46 A5
  STAUS PL25 ...... 65 E4
Hillside Av PAR PL24 ...... 50 B5
  SALT PL12 ...... 77 E2
Hillside Ct BODM PL31 ...... 10 B2
Hillside Gdns LOST PL22 ...... 37 F4
Hillside Meadow PENRYN TR10.. 53 E4
Hillside Pk BODM PL31 ...... 10 B2
Hillside Rd FAL TR11 ...... 22 B3
  SALT PL12 ...... 76 B4
  STAUS PL25 ...... 64 A2
Hillside Ter LOOE PL13. ...... 35 E2
  PENZ TR18 ...... 45 G2
  RED TR15 ...... 61 F3
Hill St PADS PL28 ...... 48 B3
Hobbs Crs SALT PL12 ...... 76 C4
Hockens La FOW PL23. ...... 24 C4
Hodge Cl SALT PL12 ...... 76 C4
Ho Hl FOW PL23 * 24 D2
Holcroft Cl SALT PL12 ...... 76 C3
Hollabury Rd BUDE EX23 ...... 12 D4
Hollies Cl LAUN PL15 ...... 30 D1
Hollies Rd LAUN PL15 ...... 30 D1
Hollowgutter La TOR PL11 ...... 80 B5
Hollow's Ter HAYLE TR27 ...... 27 G2
Holly Cl RTRUS TR3. ...... 82 D3
Holly Ter PENZ TR18 * 54 C2
Holman Av CAMBORNE TR14... 14 B2

Holman Rd LISK PL14 ...... 33 H2
Holmbush Arch Rd STAUS PL25.. 65 E4
Holmbush Rd STAUS PL25 ... 64 D4
Holnicote Rd BUDE EX23 ...... 12 C3
Holt Crs NEWQ TR7 * 46 A5
Holywell Rd LISK PL14. ...... 33 H2
  NEWQ TR7. ......
Homefield Pk BODM PL31 ...... 11 E4
Home Park Rd SALT PL12. ... 77 F2
Homer Pk SALT PL12. ...... 76 C1
Homer St BODM PL31. ...... 10 D3
Honeysuckle Cl SALT PL12 ... 76 B1
Honeysuckle Gdns LAUN PL15... 31 H5
Hooper La CAMBORNE TR14 ... 14 C4
Hope Ter NEWQ TR7. ...... 46 A4
Hornabrook Ct PADS PL28 *... 48 B3
Hornabrook Pl PADS PL28 *... 48 B3
Horn La LISK PL14 ...... 33 E2
Horse & Jockey La HELS TR13... 29 F4
Horsley Ri STAUS PL25 ...... 64 A4
Hosking's Rw RED TR15 ...... 61 H4
Hospital Rd BUDE EX23 ...... 13 F3
Hounster Dr MBRK/KGSD PL10.. 43 E1
Hounster Hl MBRK/KGSD PL10.. 42 D1
Howard Cl SALT PL12. ...... 76 C2
Howard La BUDE EX23 ...... 13 G5
Howards Wy BUDE EX23 ...... 13 F3
Howell's Rd BUDE EX23 ...... 13 F3
Hughville St CAMBORNE TR14... 14 C2
Hugus Rd RTRUS TR5. ...... 83 E3
Hull's La FAL TR11 ...... 23 E3
Humphry Davy La HAYLE TR27.. 27 F3
Hunkin Cl TRU TR1 ...... 85 E1
Hurdon Rd LAUN PL15 ...... 31 F5
Hurland Rd TRU TR1 ...... 85 F4
Hurlers Ct LISK PL14 ...... 33 E3
Huthnance Cl TRU TR1 ...... 85 H2

I

Ince Cl TOR PL11 ...... 81 E3
Infirmary Hl TRU TR1 ...... 85 E4
Island Crs NEWQ TR7 ...... 46 B3
Island Rd STIVES TR26 ...... 69 F2
Islington Whf PENRYN TR10 ... 53 E3
Ivey Ter LISK PL14 ...... 33 C1
Ivy La PENZ TR18. ...... 54 C4
Ivy Ter RNEWQ TR8 * 21 E5

J

Jack Bice Cl LISK PL14 ...... 33 H3
Jack La PENZ TR18 ...... 45 G2
Jackman's Meadow
  MBRK/KGSD PL10 ...... 43 H3
Jacks Cl PENRYN TR10 ...... 53 E4
Jackson Wy SALT PL12 ...... 76 D2
Jack Stephens Est PENZ TR18.. 54 D1
Jago Av TOR PL11 ...... 81 F4
Jago Cl BODM PL31 ...... 10 A4
Jamaica Pl PENZ TR18 * 54 C2
Jamaica Ter PENZ TR18 * 54 C2
James Pl TRU TR1 ...... 85 F5
Janes Ct FAL TR11 ...... 22 D1
Jeanne Rees Ct LISK PL14 ... 33 E3
Jelbert Wy PENZ TR18. ...... 55 H2
Jenkins Cl NEWQ TR7 * 46 B3
Jenkins Ter RED TR15 ...... 61 F3
Jennings Rd PENRYN TR10 ... 52 B5
Jennings St PENZ TR18 ...... 55 E4
Jeryon Cl STAUS PL25 ...... 64 B1
Jethan Dr CAMBORNE TR14 ... 14 A3
Jetty St MEVA PL26. ...... 41 H3
Johns Pk RED TR15. ...... 61 E2
John St TRU TR1 ...... 85 E3
Jon Davey Dr RTRUNW TR4... 61 E1
Josephs Ct PERRAN TR6. ... 56 B3
Joseph's La PENZ TR18. ...... 54 C1
Jubilee Cl SALT PL12. ...... 76 C3
Jubilee Ct STIVES TR26 ...... 68 D4
Jubilee Meadow STAUS PL25.. 65 F2
Jubilee Pl CAMBORNE TR14 ... 14 D3
Jubilee Rd FAL TR11 ...... 22 C1
  RTRUS TR3. ...... 82 D3
  WADE PL27 ...... 86 D3
Jubilee St NEWQ TR7 ...... 46 A3
Jubilee Ter BODM PL31 ...... 10 A2
Julias Pl BUDE EX23 * 12 B3

K

Karensa Gn FAL TR11 ...... 22 A1
Kay Crs BODM PL31 ...... 10 A4
Kay Gdns WADE PL27 ...... 87 F3
Keeble Pk RTRUS TR3. ...... 18 C3
Kel Avon Cl TRU TR1 ...... 85 H2
Kellaway Pk HELS TR13 ...... 29 H4
Kelley Rd FAL TR11 ...... 22 A1
Kemp Cl TRU TR1 ...... 85 F3
Kempton Ter TOR PL11 ...... 81 G4
Kenidjack Ct STIVES TR26 ... 71 G2
Kenna Pk TRU TR1 ...... 84 B3

Kennerley Ter
  RTRUE/STMW TR2. ...... 74 C2
Kensey Pl LAUN PL15 * 31 F3
Kensey Valley Meadow
  LAUN 31 G3
Kensey Vw LAUN PL15 ...... 31 G4
Kenstella Rd PENZ TR18 ...... 45 G2
Kent Av STAUS PL25 ...... 65 F4
Kenwyn Church Rd TRU TR1... 84 D1
  TRU TR1 ...... 84 D1
Kenwyn Cl BUDE EX23 ...... 12 B1
Kenwyn Hl TRU TR1 ...... 84 D1
Kenwyn Pk TRU TR1 ...... 84 D1
Kenwyn Rd TRU TR1 ...... 84 D2
Kenwyn St TRU TR1 ...... 85 E3
Kenython La LANDS TR19 ... 72 D2
Kerley Gv TRU TR1 ...... 84 B3
Kernick Rd PENRYN TR10 ... 52 B4
Kernick Wy HAYLE TR27 ...... 27 G1
Kernow Cl BODM PL31 ...... 11 E2
  TOR PL11 ...... 80 D4
  WADE PL27 ...... 86 C3
Kernow Crs BUDE EX23 ...... 12 C4
Kernyk Lowen
  CAMBORNE TR14 ...... 15 E1
Kerris Gv TRU TR1 ...... 84 D2
Keryor Cl STAUS PL25 ...... 64 C4
Kestell Pk BODM PL31 ...... 10 D5
Kestle Ct BODM PL31 * 10 B4
Kestle Dr TRU TR1 ...... 84 B3
Kew Cl NEWQ TR7 ...... 46 D5
Kew Noweth CAMBORNE TR14.. 14 C4
Kew Vean STIVES TR26 ...... 69 G5
Khyber Cl TOR PL11 ...... 81 F4
Kilhalion Woodlands PAR PL24.. 50 D3
Killerton Rd BUDE EX23 ...... 12 C3
Killigrew Av SALT PL12 ...... 76 C4
Killigrew Pl FAL TR11 * 22 C2
Killigrew Rd LISK PL14 ...... 33 F2
Killigrew St FAL TR11 ...... 22 D2
  FAL TR11 ...... 22 D2
Killivose Gdns
  CAMBORNE TR14 ...... 14 C5
Killivose Rd CAMBORNE TR14.. 14 C5
Killyvarder Wy STAUS PL25 ... 64 D1
Kilmar Rd LISK PL14 ...... 33 H2
Kiln Cl MBRK/KGSD PL10 ...... 43 H5
  MEVA PL26 ...... 41 G2
  PLYNW PL5 ...... 77 H5
Kimberley Park Rd FAL TR11... 22 C2
Kimberley Pl FAL TR11 ...... 22 C2
Kimberly Cl NEWQ TR7 ...... 46 A3
King Charles Quay FAL TR11 *.. 23 E2
King Edward Crs NEWQ TR7... 46 A2
King Edward Rd SALT PL12 ... 77 E2
Kingfisher Dr STAUS PL25 ... 64 C3
King George V Memorial Wk
  HAYLE TR27 ...... 27 E3
King's Av FAL TR11 ...... 22 B2
Kings Av STAUS PL25 ...... 64 A4
King's Hl BUDE EX23 ...... 12 C4
Kings Hill BUDE EX23 ...... 12 C4
Kingsley Av TOR PL11 ...... 81 G5
Kingsley Wy HELS TR13 ...... 29 G3
King's Rd CAMBORNE TR14 ... 14 C2
Kings Rd MARAZ TR17 ...... 38 B3
Kings Rd RTRUE/STMW TR2... 74 C2
King's St LOST PL22 ...... 37 F4
King St BUDE EX23 ...... 12 B3
  MBRK/KGSD PL10 ...... 43 F4
  NEWQ TR7 ...... 46 A3
  RED TR15 ...... 61 H4
  TRU TR1 ...... 85 F3
Kinsman Est BODM PL31 ...... 10 B4
Kinterbury Rd PLYNW PL5 ... 77 G5
Kinterbury Ter PLYNW PL5 ... 77 G5
Kirby Rd TRU TR1 ...... 84 C3
Kirland Rd RBODM PL30 ...... 10 A5
Kit Hill Crs PLYNW PL5 ...... 77 H5
Knights Cl TINT PL34 ...... 78 B3
Knights Ct LOST PL22 ...... 37 E3
Knights Hl TRU TR1 ...... 84 D1
Knight's Mdw RTRUS TR3 ... 19 F2
Knights Wy RED TR15 ...... 61 G1
Knoll Cl STIVES TR26 ...... 71 E1
Knill Cross MBRK/KGSD PL10... 43 F1
Knoll Pk TRU TR1 ...... 85 H3
Kynance Cl TOR PL11 ...... 81 E3

L

Laburnum Cl FAL TR11 ...... 53 G5
Laburnum Dr FAL TR11 ...... 22 B3
Lady St HELS TR13 ...... 29 F3
Ladywell PADS PL28 ...... 48 B3
Lafrowda Cl LANDS TR19 ...... 72 B4
Lafrowda Ter LANDS TR19 ... 72 C4
Laguna Ct RED TR15 ...... 61 E3
Laity Dr CAMBORNE TR14 * ... 15 E3
Laity Flds CAMBORNE TR14... 15 E3
Laity La STIVES TR26 ......
Lake La LISK PL14 ...... 33 G3
Lake Ms MBRK/KGSD PL10 *... 43 F1
Lambert Ter FAL TR11 * 22 C1
Lamb Pk PAR PL24 ...... 50 D4
Lambs La FAL TR11 ...... 22 C1

Lamellion Cross LISK PL14 ....32 D4
Lamellyn Dr TRU TR1 ....83 H3
Lamellyn Rd PAR PL24 ....50 B5
Lamorak Cl MEVA PL26 ....41 F3
Lamorna Pk TOR PL11 ....80 D3
Lamorne Cl PERRAN TR6 ....56 B4
Lanadwell St PADS PL28 ....48 B3
Lanaton Rd PENRYN TR10 ....52 B4
Lance Dr BODM PL31 ....10 B3
Lanchard Gn LISK PL14 ....33 E3
Lanchard La LISK PL14 ....33 E3
Lanchard Ri LISK PL14 ....33 E3
Lanchard Rd LISK PL14 ....33 E3
Lander Ct TRU TR1 * 85 E4
Lander Rd SALT PL12 ....77 E2
Landeryon Gdns PENZ TR18 ....54 D3
Landithy RPENZ TR20 ....54 A1
Landrake Cl PLYNW PL5 ....77 H5
Landreath Pl PAR PL24 ....50 C3
Landrew Rd STAUS PL25 ....64 C1
Landulph Gdns PLYNW PL5 ....77 H5
Lane Reddin Ter PENZ TR18 * 45 G2
Langarth Cl RTRUS TR3 ....83 E2
Langdon Down Wy TOR PL11 ....80 D3
Langerwell Cl SALT PL12 ....76 B2
Langerwell La SALT PL12 ....76 B2
Langorran Rd CAMBORNE TR14 ...14 A3
Lang Rd LISK PL14 ....33 E4
Langton Rd FAL TR11 ....53 H5
Langton Ter FAL TR11 * 22 C1
Langurroc Rd RNEWQ TR8 ....21 F5
Langurtho Rd FOW PL23 ....24 B2
Langweath Gdns STIVES TR26 .....26 A5
Lanhenvor Av NEWQ TR7 ....46 B4
Lankelly La FOW PL23 ....24 A2
Lannoweth Rd PENZ TR18 ....55 F3
Lanoweth PENRYN TR10 ....52 C2
Lansdown Cl BUDE EX23 ....12 B3
Lansdowne Ct PENZ TR18 ....54 C4
Lansdowne Ct PENZ TR18 * 54 B4
Lansdowne Pl PENZ TR18 ....54 C5
Lansdowne Rd FAL TR11 ....23 E3
   PENZ TR18 ....54 C4
Lansdown Rd BUDE EX23 ....12 B3
   WADE PL27 ....86 C3
Lanwithan Cl LOST PL22 ....37 C4
Lanwithan Rd LOST PL22 ....37 G4
Larch Cl SALT PL12 ....76 B2
Larcombe Rd STAUS PL25 ....64 D1
Laregan Hl PENZ TR18 ....54 C5
Lariggan Crs PENZ TR18 ....54 D5
Lariggan Rd PENZ TR18 ....54 D5
Larkfield Ri RTRUE/STMW TR2 .....74 C3
Launceston Rd BODM PL31 ....11 E3
Launceston Rd BODM PL31 ....11 E3
Laura Cl TINT PL34 ....78 D3
Laura Dr STAUS PL25 ....64 D2
Lavorrick Orchards MEVA PL26 ....41 G2
The Lawns TOR PL11 ....81 F3
The Lawn PAR PL24 ....50 C2
Lawry Cl LISK PL14 ....33 E3
Lawton Cl NEWQ TR7 ....21 G3
Leader Rd NEWQ TR7 ....47 G2
Leafield BODM PL31 ....11 F3
Leanway SALT PL12 ....76 D5
Leap Pk RTRUS TR3 ....82 D3
The Leas TRU TR1 ....85 G2
Leatfield MEVA PL26 ....41 G3
The Leats TRU TR1 ....85 E3
The Leat BUDE EX23 ....13 F3
Leat Vw SALT PL12 ....76 A2
Lea Wy BUDE EX23 ....12 D2
Ledrah Gdns STAUS PL25 ....63 G4
Ledrah Rd STAUS PL25 ....63 G4
Leggos Cl RED TR15 * 85 F2
Legion La PAR PL24 ....51 G3
Lelant Mdw STIVES TR26 ....26 A4
Lemin's Ct RED TR15 * 85 F3
Lemon Mews Rd TRU TR1 ....85 E3
Lemon Pl RED TR15 * 61 G3
Lemon Quay TRU TR1 ....85 E3
Lemon Rw TRU TR1 * 85 E4
Lemon St TRU TR1 * 85 E4
Lescudjack Crs PENZ TR18 ....55 F3
Lescudjack Rd PENZ TR18 ....55 F3
Lescudjack Ter PENZ TR18 * 55 F3
Leskinnick Pl PENZ TR18 ....55 F3
Leskinnick St PENZ TR18 ....55 F3
Leskinnick Ter PENZ TR18 ....55 F3
Lesnewth PAR PL24 ....50 B5
Lethlean La HAYLE TR27 ....27 F2
Lethlean La HAYLE TR27 ....27 F2
Lethlean Towans HAYLE TR27 ......27 F1
Levine Vw FAL TR11 ....22 A4
Lewarne Crs NEWQ TR7 ....47 F1
Lewarne Rd NEWQ TR7 ....47 F1
Lewellyn Cl CAMEL PL32 ....17 E5
Lewis Wy STAUS PL25 ....64 B1
Leys La MARAZ TR17 ....38 B3
Lidden Cl PENZ TR18 ....45 G1
Lidden Crs PENZ TR18 ....45 G1
Lidden Rd PENZ TR18 ....45 G1
The Lidden PENZ TR18 ....45 G1
Liddicoat Rd LOST PL22 ....37 G3
Lifeboat Hl STIVES TR26 ....69 F2
Lilyerne Ct STAUS PL25 ....64 B1
Limes La LISK PL14 ....33 E4
Linden Av NEWQ TR7 ....46 B4
Linden Crs NEWQ TR7 ....46 B5
Lingard Cl LISK PL14 ....32 D2

Linhay Cl STAUS PL25 ....65 G1
Link Cl FAL TR11 ....22 B3
The Links FAL TR11 ....22 B5
Links Vw BUDE EX23 ....12 C2
Linley Cl RTRUS TR3 ....83 E3
Linnet Ct SALT PL12 ....76 B3
Liscawn Ter TOR PL11 ....81 G4
Liskeard Rd SALT PL12 ....76 B2
Liskerrett Rd LISK PL14 ....33 G3
Liskey Hl PERRAN TR6 ....56 B3
Liskey Hill Crs PERRAN TR6 ....56 B3
Lister Hl FAL TR11 ....22 C2
Lister St FAL TR11 ....22 C2
Listowel Dr LOOE PL13 ....35 F2
Listry Rd NEWQ TR7 ....46 B4
Little Ash Gdns PLYNW PL5 ....77 G4
Little Ash Rd PLYNW PL5 ....77 G4
Little Bridge Pk WADE PL27 ....87 E2
Little Castle St TRU TR1 ....85 E3
Little Dean LISK PL14 ....32 D3
Little Dinas PADS PL28 ....48 B4
Little Down Pk NEWQ TR7 ....46 D5
Little Gilly Hl RED TR15 ....61 E4
Little-in-Sight STIVES TR26 * 69 E3
Little La HAYLE TR27 ....27 G2
   MBRK/KGSD PL10 ....43 H4
Little Meadow BODM PL31 ....10 C2
Little Mill La HAYLE TR27 ....67 E3
Little Oaks PENRYN TR10 ....52 B4
Little Point Crs
   MBRK/KGSD PL10 ....43 G1
Little Trelyn WADE PL27 ....49 G2
Little Woburn Cl LAUN PL15 ....31 E5
Llawnroc Cl CAMBORNE TR14 .....14 D4
Llewellyn Cl CAMEL PL32 ....17 E5
Lockyer Ter SALT PL12 * 77 E2
Lodenek Av PADS PL28 ....48 B4
Lodge Dr TRU TR1 ....85 H1
Lodge Hl LISK PL14 ....33 E3
Loe Bar Rd HELS TR13 ....58 B3
Loe Valley Rd HELS TR13 ....29 F2
Loftus Gdns PLYNW PL5 ....77 H3
Loggans Cl HAYLE TR27 ....27 G1
Loggans Rd HAYLE TR27 ....27 G1
Loggans Wk HAYLE TR27 ....27 G1
Loggans Wy HAYLE TR27 ....27 G1
Logue Rd SALT PL12 ....76 D2
Long Acre SALT PL12 ....76 A1
Longfield FAL TR11 ....22 B1
Longfield Dr CAMEL PL32 ....16 D5
Longfield Rd CAMEL PL32 ....17 E5
Longhouse La WADE PL27 ....49 G1
Long La HAYLE TR27 ....27 G2
Longmeadow SALT PL12 ....76 D2
Long Park Rd SALT PL12 ....76 C3
Longpark Wy STAUS PL25 ....64 C2
Long Steps FOW PL23 ....24 C2
Longstone Cl STIVES TR26 ....71 G2
Longstone Hl STIVES TR26 ....71 G2
Longview FAL TR11 ....22 C2
The Lookout FAL TR11 * 22 D1
Lostmarch Rd BODM PL31 ....11 E5
Lostwithiel St FOW PL23 ....24 C2
Lostwood Rd STAUS PL25 ....64 B2
Loughboro Rd PLYNW PL5 ....77 H4
Love La BODM PL31 ....11 E2
   HAYLE TR27 * 27 G2
   PENRYN TR10 ....53 E3
   PENZ TR18 ....54 C5
   STIVES TR26 ....69 F2
Lovering Rd STAUS PL25 ....64 B1
Lowarth Cl HELS TR13 ....29 F3
Lowenac Gdns
   CAMBORNE TR14 ....14 B4
Lowenek Cl FAL TR11 ....22 A1
Lowenna Gdns LOOE PL13 ....35 E2
Lowen Wy RTRUS TR3 ....82 D3
Lower Anderton Rd
   MBRK/KGSD PL10 ....43 G1
Lower Barncoose STAUS PL25 .....60 B4
Lower Bolenna PERRAN TR6 ....56 A4
Lower Boscaswell BODM PL31 .....10 C2
Lower Castle Rd
   RTRUE/STMW TR2 ....74 B3
Lower Chapel St LOOE PL13 ....35 F3
Lower Church St HAYLE TR27 ......27 F3
Lower Chywoone Hl
   PENZ TR18 ....45 G2
Lower Cleaverfield LAUN PL15 .....31 F2
Lower Fore St SALT PL12 ....77 F3
Lower Greenbanks WADE PL27 ....49 G2
Lower Green St PENZ TR18 ....45 H3
Lower Gurnick Rd PENZ TR18 ......54 C5
Lower Hl HELS TR13 ....29 G3
Lower Hillcrest HELS TR13 ....29 G3
   PERRAN TR6 ....56 A4
Lower Hugus Rd RTRUS TR3 ....82 D4
Lower Lux St LISK PL14 ....33 F2
Lower Market St LOOE PL13 ....35 F3
   PENRYN TR10 ....52 D3
Lower Merritts Hl
   RTRUNW TR4 ....60 A1
Lower Pengegon
   CAMBORNE TR14 ....15 E3
Lower Peverell Rd PENZ TR18 .....55 E2
Lower Polstain Rd RTRUS TR3 .....83 E4
Lower Port Vw SALT PL12 ....77 E3
Lower Queen St PENZ TR18 ....55 E5
Lower Redannick TRU TR1 ....85 E3
Lower Rosewin Rw TRU TR1 * 85 F3
Lower Silver Hl HELS TR13 ....29 G5

Lower St LOOE PL13 ....35 F3
   PENRYN TR10 ....52 D4
Lowertown La HELS TR13 ....29 G2
Lower Tywarnhayle
   PERRAN TR6 ....56 B3
Lower Well Gdns HELS TR13 ....29 G3
Lower Well Pk MEVA PL26 ....41 H3
Lower Woodside STAUS PL25 ......63 F3
Lowley Rd LAUN PL15 ....30 C5
Lucas Cl BODM PL31 ....10 D4
Lukes Cl TRU TR1 ....85 H2
Lusty Glaze Rd NEWQ TR7 ....47 E1
Luxon Dr TRU TR7 ....46 C5
Luxstowe LISK PL14 ....33 G2
Luxstowe Dr LISK PL14 ....33 F2
Luxstowe Gdns LISK PL14 * 33 F2
Luxulyan Rd PAR PL24 ....50 A3
Lychgate Dr TRU TR1 ....84 D1
Lyndhurst Av STAUS PL25 ....64 D3
Lyndon Cl SALT PL12 ....76 C1
Lyner Cl SALT PL12 * 77 E4
Lynher Dr SALT PL12 ....76 D4
Lyn-Meynel RED TR15 ....61 H1
Lynstone Rd BUDE EX23 ....12 B5
Lyn Ter PENZ TR18 ....45 G3
Lynwood Cl BODM PL31 ....10 D3
Lyons Rd STAUS PL25 ....65 E3
Lytton Pl STAUS PL25 ....64 C3

M

Mabbots Ct PENZ TR18 * 54 D5
Macey St TOR PL11 ....81 G4
Mackenzie St PLYNW PL5 ....77 H4
Maddever Crs LISK PL14 ....33 F3
Madeira Wk FAL TR11 ....22 C4
Madford La LAUN PL15 ....31 F4
Madison Ter HAYLE TR27 ....27 G2
Madison Vean HAYLE TR27 ....27 G2
Madron Rd PENZ TR18 ....54 C2
Maer Down Rd BUDE EX23 ....12 A1
Maiden St BUDE EX23 ....13 G3
Main St PENZ TR18 ....54 C2
Maker La MBRK/KGSD PL10 ....43 G2
Maker Rd TOR PL11 ....81 F5
Malabar Rd TRU TR1 ....84 B3
Malpas Rd TRU TR1 ....85 F3
Malt House Gdns PENZ TR18 ....45 G2
Malthouse La MARAZ TR17 ....38 C3
Manaton Cl HELS TR13 ....29 F3
Manewas Wy NEWQ TR7 ....47 E2
Manfield Wy STAUS PL25 ....65 E3
Manley Cl LISK PL14 ....33 G3
Manley Rd LISK PL14 ....33 E3
Manley Ter LISK PL14 ....33 E3
Mannor Wy HELS TR13 ....29 H1
Manor Cl FAL TR11 ....22 A1
   HELS TR13 ....29 H1
   PENZ TR18 ....54 D2
   STAUS PL25 ....64 C3
Manor Crs FAL TR11 ....22 A1
Manor Dr STIVES TR26 ....69 G5
Manor Farm Cl RPENZ TR20 ....39 H3
Manor Gdns CAMEL PL32 ....17 F4
   HAYLE TR27 ....67 F3
   RED TR15 ....60 D3
   TRU TR1 ....85 G2
Manor Pk SALT PL12 * 76 C3
Manor Pl PENZ TR18 ....54 D5
Manor Rd BUDE EX23 ....12 D4
   CAMBORNE TR14 ....14 B4
   FAL TR11 ....22 A1
   NEWQ TR7 ....46 B5
Manor Ter RED TR15 * 61 E2
Manor Vw PAR PL24 ....50 C5
Manor Wy PENZ TR18 ....54 D2
Manse Rd RTRUS TR3 ....19 F2
Maple Av CAMEL PL32 ....17 G3
   TOR PL11 ....81 F4
Maple Cl BODM PL31 ....10 A3
Marconi Cl HELS TR13 ....29 F3
Marcus Hl NEWQ TR7 ....46 B3
Margaret Av STAUS PL25 ....64 B4
Margaret Crs BODM PL31 ....10 B3
Margaret Gdns WADE PL27 ....87 E3
Margate La RBODM PL30 ....11 H5
Marine Crs FAL TR11 ....23 E3
Marine Dr FAL TR11 ....22 D3
Marine Pde RTRUE/STMW TR2 ....74 B3
Marine Ter PENZ TR18 * 55 E5
   STIVES TR26 ....69 E2
   TOR PL11 ....81 G5
Market Hl STAUS PL25 ....63 H3
Market Jew St PENZ TR18 ....55 E4
Market Pl CAMEL PL32 ....17 F4
   HELS TR13 ....29 F4
   MARAZ TR17 ....38 B3
   PADS PL28 ....48 B3
   PENZ TR18 ....55 E4
   STIVES TR26 ....69 F2
Market Sq HAYLE TR27 ....27 F3
   LANDS TR19 ....72 C4
   MEVA PL26 ....41 G3
Market Strd FAL TR11 ....22 D4
   PADS PL28 ....48 B3
   RED TR15 * 85 F2
   STIVES TR26 ....69 F2
Market St BODM PL31 ....10 D2
   BUDE EX23 ....13 G3
   FAL TR11 ....22 D2

   FOW PL23 ....24 D2
   HAYLE TR27 ....27 F3
   LANDS TR19 ....72 C4
   LAUN PL15 ....31 F3
   LISK PL14 ....33 F2
   MBRK/KGSD PL10 ....43 H5
   RTRUS TR3 ....19 E4
   STAUS PL25 ....63 H4
The Market PADS PL28 ....48 B3
Market Wy RED TR15 * 61 E4
Marks Dr BODM PL31 ....10 D4
Marks Wy NEWQ TR7 ....46 A5
Marlborough Av FAL TR11 ....22 C3
Marlborough Ct FAL TR11 ....22 C3
   SALT PL12 ....77 E4
Marlborough Cl FAL TR11 * 22 C3
Marlborough Crs FAL TR11 ....22 C3
Marlborough Gv FAL TR11 ....22 C3
Marlborough Rd FAL TR11 ....22 B3
Marriotts Av CAMBORNE TR14 .....14 A2
Marshall Av WADE PL27 ....87 E3
Marshall Rd BODM PL31 ....10 C4
Marsh La HAYLE TR27 ....27 E2
Martin Cl RED TR15 ....61 G3
Martins Cl LISK PL14 ....33 H1
Martinvale Av RED TR15 ....61 H1
Martinvale Parc RED TR15 ....61 H1
Martyn's Cl RTRUNW TR4 ....57 H4
Matela Cl FAL TR11 ....58 B2
Matthews Blds STIVES TR26 * 69 E3
Maudlin Ct LISK PL14 ....33 G3
Maybrook Dr SALT PL12 ....76 C3
Mayfield Cl BODM PL31 ....11 F2
   STAUS PL25 ....64 D5
Mayfield Crs NEWQ TR7 ....46 B4
Mayfield Rd FAL TR11 ....22 B3
   NEWQ TR7 ....46 B4
May La LOOE PL13 ....35 F2
Mayne Cl LAUN PL15 ....31 E2
Maynes Rw CAMBORNE TR14 .....14 C4
Meade Kingsley NEWQ TR7 ....47 E5
The Mead Houses PENZ TR18 .....55 F1
Meadowbank Rd FAL TR11 ....53 H5
Meadow Breeze LOST PL22 ....37 F4
Meadow Cl FOW PL23 ....24 D4
   NEWQ TR7 ....46 D5
   STAUS PL25 ....64 C1
   TRU TR1 ....83 G3
Meadow Dr BUDE EX23 ....12 D2
   CAMBORNE TR14 ....14 A2
   LOOE PL13 ....35 G1
   PAR PL24 ....50 C4
   SALT PL12 ....76 C1
Meadowhead WADE PL27 ....86 D4
Meadow La TRU TR1 ....85 F4
Meadow Pk LISK PL14 ....63 E3
   STAUS PL25 ....64 C3
Meadow Pl BODM PL31 ....10 C3
Meadowside LAUN PL15 ....30 D5
   NEWQ TR7 ....46 D5
   STAUS PL25 ....64 C1
Meadowside Cl HAYLE TR27 ....67 F1
Meadowside Rd FAL TR11 ....22 B3
The Meadows TOR PL11 ....80 D3
Meadow St MEVA PL26 ....41 G3
Meadowsweet Pk SALT PL12 ....76 B4
The Meadow STIVES TR26 * 69 F2
   TRU TR1 * 84 D3
Meadow Vw CAMBORNE TR14 .....14 D5
   RPENZ TR20 ....39 H3
Meadway LOOE PL13 ....35 F2
   SALT PL12 ....76 D4
   STAUS PL25 ....64 C2
Mead Whf MEVA PL26 ....41 H3
Mearwood La FAL TR11 ....22 B3
Medland Gdns STAUS PL25 ....63 H3
Medrose WADE PL27 ....49 F2
Medrose Ter PENZ TR18 * 55 E3
Melbourne Rd LISK PL14 ....33 E3
Melbourne Ter PENZ TR18 * 54 C2
Mellanear Cl HAYLE TR27 ....26 D5
Mellanear Rd HAYLE TR27 ....26 D5
Mellanvrane La NEWQ TR7 ....46 C5
Melliars Wy BUDE EX23 ....12 D2
Melville Crs FAL TR11 ....22 B3
Melville Rd RTRUS TR3 ....82 D3
Melville Ter LOST PL22 ....37 F3
Melvill La FAL TR11 ....22 D4
Melvill Rd FAL TR11 ....22 D3
Melyn Cl FAL TR11 ....27 G1
Menability Rd STAUS PL25 ....64 B1
Menacuddle Hl STAUS PL25 ....63 H3
Menacuddle La STAUS PL25 ....63 H3
Meneage Parc HELS TR13 ....29 G4
Meneage Rd HELS TR13 ....29 G4
Meneage St HELS TR13 ....29 G4
Meneage Vls STAUS PL25 ....63 G4
Menear Rd STAUS PL25 ....64 D2
Meneth Rd CAMBORNE TR14 ......15 E4
Menhay Gdns RED TR15 ....60 B3
Menhyr Dr STIVES TR26 ....71 E1
Mennaye Gdns RED TR15 * 60 B3
Mennaye Rd PENZ TR18 ....54 D5
Merchants Quay LAUN PL15 ....30 C5
Merlins Wy TINT PL34 ....78 D4
Merrick Av TRU TR1 ....85 G1
Merrifield Cl TRU TR1 ....84 D2
Merrill Pl FAL TR11 ....22 C3
Merritts Hl RTRUNW TR4 ....60 A1
Messack Cl FAL TR11 ....22 A4
Methleigh Parc HELS TR13 ....58 A1

The Mews *PAR* PL24 .... 50 C2
Mexico La *HAYLE* TR27 .... 27 E1
Mexico Ter *HAYLE* TR27 .... 27 E1
Michell Av *NEWQ* TR7 * 46 B3
Middlefield Cl *SALT* PL12 .... 76 A3
Middle Market St *LOOE* PL13 .... 35 F3
Middle Rd *RED* TR15 .... 61 H1
Middle Rosewin Rw *TRU* TR1 * 85 F2
Middle Rw *RED* TR15 .... 61 G1
Middle St *PADS* PL28 .... 48 B3
Middleton Crs *NEWQ* TR7 .... 46 C5
Middleway *PAR* PL24 .... 50 C2
Midway Dr *TRU* TR1 .... 85 G2
Midway Rd *BODM* PL31 .... 10 A2
Miers Cl *PLYNW* PL5 .... 77 H5
Miers Ct *PLYNW* PL5 .... 77 H5
Milch Pk *SALT* PL12 * 76 B2
Military Rd *MBRK/KGSD* PL10 .... 42 C2
RTRUE/STMW TR2 .... 74 D5
Mill La *HELS* TR13 .... 58 A1
WADE PL27 .... 87 F3
Millet Cl *MARAZ* TR17 .... 38 D3
Millfield *PENZ* TR18 * 55 G2
Mill Gdns *LOST* PL22 * 37 F4
Millham La *LOST* PL22 .... 37 H3
Mill Hl *HAYLE* TR27 .... 66 C1
LOST PL22 .... 37 G4
Millhouse Pk *TOR* PL11 .... 81 F5
Mill La *CAMEL* PL32 .... 17 E3
HELS TR13 .... 58 A1
TOR PL11 .... 81 F5
Millpond Av *HAYLE* TR27 .... 26 D5
Millpool Head
MBRK/KGSD PL10 .... 43 F1
Mill Rd *CAMBORNE* TR14 .... 14 A5
MBRK/KGSD PL10 .... 43 G1
PADS PL28 .... 48 B3
PERRAN TR6 .... 56 C5
Mill Sq *PADS* PL28 .... 48 B3
Mill St *BODM* PL31 .... 10 D2
Mill View Gdns
MBRK/KGSD PL10 * 43 G1
Mill View Rd *MBRK/KGSD* PL10 .... 43 G1
Miners Ct *PERRAN* TR6 .... 56 B4
RED TR15 .... 61 F3
Miners Rw *RED* TR15 .... 61 F3
Miners Wy *LISK* PL14 .... 33 G1
Minnie Pl *FAL* TR11 .... 22 D3
Minster Av *BUDE* EX23 .... 12 D4
Minton Cl *STAUS* PL25 .... 64 D3
Mitchell Cl *TRU* TR1 * 85 F1
Mitchell Hl *TRU* TR1 * 85 F3
Mitchell Hill Ter *TRU* TR1 * 85 F2
Mitchell La *CAMBORNE* TR14 .... 14 D3
Mitchell Rd *CAMBORNE* TR14 .... 14 A3
FAL TR11 .... 22 C1
STAUS PL25 .... 64 C3
Molesworth Ct *WADE* PL27 * 86 C4
Molesworth St *TINT* PL34 .... 86 C4
WADE PL27 * 86 C4
Molesworth Ter
MBRK/KGSD PL10 * 43 G1
Mongleath Av *FAL* TR11 .... 22 A3
Mongleath Cl *FAL* TR11 .... 22 A4
Mongleath Rd *FAL* TR11 .... 22 A3
Monks Pk *LAUN* PL15 .... 31 G3
Monmouth La *LOST* PL22 .... 37 F4
Montague Av *RED* TR15 .... 60 D2
Monterey Cl *BUDE* EX23 .... 12 C4
Monterey Gdns *TRU* TR1 .... 85 G2
Montgomery Cl *SALT* PL12 .... 76 C2
Monument Rd *HELS* TR13 .... 29 F4
Monument Wy *BODM* PL31 .... 10 B3
Moorland Cl *LISK* PL14 .... 33 G1
Moorland Ct *STAUS* PL25 .... 63 H4
Moorland Rd *LAUN* PL15 .... 31 E4
PAR PL24 .... 50 C3
STAUS PL25 .... 63 H4
Moorlands La *SALT* PL12 .... 76 B1
Moorland Vw *LISK* PL14 .... 33 F1
SALT PL12 .... 77 E2
Moorland Wk *CAMEL* PL32 .... 17 F5
The Moors *LOST* PL22 .... 37 F5
Moor St *CAMBORNE* TR14 .... 14 C3
Moorswater Viad *LISK* PL14 .... 32 C4
The Moor *FAL* TR11 * 22 D2
Moor Vw *BODM* PL31 .... 11 E5
TOR PL11 .... 81 E4
Morcom Cl *STAUS* PL25 .... 64 D2
Morcom Garth *LISK* PL14 .... 33 E3
Moresk Cl *TRU* TR1 .... 85 F1
Moresk Gdns *TRU* TR1 .... 85 F2
Moresk Rd *TRU* TR1 .... 85 E1
Morlaix Av *TRU* TR1 .... 85 E5
Morla La *STAUS* PL25 .... 60 D2
Morleigh Cl *STAUS* PL25 .... 64 C4
Morrab Pl *PENZ* TR18 .... 55 E4
Morrab Rd *CAMBORNE* TR14 .... 14 B3
PENZ TR18 .... 55 E4
Morrab Ter *PENZ* TR18 .... 55 E4
Morris Gdns *NEWQ* TR7 * 46 A5
Mortimore Cl *SALT* PL12 .... 76 C3
Morven Rd *STAUS* PL25 .... 64 C3
Morwenna Gdns *PERRAN* TR6 .... 56 D3
Morwenna Ter *BUDE* EX23 * 12 C4
Moss Ter *FOW* PL23 .... 24 D3
Mote Pk *SALT* PL12 .... 76 B2
Mount Agar Rd *STAUS* PL25 .... 19 G2
Mount Ambrose *RED* TR15 .... 61 G1
Mountbatten Av *NEWQ* TR7 .... 47 G2

Mount Bennett Rd *PAR* PL24 .... 51 G3
Mount Camel *CAMEL* PL32 .... 17 E4
Mount Carbis Rd *RED* TR15 .... 61 F5
Mount Charles St *STAUS* PL25 .... 64 C4
Mount Cl *NEWQ* TR7 * 46 A5
Mount Crs *PAR* PL24 .... 50 D5
Mount Edgcumbe Ter
FAL TR11 * 22 D2
Mountfield Ter *PAR* PL24 .... 50 D4
Mount Folly Sq *BODM* PL31 * 10 D3
Mountlea Country Pk
PAR PL24 .... 50 D5
Mountlea Dr *PAR* PL24 .... 50 C5
Mount Lidden *PENZ* TR18 .... 54 C5
Mount Madford *LAUN* PL15 * 31 F4
Mount Pleasant *BODM* PL31 .... 10 D2
FAL TR11 .... 22 A5
HAYLE TR27 .... 27 E3
MBRK/KGSD PL10 .... 43 F1
PAR PL24 .... 50 C1
PENZ TR18 .... 54 B5
RED TR15 * 61 H1
STIVES TR26 .... 69 F2
Mount Pleasant Cl
CAMBORNE TR14 .... 14 C5
Mount Pleasant Gdns
HAYLE TR27 .... 27 E3
Mount Pleasant Pl *LOST* PL22 * 37 F3
Mount Pleasant Rd
CAMBORNE TR14 .... 14 C4
RTRUS TR3 .... 83 F3
Mount Pleasure
CAMBORNE TR14 .... 14 D5
Mount Prospect Ter
.... 45 G1
Mount Royal Cl *PENZ* TR18 .... 55 F3
Mounts Bay Rd *PENZ* TR18 .... 54 C5
Mount's Bay Ter *HELS* TR13 .... 58 B3
Mounts Bay Village
PENZ TR18 * 55 G2
Mount's Rd *HELS* TR13 .... 58 B3
Mount Stamper Rd
STAUS PL25 .... 64 A1
Mountstephen Cl *STAUS* PL25 .... 63 F4
Mount Stephens La *FAL* TR11 .... 22 B2
Mount St *MEVA* PL26 .... 41 H2
PENZ TR18 .... 55 E4
Mount Ter *PAR* PL24 .... 50 B4
The Mount *PAR* PL24 .... 50 D5
Mount View Ter *MARAZ* TR17 .... 38 D3
PENZ TR18 .... 45 G2
Mount Wise *LAUN* PL15 .... 31 F4
NEWQ TR7 .... 46 B4
Mount Wise Cots *NEWQ* TR7 .... 46 B4
Mount Zion *STIVES* TR26 * 69 F2
Mowhay Cl *NEWQ* TR7 .... 46 D5
Mowhay Meadow *WADE* PL27 .... 86 C4
Moyle Rd *PADS* PL28 .... 48 C4
Mulberry Quay *FAL* TR11 * 22 D1
Mulberry Rd *SALT* PL12 .... 76 D3
Mullion Cl *TOR* PL11 .... 81 E3
Murdoch Cl *RED* TR15 .... 61 E2
.... 85 G1
Murdock Rd *TOR* PL11 .... 81 E4
Mutton Rw *PENRYN* TR10 .... 52 D3
Myrtle Cl *SALT* PL12 .... 76 D3
Myrtles Ct *SALT* PL12 .... 54 C2
Mython Ct *PENZ* TR18 .... 54 C2

N

Nalders Ct *TRU* TR1 * 85 E3
Nampara Cl *STIVES* TR26 .... 71 G1
Nampara Wy *TRU* TR1 .... 85 H3
Nancealverne *RPENZ* TR20 .... 54 C3
Nancemere Rd *TRU* TR1 .... 85 F1
Nancevallion *CAMBORNE* TR14 .... 15 D3
Nancherrow La *LANDS* TR19 .... 72 B3
Nancherrow Rw *LANDS* TR19 .... 72 C2
Nancherrow Ter *LANDS* TR19 .... 72 C2
Nanjivey Pl *STIVES* TR26 * 69 E3
Nanjivey Ter *STIVES* TR26 * 69 E3
Nanpusker Rd *HAYLE* TR27 .... 27 G3
Nansavallon Rd *TRU* TR1 .... 83 H3
Nanscober Pl *HELS* TR13 .... 29 F1
Nans Kestenen *HELS* TR13 .... 29 F4
Nansloe Cl *HELS* TR13 .... 29 G5
Narrowcliff *NEWQ* TR7 .... 46 D2
Nathan Cl *NEWQ* TR7 * 46 C3
Navy Inn Ct *PENZ* TR18 * 45 G3
Netherton Rd *PADS* PL28 .... 48 B4
Nettell's Hl *HELS* TR13 .... 61 E3
Nettles Hl *HELS* TR13 * 29 F1
Nevada Pl *HELS* TR13 * 54 C2
Nevada St *PENZ* TR18 .... 54 C2
Nevada Vls *PAR* PL24 .... 50 D5
Newbridge La *RTRUS* TR3 .... 83 H4
New Bridge St *TRU* TR1 .... 85 F3
Newbridge Wy *TRU* TR1 .... 83 H3
New Connections St
CAMBORNE TR14 .... 14 C3
New Cross Rw *FAL* TR11 * 22 D2
New Cut *RED* TR15 .... 61 E3
New Dairy La *MARAZ* TR17 .... 38 B1
New Guineaport *WADE* PL27 .... 86 D4
Newham La *HELS* TR13 .... 29 E1
Newham Rd *TRU* TR1 .... 85 H4
New La *RED* TR15 .... 61 H1

Newman Rd *SALT* PL12 .... 77 E2
Newmills Cl *TRU* TR1 .... 84 C1
New Mills La *RTRUNW* TR4 .... 84 B1
New Pk *WADE* PL27 .... 86 D4
New Park Rd *WADE* PL27 .... 86 D4
Newport Sq *LAUN* PL15 .... 31 E2
Newport St *MBRK/KGSD* PL10 .... 43 F1
Newquay Rd *RTRUNW* TR4 .... 57 H4
New Rd *BUDE* EX23 .... 13 F5
CAMBORNE TR14 .... 15 G4
LANDS TR19 .... 72 C3
LISK PL14 .... 32 C3
MBRK/KGSD PL10 .... 43 H4
PENZ TR18 .... 45 G3
PERRAN TR6 .... 56 C3
SALT PL12 .... 76 C2
New Road *MBRK/KGSD* PL10 .... 43 H4
New Road Hl *FOW* PL23 .... 24 C2
New St *FAL* TR11 .... 22 D2
MBRK/KGSD PL10 .... 43 F1
PADS PL28 .... 48 B3
PENRYN TR10 .... 53 E4
PENZ TR18 .... 55 E4
Newton Pk *RTRUE/STMW* TR2 .... 74 B3
Newton Rd *RTRUE/STMW* TR2 .... 74 C1
New Town La *PENZ* TR18 .... 55 E4
New Windsor Ter *FAL* TR11 .... 22 C3
Nicholas Parc *PENZ* TR18 .... 54 C2
Nilch Pk *SALT* PL12 76
No Go by HI *LANDS* TR19 .... 72 C3
Norfolk Rd *FAL* TR11 .... 22 D2
Normandy Hl *PLYNW* PL5 .... 77 G3
Normandy Wy *BODM* PL31 .... 11 E5
CAMBORNE TR14 .... 15 G4
PLYNW PL5 .... 77 H3
North Cnr *PENZ* TR18 .... 45 G2
Northey Rd *BODM* PL31 .... 10 C3
Northfield Dr *TRU* TR1 .... 85 E4
Northgate Pl *LAUN* PL15 * 31 F3
Northgate St *LAUN* PL15 * 31 F3
North Hill Pk *STAUS* PL25 .... 63 H4
North Pde *CAMBORNE* TR14 .... 14 C3
HELS TR13 .... 53 H5
PENZ TR18 .... 55 E4
North Parade Rear
CAMBORNE TR14 .... 14 C3
North Park Vls *SALT* PL12 .... 76 B1
North Pl *STIVES* TR26 * 69 F2
North Quay *HAYLE* TR27 .... 26 C3
PADS PL28 .... 48 B3
North Quay Hl *NEWQ* TR7 .... 46 A2
North Quay Pde *PADS* PL28 .... 48 C2
North Rd *CAMBORNE* TR14 .... 14 D3
LOOE PL13 .... 35 G2
RPENZ TR20 .... 39 H3
SALT PL12 .... 77 E2
TOR PL11 .... 81 G5
North Roskear Meadow
CAMBORNE TR14 .... 14 D1
North Roskear Rd
CAMBORNE TR14 .... 14 D2
North Rw *LANDS* TR19 .... 72 C3
North St *FOW* PL23 .... 24 D2
LAUN PL15 .... 30 D1
LOST PL22 .... 37 F4
MARAZ TR17 .... 38 D3
PAR PL24 .... 51 F3
RED TR15 .... 61 E2
STAUS PL25 .... 63 H5
North Ter *STIVES* TR26 * 69 F3
North Vw *LOOE* PL13 .... 35 F2
Norton Ter *PENZ* TR18 * 54 D5
Norway Cl *STIVES* TR26 .... 69 F2
Norway La *STIVES* TR26 .... 69 F2
Norway Sq *STIVES* TR26 * 69 F2
Noweth Pl *FAL* TR11 .... 22 A1
Nursery Cl *PAR* PL24 .... 51 F3
TRU TR1 .... 85 F2
Nut La *HAYLE* TR27 .... 66 D1

O

Oak Apple Cl *SALT* PL12 .... 76 C1
Oak Dr *LISK* PL14 .... 33 E3
Oakfield Rd *FAL* TR11 .... 22 B1
Oaklands Dr *SALT* PL12 .... 76 B2
Oaklands Gn *SALT* PL12 .... 76 C2
Oaklands Rd *LISK* PL14 .... 33 G2
Oak La *TRU* TR1 .... 85 H2
Oakleigh Ter *NEWQ* TR7 .... 46 C5
Oak Park Ter *LISK* PL14 .... 33 E2
Oak Tree Cl *STAUS* PL25 .... 65 E4
Oak Wy *TRU* TR1 .... 85 E2
Oakwood Pk *BODM* PL31 .... 11 E5
Oakwood Ri *CAMEL* PL32 .... 17 G4
Oates Rd *HELS* TR13 .... 29 G3
MARAZ TR17 .... 38 C3
Observer Cl *TRU* TR1 .... 85 E4
Ocean Crs *HELS* TR13 .... 58 B3
Ocean Vw *FOW* PL23 .... 24 D3
Ocean View Rd *BUDE* EX23 .... 12 B3
Ocean View Ter *STIVES* TR26 * 69 E2
Old Barn Cl *NEWQ* TR7 .... 46 A5
Old Boatyard *PADS* PL28 .... 48 C2
Old Brewery Yd *FAL* TR11 * 22 D1
PENZ TR18 .... 55 E4
Old Bridge St *TRU* TR1 .... 85 F3
Old Carnon Hl *RTRUS* TR3 .... 19 G3
Old Drovers Wy *BUDE* EX23 .... 13 G5

Old Farm Rd *PLYNW* PL5 .... 77 H5
Old Ferry Rd *SALT* PL12 .... 77 F2
Old Foundry Cl *LANDS* TR19 .... 72 B2
Old Foundry Cl *LANDS* TR19 .... 72 C3
Old Grammar School Ct
LOST PL22 .... 37 F4
Old Hl *FAL* TR11 .... 22 C1
.... 29 E3
Old Hill Crs *FAL* TR11 .... 22 B1
Old Lawn *STAUS* PL25 .... 63 G4
Old Market Pl *BODM* PL31 .... 10 A3
Old Nursery Cl *HELS* TR13 .... 58 A1
Old Paul Hl *PENZ* TR18 .... 45 G2
Old Portreath Rd *RTRUNW* TR4 .... 60 C1
Old Post Office HI *BUDE* EX23 * 13 G3
Old Rd *LISK* PL14 .... 32 C3
Old Roselyon Crs *PAR* PL24 .... 50 C4
Old Roselyon Rd *PAR* PL24 .... 50 C4
Old School Ct *WADE* PL27 .... 86 C3
Old School Rd *PLYNW* PL5 .... 77 H5
Old Smithy Cl *MARAZ* TR17 .... 38 D3
Old Station Rd *LISK* PL14 .... 32 C3
Old Tram Rd *RTRUS* TR3 .... 19 G4
Old Vicarage Ga *HAYLE* TR27 .... 67 F3
Old Vicarage Pl *STAUS* PL25 .... 63 H4
Old Well Gdns *PENRYN* TR10 .... 52 D3
Olivers Quay *MEVA* PL26 * 41 G3
Oliver's Ter *HELS* TR13 .... 29 G4
Omaha Rd *BODM* PL31 .... 11 E5
Omil Ct *WADE* PL27 * 86 C3
Opies Cl *BODM* PL31 .... 10 B2
Orange La *STIVES* TR26 .... 69 E2
Orchard Cl *HELS* TR13 .... 29 F2
STAUS PL25 .... 64 B3
TRU TR1 .... 84 B3
Orchard Ct *PENZ* TR18 .... 54 C4
Orchard Gv *STAUS* PL25 .... 63 G3
Orchard Pl *PENZ* TR18 .... 45 G2
Orchard Ter *PENZ* TR18 * 45 G2
The Orchard *HAYLE* TR27 .... 67 E3
Orchard Wy *RPENZ* TR20 .... 39 H3
Osborne Parc *HELS* TR13 .... 29 F2
Owen Sivell Cl *LISK* PL14 .... 33 H2

P

Paardeburg Rd *BODM* PL31 .... 11 F5
Packsaddle *PENRYN* TR10 .... 52 B2
Packsaddle Cl *PENRYN* TR10 .... 52 B2
Paddock Cl *SALT* PL12 .... 76 C1
The Paddocks *HELS* TR13 .... 29 F2
RED TR15 .... 61 G5
Palace Rd *STAUS* PL25 .... 64 A3
Palmers Wy *WADE* PL27 .... 87 E2
Pannier La *STIVES* TR26 .... 71 E1
Parade Pas *PENZ* TR18 * 55 E4
Parade Sq *LOST* PL22 .... 37 G4
Parade St *PENZ* TR18 .... 55 E4
The Parade *HELS* TR13 .... 29 G4
LISK PL14 .... 33 E2
MBRK/KGSD PL10 .... 43 F1
TRU TR1 .... 85 G3
Parc-an-Bal Ct
CAMBORNE TR14 .... 14 D2
Parc-an-Banns
CAMBORNE TR14 .... 14 D5
Parc-an-Challow *PENRYN* TR10 .... 52 C4
Parc An Creet *STIVES* TR26 .... 68 D3
Parc-an-Creet *STIVES* TR26 .... 68 D3
Parc-an-Dix La *HAYLE* TR27 .... 27 E2
Parc-an-Dower *HELS* TR13 .... 29 G4
Parc-an-Forth *STIVES* TR26 .... 68 D3
Parc-an-Gwarry *RTRUS* TR3 .... 19 F1
Parc-an-Maen *HELS* TR13 .... 58 B2
Parc An Stamps *STIVES* TR26 .... 68 D3
Parc Av *STIVES* TR26 * 69 F3
Parc Bean *STIVES* TR26 * 69 E2
Parc-Bracket St
CAMBORNE TR14 .... 14 C3
Parc Briwer *PENRYN* TR10 .... 53 E4
Parc Eglos *HELS* TR13 .... 29 F3
Parc Fer Cl *BUDE* EX23 .... 13 G3
Parc Godrevy *NEWQ* TR7 .... 21 H3
Parc Holland *HELS* TR13 .... 29 G3
Parc Ledran *HELS* TR13 .... 29 G3
Parc Ledrak *HELS* TR13 .... 29 F1
Parc Letta *PENZ* TR18 .... 54 C2
Parc Mellan *CAMBORNE* TR14 .... 14 C4
Parc Owles *STIVES* TR26 .... 71 F1
Parc Ter *PENZ* TR18 * 45 G3
Parc Vean *RED* TR15 * 61 E4
Parc Venton Cl
CAMBORNE TR14 .... 14 E4
Parc Wartha Av *PENZ* TR18 .... 54 D3
Parc Wartha Crs *PENZ* TR18 .... 54 D3
Pargolla Rd *NEWQ* TR7 .... 46 C3
Par Gn *PAR* PL24 .... 51 E4
Park-an-Bans
CAMBORNE TR14 .... 14 D5
Parkancreeg *RTRUS* TR3 .... 19 F2
Park An Gonwyn *STIVES* TR26 .... 71 G2
Park An Gorsaf
CAMBORNE TR14 .... 14 C4
Park An Harvey *HELS* TR13 .... 29 G2
Park-an-Mengleth *RED* TR15 .... 61 F4
Park-an-Tansys
CAMBORNE TR14 .... 15 E5
Park Av *STIVES* TR26 .... 69 E3
Park Cnr *PENZ* TR18 .... 55 E4

Park Crs *FAL* TR11 ....22 C2
  HELS TR13......................29 F4
Park Dr *BODM* PL31....................10 A3
Parkenbutts *NEWQ* TR7................47 G2
Parkengue *PENRYN* TR10.............52 B4
Parkesway *SALT* PL12...................76 C4
Park Fenton *LISK* PL14.................33 C3
Park Hl *FAL* TR11.........................22 C2
Park Holly *CAMBORNE* TR14........14 A4
Parkins Ter *TRU* TR1 * 85 F2
Parklands Cl *NEWQ* TR7...............47 G3
Park La *CAMBORNE* TR14............14 D4
  FAL TR11.......................22 C2
Park Leven *RTRUNW* TR4.............60 A2
Park Lowen *STIVES* TR26.............71 E4
Park Pl *WADE* PL27 * 86 C3
Park Ri *FAL* TR11........................22 C1
Park Rd *CAMBORNE* TR14............14 D3
  FOW PL23........................24 C2
  LISK PL14.......................33 F2
  LOST PL22.......................37 F4
  PENZ TR18.......................45 G3
  RED TR15.........................61 F4
  STAUS PL25......................63 H4
  TOR PL11.........................81 G4
  WADE PL27.......................86 C5
Park Ter *FAL* TR11......................22 C2
The Park *PENRYN* TR10 * 52 C3
Parkvedras Ter *TRU* TR1 * 84 D3
Park Vw *CAMBORNE* TR14 * 14 C2
  LISK PL14.......................33 F2
  TRU TR1..........................85 E4
Park View Cl *RTRUS* TR3..............19 F2
Park View Rd *HELS* TR13.............29 F4
Park View Ter *WADE* PL27............86 C4
Park Vue *LAUN* PL15...................31 E4
Park Wy *STAUS* PL25...................64 C2
The Parkway *SALT* PL12...............77 F3
Par La *PAR* PL24........................50 C4
Par Moor Rd *STAUS* PL25.............65 H3
Pascoe Cl *RTRUS* TR3..................83 E2
Passage La *FOW* PL23.................24 B1
Pathfields *BUDE* EX23.................12 B3
The Pathway Flds *HAYLE* TR27......27 E4
Paull Rd *BODM* PL31...................10 A3
Paulls Rw *RED* TR15 * 61 G4
Pauls Rw *TRU* TR1 * 85 F2
Paul's Ter *TRU* TR1 * 85 E1
Pavilion Pk *CAMBORNE* TR14........15 E2
Pavlova Ct *LISK* PL14..................33 F3
Peacock Av *TOR* PL11..................81 F4
Pearce's La *STIVES* TR26.............69 E4
Pearces Rw *PAR* PL24.................50 D4
Pednandrea *LANDS* TR19..............72 B3
  RED TR15.........................61 F3
Pedn-moran
  RTRUE/STMW TR2..............74 D2
Pednolva Wk *STIVES* TR26............69 F2
Pellew Cl *PADS* PL28...................48 A3
Pellew Crs *HELS* TR13.................29 G4
Pellew Rd *FAL* TR11....................22 C1
Pembroke Cl *PAR* PL24................50 D5
Pembroke Rd *NEWQ* TR7.............47 H2
Pemros Rd *PLYNW* PL5................77 H4
Penair Crs *TRU* TR1....................85 H1
Penair Vw *TRU* TR1....................85 H2
Penalverne Av *PENZ* TR18............54 D4
Penalverne Crs *PENZ* TR18...........54 D4
Penalverne Dr *PENZ* TR18............54 D4
Penalverne Pl *PENZ* TR18............54 D4
Penameyne Ct *STIVES* TR26.........69 F2
Pen An Drea *HELS* TR13...............29 H1
Pen-an-Gwel *STIVES* TR26............69 E4
Penare Gdns *PENZ* TR18 * 55 E3
Penare Ter *PENZ* TR18.................55 E3
Penarrow Cl *FAL* TR11.................22 A4
Penarth *LOOE* PL13.....................34 D3
Penarth Rd *FAL* TR11..................22 C1
Penarwyn Crs *PENZ* TR18............54 B2
Penarwyn Rd *PAR* PL24...............50 B4
Penarwyn Woods *PAR* PL24..........50 C4
Penbeagle Cl *STIVES* TR26...........68 D4
Penbeagle Cres *STIVES* TR26.......68 D4
Penbeagle La *STIVES* TR26...........68 D4
Penbeagle Ter *STIVES* TR26.........68 D4
Penbeagle Wy *STIVES* TR26.........68 D4
Penberthy Rd *HELS* TR13.............29 G4
Pen-Brea *RTRUE/STMW* TR2.........74 C1
Pen Brea *RTRUE/STMW* TR2.........74 D1
Penbrea Rd *PENZ* TR18................54 B3
Penbugle La *BODM* PL31..............10 D1
Pencair Av *TOR* PL11...................80 D5
Pencarrick Cl *TRU* TR1.................84 D3
Pendale Sq *TRU* TR1...................84 D3
Pendarves
  CAMBORNE TR14................14 B5
  FAL TR11.........................53 G5
  PENZ TR18.......................54 D3
  TRU TR1..........................85 E1
Pendarves St *CAMBORNE* TR14.....15 E2
Pendarves Vw
  CAMBORNE TR14................14 B5
Pendean Av *LISK* PL14.................33 E2
Pendean Cl *LISK* PL14.................33 E2
Pendean Ct *LISK* PL14.................33 E2
Pendean Dr *LISK* PL14.................33 E2
Pendeen Cl *RTRUS* TR3................83 E3
Pendeen Crs *RTRUS* TR3..............83 E3
Pendeen Parc *HELS* TR13.............29 F1
Pendeen Pk *HELS* TR13................29 F1

Pendeen Rd *RTRUS* TR3...............83 E3
  TRU TR1..........................85 G4
Pendennis Cl *PENZ* TR18..............55 E2
  TOR PL11.........................81 E4
Pendennis Pl *PENZ* TR18..............55 F2
Pendennis Ri *FAL* TR11.................23 F3
Pendennis Rd *FAL* TR11................23 F3
  LOOE PL13.......................35 F2
  PENZ TR18.......................55 E2
Pender's La *RED* TR15..................61 E3
Pendilly Av *TOR* PL11...................81 E5
Pendour Pk *LOST* PL22.................37 H4
Pendower Rd *LOOE* PL13...............35 G2
Pendower Ter
  CAMBORNE TR14 * 14 D5
Pendragon Rd *LISK* PL14..............33 G3
Pendrea Cl *PENZ* TR18.................55 F2
Pendrea Pk *CAMBORNE* TR14.......15 E1
Pendrea Rd *PENZ* TR18.................55 F2
Pendrim Rd *LOOE* PL13................35 F2
Penforth *CAMBORNE* TR14............14 D4
Pengannel Cl *NEWQ* TR7..............46 A5
Pengarth Cl *TRU* TR1...................85 E4
Pengarth Ri *FAL* TR11..................22 C3
Pengarth Rd *FAL* TR11.................22 C3
Pengegon Moor
  CAMBORNE TR14................15 E4
Pengegon Parc
  CAMBORNE TR14................15 E4
Pengegon Wy
  CAMBORNE TR14................15 E4
Pengelly Hl *TOR* PL11..................81 E2
Pengelly Pk *TOR* PL11.................81 E2
Pengelly Pl *FAL* TR11...................22 A1
Pengellys Rw *CAMBORNE* TR14.....15 F1
Pengegar Wy *RTRUS* TR3.............83 E3
Pengover Cl *LISK* PL14.................33 G2
Pengover Hts *LISK* PL14...............33 G2
Pengover Parc *RED* TR15..............61 F2
Pengover Rd *LISK* PL14.................33 G2
Pengwarras Rd
  CAMBORNE TR14................14 B3
Pengwel *PENZ* TR18....................45 G2
Penhale Est *PENZ* TR18................61 E2
Penhale Rd *FAL* TR11...................22 B5
Penhaligon Cl *RED* TR15...............61 G4
Penhaligon Ct *TRU* TR1................85 G2
Penhaligon Wy *STAUS* PL25..........64 C2
Penhallick *RED* TR15....................15 H2
Penhallick Rd *RED* TR15...............15 G2
Penhallow Rd *NEWQ* TR7.............47 E2
Penhaven Ct *NEWQ* TR7...............46 B3
Penhellaz Hl *HELS* TR13...............29 F3
Penhellaz Rd *HELS* TR13..............29 F3
Penina Av *NEWQ* TR7..................46 C5
Penkernick Cl *PENZ* TR18.............45 F3
Penknight La *LOST* PL22...............36 D4
Penlean Cl *RED* TR15...................61 G1
Penlee Manor Dr *PENZ* TR18.........55 E4
Penlee Pk *PENZ* TR18..................54 D4
  TOR PL11.........................80 D4
Penlee St *PENZ* TR18..................55 E3
Penlee View Ter *PENZ* TR18 * 55 E3
Penlu *CAMBORNE* TR14................15 E1
Penmare Cl *HAYLE* TR27...............27 G2
Penmare Ter *HAYLE* TR27.............27 G2
Penmelen *CAMEL* PL32.................17 E4
Penmere Cl *HELS* TR13.................29 F2
  PENZ TR18.......................55 E2
Penmere Ct *FAL* TR11..................22 C3
Penmere Crs *FAL* TR11.................22 B3
Penmere Dr *NEWQ* TR7................21 H3
Penmere Hl *FAL* TR11...................22 C3
Penmere Pl *PENZ* TR18.................55 E2
Penmere Rd *PENZ* TR18................55 E2
  STAUS PL25......................64 D3
Penmerrin Ct *NEWQ* TR7..............46 B4
Penmeva Vw *MEVA* PL26..............41 F3
Penmorvah *FAL* TR11...................53 H1
Penmorvah Pl
  CAMBORNE TR14................14 D4
Penmorvah Rd *TRU* TR1...............85 G1
Pennance Rd *FAL* TR11.................22 C4
Penn Kernow *LAUN* PL15..............31 H5
Pennor Dr *STAUS* PL25.................64 C1
Pennygillam Wy *LAUN* PL15..........30 C5
Pennys La *PAR* PL24.....................50 A5
Penoweth *FAL* TR11.....................53 H1
Penpol Av *HAYLE* TR27.................27 E4
Penpol Hl *RNEWQ* TR8.................21 G4
Penpol Rd *HAYLE* TR27.................26 D4
Penpol Ter *HAYLE* TR27................26 D3
Penpol Vean *HAYLE* TR27.............27 E4
Penponds Rd *HELS* TR13...............58 A1
Penpons Cl *PENZ* TR18.................54 C5
Penpont Rd *RED* TR15..................61 F2
Pen Porth Av *STIVES* TR26...........68 D3
Penquite Dr *BODM* PL31...............11 E2
Penrice Parc *STAUS* PL25..............64 D4
Penrose Rd *HELS* TR13.................58 A1
  HELS TR13.......................29 F3
Penrose Ter *PENZ* TR18................55 F3
Penruan La *RTRUE/STMW* TR2.......74 D2
Penryn St *RED* TR15....................61 E4
Pensilva *PERRAN* TR6...................56 B4
Pensilva Rd *TRU* TR1...................85 G1
Penstrasse Pl *PAR* PL24...............51 G3
Pensylva *STAUS* PL25...................64 B4

Pentalek Rd
  CAMBORNE TR14................14 D5
Pentillie Wy *MEVA* PL26...............41 H2
Pentire Av *NEWQ* TR7..................21 F3
Pentire Crs *NEWQ* TR7.................21 E5
Pentire Gn *RNEWQ* TR8...............21 E5
Pentire Rd *NEWQ* TR7..................21 F3
  PENRYN TR10...................52 C3
  TOR PL11.........................81 E4
Pentowan Rd *HAYLE* TR27............27 F1
Pentreath *FOW* PL23....................24 B1
  PENZ TR18.......................54 D2
Penvale Ct *FAL* TR11 * 22 C2
Penvale Crs *PENRYN* TR10...........52 C3
Penvale Dr *PENRYN* TR10.............52 C3
Penvean La *FAL* TR11...................22 A1
Penventinnie La *TRU* TR1..............83 H2
Penventon Ter *RED* TR15..............60 D4
Penventon Vw *HELS* TR13.............29 F4
Penview Crs *HELS* TR13................29 F4
Penware Parc
  CAMBORNE TR14................14 B5
Penwarne La *MEVA* PL26..............41 G4
Penwartha Cl *NEWQ* TR7.............47 G3
Penweathers La *RTRUS* TR3.........84 D1
Penwerris La *FAL* TR11.................53 H5
Penwerris Ter *FAL* TR11 * 22 C1
Penwinnick Rd *STAUS* PL25..........63 G4
Penwith Cl *STIVES* TR26...............68 D4
Penwithian Cl *HAYLE* TR27............27 G3
Penwithian Rd *STIVES* TR26.........68 D4
Penwith St *PENZ* TR18.................55 E2
Penworth Cl *LAUN* PL15................31 F4
Penzance Rd *HELS* TR13...............29 E3
Peoples Palace *TRU* TR1 * 85 E3
Peppers Park Rd *LISK* PL14..........33 H2
Percuil Vw *RTRUE/STMW* TR2.......74 D2
Percy Davy Cl *PERRAN* TR6..........56 B2
Permarin Rd *PENRYN* TR10..........52 C4
Perran Cl *RTRUS* TR3...................19 E4
Perrancombe Garden Ct
  PERRAN TR6.....................56 A5
Perranwell Rd *RTRUNW* TR4.........57 G4
Perrily Mt *BUDE* EX23..................12 C4
Petherick Rd *PENZ* TR18..............54 C5
Pethericks Mi *BUDE* EX23.............12 B4
Pethybridge Dr *BODM* PL31..........10 A4
Peverell Rd *HELS* TR13.................58 A2
  PENZ TR18.......................55 E3
Peverell Ter *HELS* TR13................58 A2
Phernyssick Rd *STAUS* PL25..........64 B1
Philgray Cl *HAYLE* TR27................27 G2
Phillack Hl *HAYLE* TR27................27 G2
Phillips Ter *CAMBORNE* TR14 * 15 E1
Piala Pl *HAYLE* TR27....................27 G2
Pickard Wy *BUDE* EX23.................12 D3
Pickets Yd *PENRYN* TR10..............53 E4
Pier La *MBRK/KGSD* PL10............43 H5
Pigmeadow La *LISK* PL14..............33 F2
Pike's Hl *FAL* TR11......................22 D3
Pikes Hl *FOW* PL23.....................24 C2
Pike St *LISK* PL14.......................33 F2
Pill La *SALT* PL12.......................76 D1
Pillmere Dr *SALT* PL12..................76 B3
Pine Cl *HELS* TR13.......................29 H4
Pine Rd *PENZ* TR18.....................54 B5
Pintail Av *HAYLE* TR27..................66 D1
Pipers Ct *LAUN* PL15...................30 B5
Pit Meadow *FAL* TR11...................22 A3
Place Parc *NEWQ* TR7..................47 G2
Place Rd *FOW* PL23.....................24 C2
Place Vw *FOW* PL23 * 24 C2
Place View Rd
  RTRUE/STMW TR2..............74 C2
Plaidy La *LOOE* PL13....................35 G2
Plaidy Park Rd *LOOE* PL13............35 G2
Plain-an-Gwarry *RED* TR15...........61 E3
Plas Newydd Av *BODM* PL31.........10 D4
The Platt *WADE* PL27...................86 C3
Pleasant La *LANDS* TR19..............72 B4
Plestin Cl *LAUN* PL15...................31 F2
Pleyber Christ Wy *LOST* PL22.......37 F3
Plougastel Dr *SALT* PL12..............76 B2
Plough Gn *SALT* PL12...................76 B2
Plymouth Rd *LISK* PL14................33 G3
Point Rd *RTRUS* TR3....................19 G3
Polbathic Rd *RED* TR15................61 F3
Poldark Gdns *PAR* PL24...............50 B4
Poldhu Cl *STIVES* TR26................71 F2
Poldhu Rd *LISK* PL14...................33 G2
Poldrea *PAR* PL24.......................51 G3
Poldue Cl *RED* TR15....................61 G2
Polean La *LOOE* PL13...................34 D2
Polgarth *PENZ* TR18....................45 F1
Polgarth Cl *STIVES* TR26..............71 F2
Polglaze *PENZ* TR18....................54 D2
Polgoon Cl *PENZ* TR18.................54 C4
Polgooth Cl *RED* TR15.................61 F2
Polgover Wy *PAR* PL24.................50 C4
Polkerris Parc *PAR* PL24..............50 D5
Polkirt Hl *MEVA* PL26...................41 G3
Polkyth Rd *STAUS* PL25................64 B3
Pollards *BUDE* EX23 * 13 G2
Pollards Cl *RTRUNW* TR4.............57 H4
Pollards Wy *SALT* PL12................76 B2
Polmarth Cl *STAUS* PL25..............64 C1
Polmear Ct *WADE* PL27 * 86 C3

Polmear Hl *PAR* PL24...................51 H5
Polmear Parc *PAR* PL24...............51 F4
Polmear Rd *PAR* PL24.................51 F4
  STAUS PL25......................64 C4
Polmeere Rd *PENZ* TR18..............55 E3
Polmena La *LOST* PL22................37 H5
Polmennor Dr *STIVES* TR26..........71 F2
Polmennor Rd *FAL* TR11...............22 B5
  PENZ TR18.......................54 C1
Polmeor Cl *STIVES* TR26..............71 F2
Polmorla Rd *WADE* PL27..............86 C3
Polmorla Wk *WADE* PL27 * 86 C3
Polperro Rd *LOOE* PL13................34 C3
Polpey La *PAR* PL24.....................51 G3
Polruan Cl *STIVES* TR26...............71 F3
Polruan Rd *RED* TR15...................61 G2
  TRU TR1..........................85 E2
Polsethow *PENRYN* TR10.............52 C4
Polstain Crs *RTRUS* TR3...............83 F3
Polstain Rd *RTRUS* TR3................83 E3
Poltair Av *STIVES* TR26................64 B3
Poltair Cl *PENZ* TR18...................54 C2
Poltair Ct *STAUS* PL25.................64 B2
Poltair Crs *STAUS* PL25................64 A3
Poltair Meadow
  PENRYN TR10...................52 C4
Poltair Rd *PENRYN* TR10..............52 C4
  STAUS PL25......................64 A3
Poltair Ter *PENZ* TR18.................54 B2
Poltamar *LAUN* PL15....................31 G2
Poltisko Rd *PENRYN* TR10............52 C4
Poltisko Ter *PENRYN* TR10...........52 C4
Poltreen Cl *STIVES* TR26..............71 F2
Polvarth Est
  RTRUE/STMW TR2..............74 C2
Polvarth Rd
  RTRUE/STMW TR2..............74 C1
Polvella Cl *NEWQ* TR7..................21 G3
Polvelyn Parc *HAYLE* TR27............27 G3
Polventon Cl *FAL* TR11.................54 C2
  PENZ TR18.......................54 C2
Polvillion Rd *FOW* PL23................24 B2
Polweath Rd *PENZ* TR18...............55 E2
Polwhele Rd *TRU* TR1..................85 H1
Polwhaveral Ter *FAL* TR11 * 22 C1
Polwhele Rd *FAL* TR11.................22 C1
Polwithen Dr *STIVES* TR26...........71 E1
Polwithen Gdns *STIVES* TR26.......71 E2
Polwithen Rd *FAL* TR11................22 C2
  PENRYN TR10...................52 C3
  PENZ TR18.......................54 D4
Polwyn Cl *PENZ* TR18..................54 B2
Pondbridge Hl *LISK* PL14..............33 F3
Pondfield Rd *SALT* PL12................76 A2
Pondhu Crs *STAUS* PL25...............63 G4
Pondhu Rd *STAUS* PL25................63 G4
Pond La *PENZ* TR18.....................55 E2
Pond Lanes End *RED* TR15...........61 E2
Pond Wk *HAYLE* TR27..................27 E2
Ponsmere Ct *PERRAN* TR6 * 56 B3
Ponsmere Rd *PERRAN* TR6..........56 B3
Poole Park Rd *PLYNW* PL5............77 H5
Pool's Ct *HAYLE* TR27..................27 F2
Pool St *BODM* PL31.....................10 D2
Pordenack Cl *STIVES* TR26...........71 G1
Porhan Gn *FAL* TR11...................53 F5
Portbyhan Rd *LOOE* PL13.............34 D3
Porter Wy *SALT* PL12...................76 B2
Porth Beach Rd *NEWQ* TR7..........47 E1
Porth Bean Rd *NEWQ* TR7...........47 E1
Porthgwidden *STIVES* TR26..........69 G1
Porthia Cl *STIVES* TR26................69 E4
Porthia Crs *STIVES* TR26.............69 E4
Porthia Rd *STIVES* TR26...............68 D4
Porthilly La *WADE* PL27...............49 F2
Porthilly Vw *PADS* PL28................48 C4
Porthleven Rd *HELS* TR13.............29 E5
Porthmeor Hl *STIVES* TR26...........65 E4
Porthmeor Rd *STAUS* PL25...........65 E4
Porthmeor Sq *STIVES* TR26.........69 F2
Porthminster Point
  STIVES TR26.....................69 G4
Porthminster Ter
  STIVES TR26.....................69 F3
Porth Pde *NEWQ* TR7..................47 F1
Porthpean Rd *STAUS* PL25...........64 C4
Porthrepta Rd *STIVES* TR26.........71 G2
Porth Vw *RTRUE/STMW* TR2.........74 D1
Porth Wy *NEWQ* TR7...................47 E2
Portisco Cl *TRU* TR1....................85 G4
Portland Cl *LISK* PL14..................33 F1
Portland Ter *LISK* PL14................33 F1
Portmellon Pk *MEVA* PL26............41 G4
Portmellon Rd *MEVA* PL26............41 H4
Portuan Rd *LOOE* PL13................35 E5
Posses La *PENZ* TR18..................55 C1
Post Box Rw
  CAMBORNE TR14................15 F3
Poughill Rd *BUDE* EX23................12 C1
Pound Dean *LISK* PL14.................32 D3
Poundfield *BUDE* EX23.................13 F2
Poundfield Hl *BUDE* EX23.............13 F2
Poundfield La *BUDE* EX23.............13 F2
Pound La *BODM* PL31..................10 D2
Pounds Pk *SALT* PL12..................77 E2
Pound St *LISK* PL14.....................33 F2
Praed Pl *STIVES* TR26..................26 B3
Praed's La *MARAZ* TR17...............38 C3

Praze An Creet STIVES TR26 *....68 D3
Praze Meadow PENRYN TR10....52 D3
Praze Rd HELS TR13....58 B1
　NEWQ TR7....47 E2
The Praze PENRYN TR10....52 D3
Prideaux Rd PAR PL25....50 C1
Pridmouth Rd STAUS PL25....64 B1
Priesthood Ter
　MBRK/KGSD PL10....43 F1
Primitive Rw
　CAMBORNE TR14....15 F2
Primrose Cl CAMBORNE TR14....14 A2
　RPENZ TR20....80 D3
　TOR PL11....85 E3
Primrose La RPENZ TR20....39 G4
Primrose La PENZ TR20....39 G3
Primrose Rd BUDE EX23....12 D3
Primrose Ter PENZ TR18....45 H3
Primrose Va STIVES TR26....69 F4
Primrose Wk SALT PL12....76 C1
Prince Charles Cl LAUN PL15....31 F2
Prince Charles Pk
　STAUS PL25....64 B2
Prince Charles Rd
　STAUS PL25....64 B2
Prince of Wales Pier
　FAL TR11 *....22 D2
Prince Philip Rd LAUN PL15....31 F2
Princes Sq LOOE PL13....35 E3
Princess St LANDS TR19....72 B4
Princes St BUDE EX23....12 B2
　PENZ TR18....35 E3
Prince's St TRU TR1 *....85 F3
Priors Barn BODM PL31....11 E4
Priors Cl STIVES TR26....68 D4
Priory Cl PAR PL24....51 E3
Priory La LAUN PL15....31 E2
Priory Park Rd LAUN PL15....31 E3
Priory Rd BODM PL31....10 D3
　NEWQ TR7....47 H3
　STAUS PL25....63 H3
Prislow Cl FAL TR11....22 A4
Prislow Flds FAL TR11....22 A4
Prislow La FAL TR11....22 A4
Promenade PENZ TR18....55 E5
Prospect Cl HAYLE TR27....27 F3
Prospect Gdns TRU TR1 *....85 F1
Prospect La SALT PL12....76 B2
Prospect Pl FAL TR11 *....22 C1
　HAYLE TR27....27 F3
　HELS TR13....29 G4
　MEVA PL26....41 G2
　PENZ TR18....55 E5
　TRU TR1 *....85 F1
Prospect Ter MEVA PL26....41 G2
Prospect Wk SALT PL12....76 B2
Prouse Ri SALT PL12....76 D3
Prouts Ct LAUN PL15....31 F3
Provis Rd PENZ TR18....54 C5
Putnam Cl LISK PL14....33 G3
Pydar Cl NEWQ TR7....47 E3
Pydar Ms TRU TR1 *....85 E2
Pydar St TRU TR1....85 E2
Pyramid Cl STAUS PL25....62 C2

Q

Quarry Cl BUDE EX23....12 C1
Quarry Gdns PENZ TR18....54 C4
Quarry HI FAL TR11....22 D2
Quarry Park Rd NEWQ TR7....46 C3
Quarry Park Ter BODM PL31....10 D2
Quarry Rd PERRAN TR6....56 C5
Quarry St TOR PL11....81 H4
Quay HI FAL TR11 *....23 E2
　PENRYN TR10....53 E4
Quay Ms FAL TR11 *....85 F3
Quay Rd NEWQ TR7....47 D2
　RTRUS TR3....19 E5
　STAUS PL25....65 E5
Quay St FAL TR11....23 E2
　LOOE PL13....35 E3
　LOST PL22....37 F4
　PENZ TR18....55 E4
　STIVES TR26 *....69 G2
　TRU TR1....85 F3
The Quay FOW PL23....24 D3
　LOOE PL13....35 E3
　MEVA PL26....41 H3
　PENZ TR18....55 F4
　RTRUE/STMW TR2....74 C2
Queen Anne Gdns FAL TR11....22 A3
Queen Elizabeth Rd
　LAUN PL15....31 F2
Queen Mary Ct FAL TR11....22 D4
Queen Mary Rd FAL TR11....22 D4
Queen's Crs BODM PL31....10 A4
Queens Pk WADE PL27....86 D4
Queens Rd STAUS PL25....64 B4
Queen St BUDE EX23....12 B2
　LANDS TR19....72 B4
　LOST PL22....37 F4
　PENZ TR18....55 E4
　RPENZ TR20....39 G3
Queen's Wy HAYLE TR27....27 F4
　RPENZ TR20....39 G3
Quenchwell Rd RTRUS TR3....19 G1
Quillet Rd PENZ TR18....45 F1

Quimperle Wy LISK PL14....33 H2
Quintrell Rd NEWQ TR7....47 H4

R

Race HI LAUN PL15....31 F4
Race Hill Ter LAUN PL15....31 F4
Radford La MBRK/KGSD PL10....43 E2
Radnor Cl BODM PL31....11 E3
Railway Cots FAL TR11 *....23 F5
Railway Ter BODM PL31 *....10 C2
Rainfields Cl PADS PL28....48 B3
Rainy Fields Cl PADS PL28....48 B3
Raleigh Av PADS PL28....48 A3
Raleigh Cl FAL TR11....22 C2
Raleigh Pl FAL TR11....22 C2
Raleigh Rd PADS PL28....48 A3
Rame Vw LOOE PL13....35 G1
Ramoth PERRAN TR6....56 C3
Ranch Vw LAUN PL15....30 D4
Ranelagh Ms BODM PL31....10 C3
Ranelagh Rd STAUS PL25....64 B3
Rapson Rd LISK PL14....33 G2
Rashleigh Av SALT PL12....76 C4
Rashleigh Ct STAUS PL25....65 F3
Rashleigh La FOW PL23....24 A3
Rashleigh Ms STAUS PL25....64 A3
Rashleigh Pl STAUS PL25....64 A3
Rashleigh V TRU TR1....85 G3
Ratcliffes La HELS TR13....28 D4
Rawley La NEWQ TR7....46 B4
Rawlings La FOW PL23....24 C1
Raymond Rd RED TR15....61 F4
Read Cl PENRYN TR10....52 C4
Readymoney Rd FOW PL23....24 B3
Rebecca Ct PAR PL24....50 C1
Rectory Gdns CAMBORNE TR14....14 B3
Rectory Rd CAMBORNE TR14....14 B4
Redannick Crs TRU TR1....84 D4
Redannick La TRU TR1....84 D4
Redbrooke Rd
　CAMBORNE TR14....14 D4
Redbrooke Ter
　CAMBORNE TR14 *....14 D4
Redenek Enys
　CAMBORNE TR14....15 E1
Redinnick PENZ TR18 *....55 E5
Redinnick Gdns PENZ TR18 *....55 E5
Redinnick Pl PENZ TR18....54 D5
Redinnick Ter PENZ TR18....54 D5
Redruth Hwy RED TR15....61 H1
Redruth Rd HELS TR13....29 G1
Redvers Hts RED TR15....61 E5
Redwood Cl BUDE EX23....12 C3
Redwood Gv BUDE EX23....12 C3
Reeds Pk LOST PL22....37 G4
Reeds Wy NEWQ TR7....46 A4
Reen Hl PERRAN TR6....56 D5
Reens Crs PENZ TR18....54 C5
Reens Rd PENZ TR18....54 C5
Reeves Cl LISK PL14....33 H1
Regal Ct SALT PL12 *....77 E3
Regent Blds PENZ TR18 *....55 E5
Regent Sq PENZ TR18....55 E5
Regent Ter LANDS TR19....72 B4
　PENZ TR18....55 E5
Rennie Av PLYNW PL5....77 H4
Reskadinnick Rd
　CAMBORNE TR14....14 C1
Respryn Cl LISK PL14....33 G2
Restormel Rd LOOE PL13....35 F2
　LOST PL22....37 F2
Restormel Ter FAL TR11....22 D3
Retallack Gdns RPENZ TR20 *....39 H3
Retallick Mdw STAUS PL25....65 F3
The Retreat PENRYN TR10 *....53 E4
Reynolds Gv PLYNW PL5....77 H5
Rhind St BODM PL31....10 D2
Rialton Hts NEWQ TR7....47 D2
Rialton Rd NEWQ TR7....47 D2
Richards Crs TRU TR1....84 B3
Richards La RTRUNW TR4....60 A1
Richards Ter
　MBRK/KGSD PL10....43 F1
Richmond HI TRU TR1....84 D3
Richmond Pl STIVES TR26 *....69 F2
　TRU TR1....84 D3
Richmond St PENZ TR18....55 E4
Richmond Ter TRU TR1....84 D3
Richmond Wy STIVES TR26....71 F2
Ridgegrove HI LAUN PL15....31 F3
Ridgegrove La LAUN PL15....31 F2
Ridgeovean PENZ TR18....55 F1
Ridgevale Cl PENZ TR18....54 C3
Ridgevale La PENZ TR18....55 F1
Ridgeway PERRAN TR6....56 B3
　SALT PL12....76 C4
Ringway BODM PL31....10 C2
Ringwell HI RTRUS TR3 *....19 E1
Rivendell WADE PL27....86 D4
Riversdale WADE PL27 *....86 C3
Riverside LAUN PL15....31 E3
　PADS PL28....48 B3
　STIVES TR26....26 B4
Riverside Av NEWQ TR7....21 F3
Riverside Crs NEWQ TR7....21 E3
Riverside Ms SALT PL12....77 E2
Riverside Vw TRU TR1....85 G1
The Rivers SALT PL12....76 D4

River St MEVA PL26....41 G3
　TRU TR1....85 E3
Riverview FAL TR11 *....53 H5
River Vw LOOE PL13....35 E2
　SALT PL12....77 E2
River Wk STAUS PL25....63 G4
Riviera La RTRUE/STMW TR2....74 B2
Roach's Rw RED TR15....61 E5
Robartes Ct TRU TR1 *....85 E3
Robartes Gdns STAUS PL25....64 B3
Robartes Pl STAUS PL25....64 B3
Robartes Rd BODM PL31....10 C3
　NEWQ TR7....46 C4
Robartes Ter LOST PL22....37 F3
Robert Eliot Ct STAUS PL25....63 G4
Robert Hichens Rd FAL TR11....22 C1
Roberts Av TOR PL11....81 G4
Roberts Rd PLYNW PL5....77 H5
Robin Dr LAUN PL15....31 H5
Robins Cl PAR PL24....50 B5
Rock Cl CAMBORNE TR14....15 E4
Rock La BODM PL31....10 B3
Rock Rd PENZ TR18....45 G1
　WADE PL27....49 F2
Rock Ter PENZ TR18....54 C2
Rock Vls WADE PL27....49 F2
Rodwell Cl RED TR15....60 A4
Roekindale Cl RED TR15....61 E5
Roeselare Av TOR PL11....81 E4
Roeselare Cl TOR PL11....81 E4
Rogers Dr SALT PL12....76 C1
Roma Cl NEWQ TR7....47 F2
Roma Ct NEWQ TR7....47 F2
Roman Dr BODM PL31....11 E5
Ropehaven Cl STAUS PL25....64 B1
Ropehaven Rd STAUS PL25....64 B1
Rope Wk PADS PL28....48 A3
The Ropewalk PENZ TR18....54 C5
The Rope Wk
　RTRUE/STMW TR2....74 C2
　STIVES TR26....69 F3
Roscadghill Parc PENZ TR18....54 B2
Roscadghill Rd PENZ TR18....54 B3
Roscarrack Cl FAL TR11....22 A4
Roscarrack Rd FAL TR11....22 A4
Rose Cots CAMBORNE TR14....14 D3
Rosedale Gdns BODM PL31....11 E5
Rosedale Rd TRU TR1....85 F2
Rosehill MARAZ TR17....38 D2
　FAL TR11....53 H1
Rose HI FOW PL23....24 C2
　LOST PL22....37 F5
　PAR PL24....50 C3
　RED TR15....61 E3
Rosehill Cl LOST PL22....37 F4
Rosehill Gdns PENZ TR18....54 B3
Rosehill Meadow PENZ TR18....54 B3
Rose Hill Rd PAR PL24....50 C4
Roseland Gdns BODM PL31....10 D1
　RED TR15....61 F3
Roseland Pk CAMBORNE TR14....14 C2
Roselands Rd BODM PL31....10 D1
Rose La STIVES TR26....69 F2
Roselidden Parc HELS TR13....29 F2
Roselyon Pk PAR PL24....50 D3
Rose Mdw RTRUNW TR4....57 H4
Rosemellen Ter LISK PL14....33 H4
Rosemellin CAMBORNE TR14 *....14 D2
Rose Rw RED TR15....61 E3
Rose Ter PENZ TR18....55 E3
Rosevale Crs CAMBORNE TR14....14 D2
Rosevale Est PENZ TR18....54 B5
Rosevalley RTRUS TR3....83 E3
Rosevallon La BODM PL31....10 B2
Rosevean Av
　CAMBORNE TR14....14 D3
Rosevean Cl CAMBORNE TR14....14 C3
　PENZ TR18....55 E3
Rosevean Ter PENZ TR18....55 E3
Rosewall Ter STIVES TR26 *....69 E3
Rosewarne Cl CAMBORNE TR14....14 B2
Rosewarne Gdns
　CAMBORNE TR14....14 C1
Rosewarne Mdw
　CAMBORNE TR14....14 C1
Rosewarne Ms
　CAMBORNE TR14....14 C2
Rosewarne Pk
　CAMBORNE TR14....14 C2
Rosewarne Rd
　CAMBORNE TR14....14 C3
Rosewarne Ter
　CAMBORNE TR14....14 C1
Rosewin Rw TRU TR1 *....85 F2
Roskear CAMBORNE TR14....14 D1
Roskear Flds CAMBORNE TR14....14 D1
Roskear Parc CAMBORNE TR14....14 D1
Roskear Rd CAMBORNE TR14....14 D1
Roskilling HELS TR13....29 H2
Roskilling Wartha HELS TR13....29 H1
Roskruge Cl HELS TR13....29 H1
Ros Lyn STIVES TR26....71 E2
Roslyn Ct STAUS PL25....64 C2
Rosparvah Gdns PENZ TR18....54 C2
Rossett Gdns BODM PL31....11 F5
Roughtor Dr CAMEL PL32....17 H4
Roughtor Rd CAMEL PL32....17 H4
Round Ring PENRYN TR10....53 E3
Round's La TINT PL54....78 D4
Rowan Cl BODM PL31....10 A3

Rowan Ct SALT PL12....76 B3
The Rowans BUDE EX23....12 C4
Rowe St TOR PL11....81 G4
Royalist Ct FAL TR11 *....23 E3
Royal Sq STIVES TR26 *....69 F3
Roydon Cl LAUN PL15....31 E1
Roydon La LAUN PL15....31 E1
Roydon Rd LAUN PL15....31 E1
Royffe Wy BODM PL31....10 B2
Rundle Ct LISK PL14....33 E4
Russell Cl SALT PL12....76 B2
Russell Pl BODM PL31 *....10 B2
Russell St LISK PL14....33 F3
Russells Wy PENRYN TR10....52 D4
Ruthy's La PADS PL28....48 B3
Rye HI SALT PL12....76 B3

S

Saffron Cl FOW PL23....24 C2
St Ambrusca Rd RNEWQ TR8....21 F5
St Andrews Cl SALT PL12....76 B3
St Andrew's Pl
　MBRK/KGSD PL10....43 H5
St Andrew's Rd BUDE EX23....13 F5
　PAR PL24....51 E3
St Andrew's St
　MBRK/KGSD PL10....43 H5
　STIVES TR26....69 F3
St Andrews Ter PAR PL24....50 D2
St Andrew St
　MBRK/KGSD PL10....43 H5
St Annes Cl STIVES TR26....26 B4
St Anne's Rd NEWQ TR7....46 D3
St Annes Rd PAR PL24....50 B5
St Anne's Rd SALT PL12....76 B3
　STAUS PL25....62 D3
St Anta Rd STIVES TR26....71 G2
St Anthony La FAL TR11....22 C4
St Aubyns Crs RPENZ TR20....46 D3
St Aubyns RPENZ TR20....39 G3
St Aubyn's Rd FAL TR11....85 E3
St Aubyns Vean TRU TR1 *....85 H1
St Austell Rd PAR PL24....65 H2
St Austell Rw
　RTRUE/STMW TR2....74 C2
St Benedicts La PAR PL24....51 F3
St Benedicts Pl PAR PL24....51 F3
St Blazey Rd PAR PL24....51 F3
St Catherines Cove FOW PL23....24 B3
St Catherines Hl LAUN PL15....30 D3
St Clare St PENZ TR18....54 D3
St Cleer Dr WADE PL27....87 E2
St Clement's Hi TRU TR1....85 G3
St Clement's Hl TRU TR1....85 G3
St Clements Parc TRU TR1....85 G3
St Clements Ter TRU TR1....85 F2
St Clement St TRU TR1....85 F2
St Clements Vean TRU TR1....85 H1
St Cuthbert La LAUN PL15....31 E2
St Cuthbert's Rd NEWQ TR7....46 A4
St Day Rd RED TR15....61 G3
　RTRUNW TR4....61 G5
St Dominic Cl BODM PL31....10 D2
St Dominic Sq TRU TR1....85 E3
St Dominic St PENZ TR18....55 E3
　TRU TR1....85 E3
St Edmunds La PADS PL28....48 B3
St Eia St STIVES TR26....69 G3
St Elwyns Ri HAYLE TR27....26 D3
St Enodoc Cl WADE PL27....87 E2
St Erth Hl HAYLE TR27....67 G4
St Fimbarrus Rd FOW PL23....24 C3
St Francis St PENZ TR18....55 E3
St Georges Ar FAL TR11....22 D2
St Georges Ct LOOE PL13....35 F4
St George's Crs BODM PL31....10 B4
St Georgeshill Cl PERRAN TR6....56 A4
St Georges Pk LOST PL22....37 F3
St George's Rd HAYLE TR27....35 F2
　LOOE PL13....35 F2
　NEWQ TR7....46 A3
St Georges Rd SALT PL12....76 C2
St Georges Rd TRU TR1....84 D2
St Georges Sq MEVA PL26....41 G3
St Giles Dr WADE PL27....86 D2
St Giles Ms WADE PL27....86 D2
St Gluvias Parc PENRYN TR10....53 E3
St Gluvias St PENRYN TR10....53 E4
St Golder Rd PENZ TR18....45 F1
St Henry St PENZ TR18....55 E3
St Ives Rd STIVES TR26....69 E3
St James Ct TOR PL11....81 G4
St James Rd TOR PL11....81 G4
St James' St PENZ TR18....55 E3
St James Ter PENRYN TR10 *....52 C4
St John's Cl HELS TR13....29 E3
St John's Rd
　MBRK/KGSD PL10....43 F1
St John's Rd HELS TR13....29 F3
St Johns Rd NEWQ TR7....46 A3
St John's Rd LAUN PL15....30 D3
St John's St HAYLE TR27....27 F3
St John's Ter RTRUS TR3....19 E4
St Johns Wk STIVES TR26....68 D3
St Joseph's Rd LAUN PL15....31 E1
St Keyne Cl TRU TR1....85 E1
St Leonards BODM PL31....10 D3
St Leonard's Rd LAUN PL15....31 E1
St Leonards Ter BODM PL31 *....10 D3

St Levan Cl *MARAZ* TR17 ....**38** D3
St Levan Rd *MARAZ* TR17 ....**38** D3
St Martins Cl
  CAMBORNE TR14 * **14** B4
  LOOE PL13 ....**35** F1
St Martin's Crs
  CAMBORNE TR14 ....**14** B3
St Martins Rd *BUDE* EX23 ....**13** F4
St Martin's Ter
  CAMBORNE TR14 ....**14** B3
St Marys Cl *BODM* PL31 ....**10** B3
St Marys St *NEWQ* TR7 * **46** A4
St Mary's Crs *BODM* PL31 ....**10** B3
St Marys Gdns *BODM* PL31 ....**10** B3
St Mary's Rd *BODM* PL31 ....**10** A4
  LAUN PL15 ....**31** F1
  NEWQ TR7 ....**46** A4
St Marys Rd *PAR* PL24 ....**50** A5
St Mary's St *PENZ* TR18 ....**55** E4
  TRU TR1 ....**85** F3
St Mary's Street Ms *TRU* TR1 * **85** F3
St Marys Ter *TRU* TR1 * **85** E2
St Matthews Hl *WADE* PL27 ....**87** D3
St Mawgan Cl *BODM* PL31 ....**11** E2
St Meriadoc Rd
  CAMBORNE TR14 ....**14** B3
St Mewan La *STAUS* PL25 ....**63** E4
St Michael's Cl *HAYLE* TR27 ....**26** D5
St Michael's Rd *BUDE* EX23 ....**13** F5
  NEWQ TR7 ....**46** B3
  PERRAN TR6 ....**56** B4
St Michael's St *PENZ* TR18 ....**55** E3
St Michaels Ter *HELS* TR13 ....**29** C4
St Michael's Ter *PENZ* TR18 ....**54** D3
St Michael's Wy *MARAZ* TR17 ....**38** B4
  STIVES TR26 ....**69** G3
St Nicholas Cl *LOST* PL22 ....**37** F1
St Nicholas Pk *SALT* PL12 ....**37** G5
St Nicholas St *BODM* PL31 ....**10** D3
  TRU TR1 ....**85** F3
St Olaf's Rd *BUDE* EX23 ....**13** F3
St Peter's Hl *PENZ* TR18 ....**45** G3
St Peters Rd *BUDE* EX23 ....**13** F3
St Peters St *STIVES* TR26 ....**69** F2
St Peters Wy *HELS* TR13 ....**58** B2
St Petroc's Cl *BODM* PL31 ....**10** D3
St Petrocs Meadow *PADS* PL28 ....**48** A3
St Petry *RPENZ* TR20 ....**39** C3
St Philip St *PENZ* TR18 ....**55** E3
St Pirans Cl *BODM* PL31 ....**10** A3
St Pirans Cl *STAUS* PL25 ....**65** F3
St Pirans Cl *TRU* TR1 ....**85** F3
St Piran's Hl *RTRUS* TR3 ....**18** B5
St Pirans Parc *HELS* TR13 ....**58** B2
St Piran's Rd *NEWQ* TR7 ....**21** H2
St Pirans Rd *PERRAN* TR6 ....**56** B3
St Pirans Wy *RPENZ* TR20 ....**39** F5
St Pol De Leon Vw *LANDS* TR19 ....**45** G5
St Sampsons Cl *PAR* PL24 ....**51** C3
St Saviour's Hl *FOW* PL23 ....**24** C4
St Saviour's La *PADS* PL28 ....**48** B2
St Smithwick Wy *FAL* TR11 ....**23** E3
St Stephen's H *LAUN* PL15 ....**31** E2
  SALT PL12 ....**76** B4
St Stephen's Rd *SALT* PL12 ....**76** D3
Saint's Wy *FOW* PL23 ....**24** A3
  PADS PL28 ....**48** B3
  PAR PL24 ....**50** D1
St Thomas Cl *TRU* TR1 ....**84** A2
St Thomas Hl *LAUN* PL15 ....**31** E3
St Thomas Rd *LAUN* PL15 ....**31** E3
St Thomas' Rd *NEWQ* TR7 ....**46** C4
St Thomas St *PENRYN* TR10 ....**53** E4
St Uny Cl *STIVES* TR26 ....**26** A5
St Uny Crs *RED* TR15 ....**60** C5
St Warren St *PENZ* TR18 ....**55** E3
St Winnolls Pk *LOOE* PL13 ....**35** F2
Salamanca St *TOR* PL11 ....**81** C4
Salisbury Rd *TRU* TR1 ....**84** D3
Salmon Rw *TRU* TR1 * **85** F3
Saltbox Cl *FAL* TR11 ....**53** H1
Saltbox Rd *FAL* TR11 ....**53** H1
Saltburn Rd *PLYNW* PL5 ....**77** H3
Salt Cellar Hl *HELS* TR13 ....**58** A2
The Saltings *STIVES* TR26 ....**26** B4
Salt Mi *SALT* PL12 ....**77** E1
Salubrious Ter *STIVES* TR26 * **69** F2
Sampson Wy *RTRUS* TR3 ....**83** E3
Samuel Bone Cl *LISK* PL14 ....**33** G2
Sanctuary Cl *CAMBORNE* TR14 ....**14** B4
Sanctuary La *BUDE* EX23 ....**13** C2
  HELS TR13 ....**29** C3
Sandfield Crs *CAMBORNE* TR14 ....**14** B4
Sandhurst Ter *TRU* TR1 * **85** E2
Sandows La *STIVES* TR26 * **69** E3
Sandra Wy *BODM* PL31 ....**10** B2
Sandyacres *HAYLE* TR27 ....**27** C1
Sandy Hl *STAUS* PL25 ....**64** C3
Sandy La *RED* TR15 ....**61** G4
Sandymoor *CAMBORNE* TR14 ....**15** D3
Sango Rd *TOR* PL11 ....**81** F5
Saracen Cl *PENRYN* TR10 ....**52** D4
Saracen Crs *PENRYN* TR10 ....**52** D4
Saracen Pl *PENRYN* TR10 ....**52** D4
Saracen Wy *PENRYN* TR10 ....**52** D4
Sarahs Cl *PADS* PL28 ....**48** B4
Sarah's Ct *PADS* PL28 ....**48** B4
Sarah's La *PADS* PL28 ....**48** B4

Sarah's Meadow *PADS* PL28 ....**48** B4
Sarah's Vw *PADS* PL28 ....**48** B4
Savage Rd *PLYNW* PL5 ....**77** H5
Sawles Rd *STAUS* PL25 ....**63** G5
Scarletts Well Pk *BODM* PL31 ....**10** B1
Scarlett's Well Rd *BODM* PL31 ....**10** A1
Scholar's La *HELS* TR13 ....**28** C1
School Cl *NEWQ* TR7 ....**47** H3
  PAR PL24 ....**50** B5
School Hl *MEVA* PL26 ....**41** F3
  PADS PL28 ....**48** B3
  RTRUS TR3 ....**18** A5
School La *PL23* **24** D4
  HAYLE TR27 ....**67** F3
  MARAZ TR17 ....**38** C3
  PENZ TR18 ....**55** C1
  RED TR15 ....**61** G3
  STAUS PL25 ....**63** G4
  STAUS PL25 ....**65** F1
  TRU TR1 ....**85** F4
School Wk *WADE* PL27 ....**87** C2
Sconner Rd *TOR* PL11 ....**81** F4
Scott Av *PLYNW* PL5 ....**77** H5
Scowbuds *CAMBORNE* TR14 ....**15** E1
Scrations La *LOST* PL22 ....**37** E4
Seacroft Rd *PLYNW* PL5 ....**77** H3
Sea Rd *STAUS* PL25 ....**65** F5
Sea View Crs
  RTRUE/STMW TR2 ....**74** C2
Sea View Pl *STIVES* TR26 ....**69** G2
Sea View Rd *FAL* TR11 ....**22** C4
Sea View Ter *CAMBORNE* TR14 ....**14** D4
  HELS TR13 * **29** F3
  PAR PL24 ....**50** C1
  PENZ TR18 * **45** G3
  RED TR15 ....**61** F4
  STIVES TR26 * **69** F3
Seawell Rd *BUDE* EX23 ....**12** D1
Seneschall Pk *HELS* TR13 ....**29** H1
Sennen Cl *TOR* PL11 ....**81** E3
Seton Gdns *CAMBORNE* TR14 ....**14** A3
Seymour Av *NEWQ* TR7 ....**46** B3
Seymour Ct *RTRUS* TR3 ....**82** D3
Shackleton Dr *NEWQ* TR7 ....**47** E4
Sharaman Cl *STAUS* PL25 ....**64** D2
Sheila's Ct *STIVES* TR26 ....**71** F2
Shelburne Ct *FAL* TR11 ....**22** B3
Shelburne Rd *FAL* TR11 ....**22** B2
Shelley Rd *STAUS* PL25 ....**65** H3
Sherwood Dr *BODM* PL31 ....**10** A2
Shilson Ter *LAUN* PL15 ....**31** F4
Shoemaker's La *SALT* PL12 ....**76** D3
Shoot Rw *RED* TR15 ....**61** F3
Shop Hl *MARAZ* TR17 ....**38** D3
Shopside *RED* TR15 ....**60** D5
Shores La *WADE* PL27 ....**49** C1
Shrubberies Hl *HELS* TR13 ....**58** B2
Shute Hl *HELS* TR13 ....**29** C3
  LOST PL22 ....**37** F4
Shute La *PENRYN* TR10 ....**52** D3
Shute Meadow *PENRYN* TR10 ....**52** D3
Shutta Rd *LOOE* PL13 ....**35** E2
The Sidings *STAUS* PL25 ....**64** B4
Sidney Ter *RED* TR15 ....**61** F3
Silvanus Jenkin Av *LISK* PL14 ....**33** H3
Silver Cl *RED* TR15 ....**60** D3
Silverdale Rd *FAL* TR11 ....**22** C4
Silver Hl *RTRUS* TR3 ....**18** B3
Silver St *SALT* PL12 ....**77** F3
Silverton Cl *BUDE* EX23 ....**12** C3
Silverton Rd *BUDE* EX23 ....**12** C3
Silver Wy *RTRUS* TR3 ....**83** C3
Sithney Common Hl *HELS* TR13 ....**28** C2
Sithney Old Hl *HELS* TR13 ....**28** C3
Sithney St *PLYNW* PL5 ....**77** H4
Skidden Hl *STIVES* TR26 ....**69** F3
Slades La *PENRYN* TR10 ....**52** D4
Slades Rd *STAUS* PL25 ....**64** B2
Slipway *WADE* PL27 ....**49** E2
Smallridge La *BUDE* EX23 ....**13** H1
Smithfield Dr *SALT* PL12 ....**76** A2
Smithick Hl *FAL* TR11 ....**22** D2
Smiths Wy *SALT* PL12 ....**76** A2
Smithy Cl *SALT* PL12 ....**76** B1
Smithy La *RTRUS* TR3 ....**19** F2
Smugglers Rw *FAL* TR11 * **22** D1
Snell Dr *SALT* PL12 ....**76** A2
Snowdrop Crs *LAUN* PL15 ....**31** H5
Socotra Dr *STAUS* PL25 ....**63** E3
Solar Rw *TRU* TR1 * **85** F2
Somerville Rd *PERRAN* TR6 ....**56** B4
Sonamerg Cl *PENZ* TR18 ....**55** C1
South Albany Rd *RED* TR15 ....**61** F5
Southbourne Rd *STAUS* PL25 ....**64** B5
Southernhaye *LAUN* PL15 * **31** F4
Southern Wy *WADE* PL27 ....**86** D3
Southleigh Pl *STIVES* TR26 * **69** E3
Southfield Rd *BUDE* EX23 ....**12** C3
Southfields Pl *STIVES* TR26 ....**69** E3
Southgate Pl *LAUN* PL15 * **31** F3
Southgate St *RED* TR15 ....**61** F5
South Harbour *PENRYN* TR10 * **53** E4
South Pde *PENZ* TR18 * **55** E4
South Pk *RED* TR15 ....**60** C4
South Park Cl *RED* TR15 ....**60** D4
Southpark Rd *PAR* PL24 ....**51** E3
South Pl *LANDS* TR19 ....**72** B4
South Place Folly *PENZ* TR18 ....**55** E5
South Place Gdns *LANDS* TR19 ....**72** B4
South Quay *PADS* PL28 ....**48** B3

South Quay Hl *NEWQ* TR7 ....**46** A2
South Rd *RPENZ* TR20 ....**39** G4
South Roskear Ter
  CAMBORNE TR14 ....**14** C3
South St *FOW* PL23 * **24** D2
  LOST PL22 ....**37** E4
  STAUS PL25 ....**63** H4
South Ter *CAMBORNE* TR14 ....**14** C4
  STAUS PL25 ....**65** E5
South Vw *HELS* TR13 ....**58** A1
  LISK PL14 ....**33** C1
  PENRYN TR10 ....**52** D3
Southview Dr *BODM* PL31 ....**10** B3
Southview Rd *PAR* PL24 ....**50** B5
South West Coast Pth
  BUDE EX23 ....**12** A4
  FAL TR11 ....**22** D5
  FOW PL23 ....**24** A4
  HAYLE TR27 ....**26** C2
  HELS TR13 ....**58** D5
  LOOE PL13 ....**35** H1
  MARAZ TR17 ....**38** A3
  MBRK/KGSD PL10 ....**42** D4
  NEWQ TR7 ....**46** C2
  PENZ TR18 ....**45** H1
  PERRAN TR6 ....**56** B2
  RTRUE/STMW TR2 ....**75** G3
  STAUS PL25 ....**65** F5
  STIVES TR26 ....**68** D1
  TINT PL34 ....**78** A4
Spargo's La *TRU* TR1 * **85** E2
Sparnon Cl *RED* TR15 ....**61** E4
  STAUS PL25 ....**63** C3
Sparnon Hl *RED* TR15 * **61** E4
Sparnon Rd *RED* TR15 ....**61** E4
Sparnon Ter *RED* TR15 ....**61** E4
Spaven Mor *CAMBORNE* TR14 ....**15** E1
The Speares *SALT* PL12 ....**76** B4
Speedwell Cl *BUDE* EX23 ....**12** D3
  MBRK/KGSD PL10 ....**43** G1
Spencer Gdns *SALT* PL12 ....**76** D4
Spernen Cl *STIVES* TR26 ....**71** E1
Spernen Wyn Rd *FAL* TR11 ....**22** C4
Spicers La *BUDE* EX23 ....**13** F3
Spire Hill Pk *SALT* PL12 ....**76** B3
The Spires *TRU* TR1 ....**85** E1
Sportsmans Cl *CAMEL* PL32 ....**16** D5
Sportsmans Rd *CAMEL* PL32 ....**16** D5
Springfield Cl *HAYLE* TR27 ....**27** C2
  LOST PL22 ....**37** G4
  STAUS PL25 ....**64** D3
Springfield Rd *FAL* TR11 ....**22** A2
  LISK PL14 ....**33** H2
  LOOE PL13 ....**35** F1
  NEWQ TR7 ....**46** D4
  RPENZ TR20 ....**39** H3
Springfield Vw *RTRUS* TR3 ....**82** D2
Spring Gdns *WADE* PL27 ....**86** D2
Springwell Vw *BODM* PL31 ....**11** E2
Spurway Rd *LISK* PL14 ....**33** G2
The Square *LOST* PL22 * **37** E4
  MARAZ TR17 ....**38** B3
  NEWQ TR7 ....**46** C2
  PENRYN TR10 ....**53** E4
  SALT PL12 * **76** D2
Squires La *HELS* TR13 ....**28** C5
Stafford Cl *NEWQ* TR7 ....**47** G3
Staggy La *RTRUS* TR3 ....**19** F2
Stamford Hl *BUDE* EX23 ....**13** F2
Stamps La *RED* TR15 ....**60** A3
Stanford Cl *PENZ* TR18 * **54** D4
Stanford Ter *PENZ* TR18 ....**54** D4
Stanharver La *NEWQ* TR7 ....**47** H3
Stanhope Rd *PLYNW* PL5 ....**77** H3
Stanlake Cl *SALT* PL12 * **76** C3
Stanley Maggs Wy *LISK* PL14 ....**33** H3
Stanley Ter *RED* TR15 ....**61** E3
Stanley Wy *RED* TR15 ....**61** G2
Stanways Rd *NEWQ* TR7 ....**47** G2
Stapleton Rd *BUDE* EX23 ....**12** C3
Statham Rd *BODM* PL31 ....**10** B3
Station Ap *HAYLE* TR27 ....**66** D2
  NEWQ TR7 ....**46** D2
Station Hl *HAYLE* TR27 ....**26** C2
  RED TR15 ....**61** E4
  STAUS PL25 ....**26** B4
Station Pde *NEWQ* TR7 ....**46** C3
Station Rd *FOW* PL23 ....**24** D1
  HELS TR13 ....**29** C2
  LAUN PL15 ....**31** E3
  LISK PL14 ....**33** E4
  LOOE PL13 ....**35** E2
  PADS PL28 ....**48** B3
  PAR PL24 ....**50** C2
  PENRYN TR10 ....**52** D4
  PERRAN TR6 ....**56** B3
  RED TR15 ....**61** G1
  RED TR15 ....**61** E4
  RTRUS TR3 ....**83** C3
  TRU TR1 ....**84** C3
Station Yd *CAMBORNE* TR14 * **14** C4
Steeple Cl *STIVES* TR26 ....**69** F5
Steeple La *STIVES* TR26 ....**70** D5
Steeple View Ct *STIVES* TR26 ....**71** E2
Stennack *STIVES* TR26 ....**69** E3
Stennack Gdns *STIVES* TR26 ....**69** E3
Stennack Rd *STAUS* PL25 ....**65** F5
The Stennack *STIVES* TR26 ....**69** E3
Stephens Rd *LISK* PL14 ....**33** H1
Stewarts Blds *PENZ* TR18 * **55** E4
Stirling Ct *PLYNW* PL5 ....**77** H4

Stirling Rd *PLYNW* PL5 ....**77** H4
Stokes Rd *TRU* TR1 ....**84** D2
Stoney Hl *STAUS* PL25 ....**63** E3
Stoney La *STAUS* PL25 ....**63** H3
Stracey Rd *FAL* TR11 ....**22** D4
Strafford Cl *BUDE* EX23 ....**12** A5
Strand *PENZ* TR18 ....**45** E4
Strand St *PADS* PL28 ....**48** B3
The Strand *BUDE* EX23 ....**12** B3
  PADS PL28 ....**48** B3
  PENZ TR18 * **45** E4
Strangways Ter *TRU* TR1 ....**85** E4
Stratton Pl *FAL* TR11 * **22** C1
Stratton Rd *BUDE* EX23 ....**12** D4
Stratton Ter *FAL* TR11 ....**53** H5
  TRU TR1 * **84** D3
Strawberry Cl *RED* TR15 ....**61** E2
Strawberry Crs *RED* TR15 ....**61** E2
Strawberry La *HAYLE* TR27 ....**67** H1
  RED TR15 ....**61** E2
  STIVES TR26 ....**26** E4
Stray Park Ct *CAMBORNE* TR14 ....**15** E4
Stray Park Rd
  CAMBORNE TR14 ....**14** D4
Stray Park Wy
  CAMBORNE TR14 ....**15** E4
Street-an-Garrow *STIVES* TR26 ....**69** F3
Street-an-Pol *STIVES* TR26 ....**69** F3
Stretyn *RTRUS* TR3 ....**82** B3
Stucley Rd *BUDE* EX23 ....**12** D3
Summerfield Cl *MEVA* PL26 ....**41** F3
Summerfield Rd *LAUN* PL15 ....**31** E2
  SALT PL12 ....**76** B4
Summerheath *PENRYN* TR10 ....**52** A4
Summerhill Rd *LAUN* PL15 ....**30** D4
Summerleaze Av *BUDE* EX23 ....**12** B1
Summerleaze Crs *BUDE* EX23 ....**12** B2
Summers St *LOST* PL22 ....**37** F4
Sun Girt La *LISK* PL14 ....**33** F3
Sunningdale *TRU* TR1 ....**84** C3
Sunningdale Rd *SALT* PL12 ....**76** C3
Sunnybank *HELS* TR13 ....**58** B3
Sunnyside *PERRAN* TR6 ....**56** B4
  RED TR15 ....**61** E4
Sunnyside Meadow
  CAMEL PL32 ....**17** F4
Sunnyside Rd *PERRAN* TR6 ....**56** B4
Sunrising Est *LOOE* PL13 ....**35** F1
Sunset Dr *HELS* TR13 ....**58** B1
Sunset Gdns *HELS* TR13 ....**58** B2
Swallow Cl *BUDE* EX23 ....**12** B3
Swallowfield Ct *PAR* PL24 ....**51** F3
Swanpool Hl *FAL* TR11 ....**22** C5
Swanpool Rd *FAL* TR11 ....**22** C5
Swanpool St *FAL* TR11 ....**23** E3
Swanvale Rd *FAL* TR11 ....**22** B3
Sweet Briar Crs *NEWQ* TR7 ....**46** D5
Sycamore Av *STAUS* PL25 ....**64** B2
Sycamore Cl *BODM* PL31 ....**10** A3
  WADE PL27 ....**49** C1
Sycamore Dr *RED* TR15 ....**60** A3
  RED TR15 ....**61** G3
  TOR PL11 ....**81** E4
Sycamore Rd *SALT* PL12 ....**76** A2
Sydney Hl *FOW* PL23 ....**24** D4
Sydney Rd *NEWQ* TR7 ....**46** A3
  TOR PL11 ....**81** F4
Sylvan Cl *STAUS* PL25 ....**64** B1
Sylverton Pl *PENZ* TR18 ....**54** C2
Symons Cl *STAUS* PL25 ....**64** D2
Symons Hl *FAL* TR11 ....**22** C1
Symons Rd *SALT* PL12 ....**77** E3
Symons Ter *RED* TR15 ....**61** E3

T

Tabernacle St *TRU* TR1 ....**85** F3
Talland Rd *STIVES* TR26 ....**69** F3
Talmena Av *WADE* PL27 ....**86** D3
Talveneth *CAMBORNE* TR14 ....**15** E3
  RED TR15 ....**61** F2
Talvenydh Ct *BODM* PL31 ....**10** C2
Tamar Br *PLYNW* PL5 ....**77** G3
Tamar St *SALT* PL12 ....**77** F3
Tamar Ter *LAUN* PL15 ....**31** G4
  SALT PL12 ....**77** F3
Tamar Vw *LAUN* PL15 ....**31** G4
Tanhouse Rd *LOST* PL22 ....**37** E4
Tannery Ct *SALT* PL12 ....**76** B3
Tanwood Vw *BODM* PL31 ....**10** B2
Taroveor Rd *PENZ* TR18 ....**55** E3
Taroveor Ter *PENZ* TR18 ....**55** E4
Tarrandean La *RTRUS* TR3 ....**18** C3
Tavern Barn *FOW* PL23 ....**24** B1
Tavistock Rd *LAUN* PL15 ....**31** F3
Tavy Rd *SALT* PL12 ....**77** F2
Taylor Rd *SALT* PL12 ....**76** B2
Teetotal St *STIVES* TR26 ....**69** G2
Tehidy Rd *CAMBORNE* TR14 ....**14** C3
  PAR PL24 ....**51** F3
Tehidy Ter *FAL* TR11 * **53** H5
Tenby Rd *PLYNW* PL5 ....**77** H4
Tencreek Av *PENZ* TR18 ....**54** D4
Tenderah Rd *HELS* TR13 ....**29** C2
Tenderah Rd *HELS* TR13 ....**29** G3
The Terrace *LOST* PL22 * **37** F4
  PENRYN TR10 ....**52** D4
  PENZ TR18 ....**55** E4
  STIVES TR26 ....**69** F3
The Terrapins *PENZ* TR18 * **55** G2

Terras HI LOST PL22 ....37 F3
Tewington Pl STAUS PL25 ....63 G3
Thanckes Dr TOR PL11 ....81 F4
Theydon Rd FAL TR11 ....22 B3
Thomas St HELS TR13 ....58 B2
Thomas Ter HELS TR13 ....58 B2
Thornberry Ter PENZ TR18 ....55 F3
Thorn La SALT PL12 ....76 B2
Thornpark Rd STAUS PL25 ....64 B3
Thorn Ter LISK PL14 ....33 E3
Timber Cl STAUS PL25 ....63 G3
Tincombe SALT PL12 ....76 B3
Tincroft Rd RED TR15 ....15 C3
Tinkers HI FOW PL23 ....24 D4
Tinners Wk FAL TR11 ....23 F3
Tinners Wy STIVES TR26 ....68 D4
Tinney Dr TRU TR1 ....85 H2
Tintagel Hts TINT PL34 ....79 E5
Tobruk Rd SALT PL12 ....76 D2
Toby Wy NEWQ TR7 ....46 A2
Tolcarne Cl STAUS PL25 ....64 B3
Tolcarne Ms NEWQ TR7 ....46 C3
Tolcarne Pl PENZ TR18 ....45 G2
Tolcarne Rd NEWQ TR7 ....46 C3
Tolcarne St CAMBORNE TR14 ....14 C4
Tolcarne Ter PENZ TR18 * 45 G1
Tolgarrick Rd CAMBORNE TR14 ....15 E1
Tolgus HI RED TR15 ....60 D3
Tolgus La RED TR15 ....60 A2
Tolgus Pl RED TR15 ....60 D3
Tolgus Vean RED TR15 ....60 D3
Tolgus Wartha RED TR15 ....60 D2
Tollgate Cl LISK PL14 ....33 E4
Tolskithy La RED TR15 ....60 B4
Toltuff Cres PENZ TR18 ....54 C5
Toltuff Rd PENZ TR18 ....54 C5
Tolvaddon Rd CAMBORNE TR14 ....15 F1
Tolver Pl PENZ TR18 ....55 E3
Tolver Rd PENZ TR18 ....55 E3
Tolview Ter HAYLE TR27 * 26 D4
Tom Lyon Rd LISK PL14 ....33 H3
Torbridge Cl SALT PL12 ....76 C4
Tor Cl HELS TR13 ....58 B1
Torleven Rd HELS TR13 ....28 A5
Tor Rd NEWQ TR7 ....46 B3
Torwood Cl BODM PL31 ....10 C3
Towan Blystra Rd NEWQ TR7 ....46 D3
Tower Ct SALT PL12 ....76 B3
Tower HI LOOE PL13 ....35 F3
    WADE PL27 ....86 B2
Tower Pk FOW PL23 ....24 B3
Tower Rd NEWQ TR7 ....21 H2
Tower St LAUN PL15 ....31 F3
Tower Vw SALT PL12 ....76 C4
Town Arms Pas BODM PL31 * 10 D2
Town End BODM PL31 * 10 B2
    PENRYN TR10 * 52 D2
Town Farm RED TR15 ....61 F5
Town Quay FOW PL23 ....24 D2
Townsend BUDE EX23 ....13 C2
    FOW PL23 ....24 D4
Trafalgar Sq FOW PL23 * 24 D2
    TRU TR1 ....85 F3
Traly Cl BUDE EX23 ....12 D4
Trannack Ter PENZ TR18 * 55 E2
Tranquil La BODM PL31 ....10 B2
Treassowe Rd PENZ TR18 ....55 E3
Treban Rd PENZ TR18 ....54 C5
Trebartha Rd TRU TR1 ....85 H2
Trebarva Cl RED TR15 ....60 D2
Trebarwith Crs NEWQ TR7 ....46 B3
Trecarn Cl LAUN PL15 ....31 E4
Trecarne FAL TR11 ....23 F1
Trecarne Ct STAUS PL25 ....65 E2
    TRU TR1 ....85 G2
Trecarrack Rd CAMBORNE TR14 ....15 E3
Trecarrel Cl LAUN PL15 ....31 F5
Trecarrell Cl LAUN PL15 ....31 F5
Tredanek Cl BODM PL31 ....10 B2
Tredarvah Dr PENZ TR18 ....54 C4
Tredarvah Rd PENZ TR18 ....54 C4
Tredavoe La PENZ TR18 ....45 F3
Tredenham Cl PAR PL24 ....50 D4
Tredenham Rd RTRUE/STMW TR2 ....74 D2
Tredinnick Wy PERRAN TR6 ....56 A4
Tredinnick Wood Cl HELS TR13 * 29 H1
Tredour Rd NEWQ TR7 ....46 B5
Tredrea Crs FAL TR11 ....22 C5
Tredrea Gdns RTRUS TR3 ....18 E5
Tredrea La HAYLE TR27 ....66 C4
Tredydan Rd LAUN PL15 ....31 E3
Tredynas Rd FAL TR11 ....23 F3
Tredyson Pl FAL TR11 ....22 C3
Tre-el-Verne Cl TRU TR1 ....84 C3
Treetop Cl SALT PL12 ....76 B3
Treffry Ct NEWQ TR7 * 46 A3
Treffry Wy PAR PL24 ....50 B5
Treforda Rd NEWQ TR7 ....46 B5
Treforest Rd WADE PL27 ....86 B2
Trefrew Rd CAMEL PL32 ....17 D3
Trefusis Cl TRU TR1 ....85 H2
Trefusis Rd RED TR15 ....61 F4
Trefusis Sq RED TR15 * 61 F3
Trefusis Ter RED TR15 ....61 F3
Treganoon Rd RED TR15 ....61 F3
Tregarland Cl CAMBORNE TR14 ....14 D5
Tregarne Ter STAUS PL25 ....63 H3

Tregarrick LOOE PL13 ....34 D3
Tregarrick Cl HELS TR13 ....29 F2
Tregartha Wy LISK PL14 ....33 G2
Tregarthen STIVES TR26 ....69 E3
Tregarth Pl PENZ TR18 ....54 B5
Tregavethan Vw RTRUS TR3 ....82 D2
Tregay La LISK PL14 ....33 F1
Tregear Gdns TRU TR1 ....85 E3
Tregenna Ct CAMBORNE TR14 ....14 B4
    FAL TR11 * 23 E3
Tregenna Flds CAMBORNE TR14 ....14 B4
Tregenna HI STIVES TR26 ....69 F3
Tregenna La CAMBORNE TR14 ....14 B4
Tregenna Parc STIVES TR26 ....69 G5
Tregenna Pl STIVES TR26 ....69 G5
Tregenna Ter STIVES TR26 ....69 F3
Tregenver Rd FAL TR11 ....22 B3
Tregenver Vls FAL TR11 ....22 B2
Tregeseal HI LANDS TR19 ....72 D2
Tregeseal Rw LANDS TR19 ....72 C3
Tregeseal Ter LANDS TR19 ....72 C3
Tregew Rd FAL TR11 ....53 H3
Tregian Cl TRU TR1 ....85 H2
Tregie PENZ TR18 ....45 F1
Treglenwith Rd CAMBORNE TR14 ....14 B4
Treglyn Cl PENZ TR18 ....45 F3
Tregolls Cl TRU TR1 ....85 G2
Tregolls Rd TRU TR1 ....85 G2
Tregoney HI MEVA PL26 ....41 F5
Tregoning Rd TOR PL11 ....81 E5
Tregonissey Cl STAUS PL25 ....64 A2
Tregonissey Rd STAUS PL25 ....64 A2
Tregonning Ct PERRAN TR6 * 56 A3
Tregonning Vw HELS TR13 ....58 B2
Tregoss Rd NEWQ TR7 ....46 C3
Tregothnan Rd FAL TR11 ....22 B3
    TRU TR1 ....85 G4
Tregrea CAMBORNE TR14 ....14 D5
Tregrea Est CAMBORNE TR14 ....15 E5
Treguddock Dr WADE PL27 ....87 E3
Tregullan Vw BODM PL31 ....10 C4
Tregullow Rd FAL TR11 ....22 A1
Tregundy Ct PERRAN TR6 ....56 A3
Tregundy La PERRAN TR6 ....56 A3
Tregundy Rd PERRAN TR6 ....56 A4
Tregunnel HI NEWQ TR7 ....46 A5
Tregunnel Pk NEWQ TR7 ....46 A5
Tregunter Ms FAL TR11 ....23 F5
Tregurra La TRU TR1 ....85 G1
Tregurtha Vw RPENZ TR20 ....39 G3
Tregurthen Cl CAMBORNE TR14 ....14 B4
Tregurthen Rd CAMBORNE TR14 ....14 B4
Tregwary Rd STIVES TR26 ....69 G3
Tregye Rd RTRUS TR3 ....19 G2
Trehane Rd CAMBORNE TR14 ....14 A3
Trehaverne La TRU TR1 ....85 E2
Trehaverne La TRU TR1 ....85 E2
Trehaverne Ter TRU TR1 * 85 E2
Trehaverne Vean TRU TR1 ....85 E2
Trehayes Meadow HAYLE TR27 ....67 E3
Trehayes Parc HAYLE TR27 * 27 C2
Trekenn Rd PENRYN TR10 ....52 C3
Trelake Rd STAUS PL25 ....63 G3
Trelan CAMBORNE TR14 ....15 E3
Trelander Barton TRU TR1 ....85 G3
Trelander East TRU TR1 ....85 H3
Trelander Hwy TRU TR1 ....85 G3
Trelander North TRU TR1 ....85 H3
Trelander South TRU TR1 ....85 H3
Trelander Vean TRU TR1 * 85 H3
Trelawne Cl RTRUS TR3 ....19 F2
Trelawne Rd RTRUS TR3 ....19 G2
Trelawney Av FAL TR11 ....22 D3
    RED TR15 ....61 H1
    STIVES TR26 ....69 E3
Trelawney Cl BODM PL31 ....10 B3
    TOR PL11 ....80 D4
Trelawney Est RPENZ TR20 ....54 A1
Trelawney Pl HAYLE TR27 ....27 E3
    PENRYN TR10 ....52 D3
Trelawney Ri TOR PL11 ....80 D2
Trelawney Rd BODM PL31 ....10 A4
    CAMBORNE TR14 ....14 C2
    FAL TR11 ....22 D2
    HELS TR13 ....29 G4
    NEWQ TR7 ....28 48
    RTRUE/STMW TR2 ....74 B2
    SALT PL12 ....76 D3
    STAUS PL25 ....64 B2
    STIVES TR26 ....69 E3
    TRU TR1 ....84 D2
Trelawney Ter LOOE PL13 * 35 E2
Trelawney Wy HAYLE TR27 ....27 E3
    TOR PL11 ....80 D4
Treleaver Wy TRU TR1 ....84 B4
Trelee Cl HAYLE TR27 ....27 C2
Treleigh Av RED TR15 ....60 D3
Treleigh Ter RED TR15 ....60 D2
Treleven Rd BUDE EX23 ....12 C4
Treliever Rd PENRYN TR10 ....52 A4
Treliske La RTRUNW TR4 ....84 B2
Treliske Rd RED TR15 ....61 G2
Trelissick Flds HAYLE TR27 ....67 G1
Trelissick Rd FAL TR11 ....22 B1
    HAYLE TR27 ....67 G1
Treloar Ter LAUN PL15 ....31 E3

Treloggan La NEWQ TR7 ....46 D5
Treloggan Rd NEWQ TR7 ....46 D5
Trelowarren St CAMBORNE TR14 ....14 C3
Treloweth Cl HAYLE TR27 ....67 E3
Treloweth La HAYLE TR27 ....66 D3
Treloyhan STIVES TR26 ....69 G5
Treloyhan Park Rd STIVES TR26 ....69 G5
Trelyn WADE PL27 ....49 G1
Trelyon Av STIVES TR26 ....69 G4
Tremaine Cl PENZ TR18 ....54 C2
Tremarle Home Pk CAMBORNE TR14 ....15 E1
Tremarren Rd WADE PL27 ....86 B3
Tremar Cl PENZ TR18 ....54 C2
Tremar Rd STIVES TR26 ....68 B3
Trematon Cl TOR PL11 ....80 D3
Tremayne Cl RTRUS TR3 ....19 E4
Tremayne Rd CAMBORNE TR14 ....15 E3
Tremayne Pk STAUS PL25 ....64 B3
    TRU TR1 ....84 D2
Trembath Crs NEWQ TR7 ....46 B4
Trembear Rd STAUS PL25 ....63 H2
Tremeadow Ter HAYLE TR27 * 26 D5
    LISK PL14 ....33 G1
Tremearne Rd HELS TR13 ....58 B2
Tremeddan La LISK PL14 ....33 F2
Tremeddan Ter LISK PL14 ....33 E4
Tremellin La HAYLE TR27 ....67 F5
Tremena Gdns STAUS PL25 ....63 H3
Tremena Rd STAUS PL25 ....63 H3
Tremenheere Av HELS TR13 ....29 H1
Tremenheere Rd PENZ TR18 ....54 D3
Tremore Rd RED TR15 ....61 F2
Tremorva HAYLE TR27 ....27 E3
Tremorvah Barton TRU TR1 ....85 G2
Tremorvah Crs TRU TR1 ....85 G2
Tremorvah Pk FAL TR11 ....22 B5
Tremorvah Wood La TRU TR1 ....85 G2
Tremough DI PENRYN TR10 ....52 C2
Trenale La TINT PL34 ....78 D4
Trenalt Ter TRU TR1 * 84 D2
Trenance Av NEWQ TR7 ....46 B4
Trenance Cl HELS TR13 ....29 F2
Trenance HI STAUS PL25 ....63 F2
Trenance La NEWQ TR7 ....46 B5
Trenance Pl STAUS PL25 ....63 G3
Trenance Rd CAMBORNE TR14 ....14 D2
    NEWQ TR7 ....46 B4
    STAUS PL25 ....63 G3
Trenant Rd LOOE PL13 ....35 F1
    PAR PL24 ....51 G3
Trenant V WADE PL27 ....87 E2
Trenarren Vw STAUS PL25 ....64 D1
Trenarth PENRYN TR10 ....52 D3
Trenarth Rd NEWQ TR7 ....46 B4
Trencher La MBRK/KGSD PL10 ....43 E4
Trencreek La RNEWQ TR8 ....47 E5
Trencreek Rd RNEWQ TR8 ....47 E5
Trencrom La STIVES TR26 ....71 F3
Trencrom Rw HAYLE TR27 * 70 D5
Trendeal Gdns PENZ TR18 * 54 D5
Trendreath Cl STIVES TR26 ....26 A5
Treneague Pk WADE PL27 ....86 C4
Trenear Cl RED TR15 ....61 G2
Treneere PENZ TR18 * 54 D2
Treneere La PENZ TR18 ....54 D2
Treneere Rd PENZ TR18 ....54 D3
Treneglos Ter PENZ TR18 ....55 G1
Trenerry Cl TRU TR1 ....85 F1
Trenethick Av HELS TR13 ....29 G1
Trenethick Cl HELS TR13 ....29 H2
Trenethick Parc HELS TR13 ....29 G4
Trengrouse Av TOR PL11 ....81 E4
Trengrouse Wy HELS TR13 ....29 G4
Trenhayle La HAYLE TR27 ....67 G2
Treningle Vw BODM PL31 ....10 B4
Treninnick HI NEWQ TR7 ....46 C4
Trennick La TRU TR1 ....85 G3
Trennick Rw TRU TR1 * 85 G4
Trennick Vls TRU TR1 * 85 G4
Trenovissick Rd PAR PL24 ....50 B4
Trenowah Rd STAUS PL25 ....65 E2
Trenoweth Av CAMBORNE TR14 ....14 A3
Trenoweth Crs PENZ TR18 ....54 B5
Trenoweth Rd FAL TR11 ....22 B4
    PENZ TR18 ....54 B5
Trenwith Br STIVES TR26 * 68 D3
Trenwith La STIVES TR26 ....69 E4
Trenwith Pl STIVES TR26 ....69 F3
Trenwith Rd CAMBORNE TR14 ....14 A3
Trenwith Sq STIVES TR26 ....69 E3
Trenwith Ter STIVES TR26 * 69 E3
Trenython Rd PAR PL24 ....50 B5
Teraven La WADE PL27 ....86 D5
Terew Rd PENZ TR18 ....54 B5
Terice Dr NEWQ TR7 ....47 E3
Terice Pl STIVES TR26 ....69 E3
Terice Rd STIVES TR26 ....69 E3
Terise Rd CAMBORNE TR14 ....14 B5
Teruffe HI RED TR15 ....61 E4
Teruffe Ter RED TR15 ....61 E4
Teryn Cl PAR PL24 ....50 C4
Tresaderns Rd RED TR15 ....61 F3
Tresahar Rd FAL TR11 ....22 C3
Tresawle Rd FAL TR11 ....53 H5
Tresawls Av FAL TR11 ....83 H1
Tresawls Rd TRU TR1 ....83 G2
Tresco Pl FAL TR11 ....22 B2
Treseder's Gdns TRU TR1 ....85 F2

Tresidder Cl FAL TR11 ....22 A2
Tresillian Rd FAL TR11 ....53 G5
Tresooth La PENRYN TR10 ....52 C3
Treswithian Park Rd CAMBORNE TR14 ....14 A3
Trethellan HI NEWQ TR7 ....21 H3
Tretherras Cl NEWQ TR7 ....46 D3
Tretherras Rd NEWQ TR7 ....46 D3
Trethewey Wy NEWQ TR7 ....46 A4
Trethew Gdns CAMBORNE TR14 ....14 D3
Treth Owan Hts TRU TR1 ....84 B4
Tretoil Vw BODM PL31 ....10 D5
Tretorvic PENZ TR18 ....54 C1
Trevail Wy STAUS PL25 ....64 B3
Trevale PENZ TR18 ....54 C1
Trevalga Cl PERRAN TR6 ....56 B4
Trevallyn Rd LAUN PL15 ....31 F5
Trevance PENRYN TR10 ....52 B4
Trevance Pk PAR PL24 ....51 F2
Trevanion Cl WADE PL27 ....86 C4
Trevanion Ct TRU TR1 ....84 B3
Trevanion HI STAUS PL25 ....62 D3
Trevanion La STAUS PL25 ....62 D2
Trevanion Pk WADE PL27 ....86 C4
Trevanion Rd LISK PL14 ....33 E3
    STAUS PL25 ....62 D3
    WADE PL27 ....86 C4
Trevanion Ter RED TR15 ....60 D5
    WADE PL27 ....86 D4
Trevanson Rd WADE PL27 ....86 B2
Trevanson St WADE PL27 ....86 C2
Trevarner Wy WADE PL27 ....86 D3
Trevarno Cl STAUS PL25 ....63 E3
Trevarrack Cl PENZ TR18 ....55 F1
Trevarrack Ct STIVES TR26 * 71 E2
Trevarrack La PENZ TR18 ....55 F1
Trevarrack Noweth PENZ TR18 ....55 G1
Trevarrack Pl PENZ TR18 ....55 F1
Trevarrack Rd PENZ TR18 ....55 F1
Trevarrack Rw PENZ TR18 ....55 G1
Trevarrick Ct STIVES TR26 ....71 E2
Trevarrick Dr STAUS PL25 ....63 G4
Trevarrick Rd STAUS PL25 ....63 G4
Trevarth Est MEVA PL26 ....41 F5
Trevarthian Rd STAUS PL25 ....64 A3
Trevarth Rd FAL TR11 ....22 A1
Trevarweneth Rd PAR PL24 ....50 B4
Trevaskis La STAUS PL25 ....62 D3
Trevassack La STAUS PL25 ....62 D2
Trevassack St HAYLE TR27 ....27 F3
Trevassack Vl HAYLE TR27 ....27 F3
Trevaylor Cl TRU TR1 ....85 F1
Trevaylor Rd FAL TR11 ....22 B1
Trevean Cl CAMBORNE TR14 * 14 A3
Trevean Gdns PENZ TR18 ....54 D4
Trevean Rd PENZ TR18 ....54 D4
    TRU TR1 ....84 A3
Trevean Wy NEWQ TR7 ....21 H3
Trevear Cl STAUS PL25 ....64 A4
Treveglos HAYLE TR27 ....26 D3
Treveglos Rd FAL TR11 ....22 A5
Trevella Rd BUDE EX23 ....12 C1
Trevelthan Rd RTRUNW TR4 ....60 A1
Trevelva Rd TRU TR1 ....85 G5
Trevelveth Rd RNEWQ TR8 ....21 E5
Trevelyan Wy PENRYN TR20 ....39 H3
Trevemper Rd NEWQ TR7 ....46 C5
Trevena Cl PENZ TR18 ....54 C5
Trevena Dr TINT PL34 ....78 C4
Trevena Rd PENZ TR18 ....54 C5
Trevena Ter NEWQ TR7 ....46 A3
Trevenen Rd HELS TR13 ....29 G4
Treveneth Crs PENZ TR18 ....45 G5
Treveneth Pl PENZ TR18 ....45 G5
Trevenner La MARAZ TR17 ....38 D3
Trevenner Ms RED TR15 * 61 E3
Trevenner Sq MARAZ TR17 ....38 D3
Trevenson La CAMBORNE TR14 ....14 C4
Trevenson Rd NEWQ TR7 ....47 E3
    RED TR15 ....15 F1
Trevenson St CAMBORNE TR14 ....14 C4
Treventon Cl FAL TR11 ....22 A2
Treverbyn Cl LISK PL14 ....33 H2
Treverbyn Gdns STAUS PL25 ....64 C3
Treverbyn Ri PENRYN TR10 ....52 B3
Treverbyn Rd FAL TR11 ....22 A5
    PADS PL28 ....48 C4
    STIVES TR26 ....69 E3
    TRU TR1 ....85 G1
Trevethan Cl FAL TR11 ....22 C2
Trevethan Gdns FAL TR11 ....22 C2
Trevethan HI FAL TR11 ....22 D1
Trevethan La FAL TR11 ....22 D1
Trevethan Rd FAL TR11 ....22 C2
Trevethan Ter FAL TR11 * 22 D1
Trevethenick Rd TRU TR1 ....85 G4
Treveth La HELS TR13 ....29 H1
Trevethlyn CAMBORNE TR14 ....15 E1
Treveth Ylyn CAMBORNE TR14 ....15 E1
Trevia Ln CAMEL PL32 ....16 C3
Trevian Cl PERRAN TR6 ....56 B4
Treviglas Cl NEWQ TR7 ....47 E2
Trevilling Rd WADE PL27 ....86 C1
Trevillis Pk LISK PL14 ....33 G4
Trevingey Cl RED TR15 ....60 D5
Trevingey Crs RED TR15 ....60 D4
Trevingey Parc RED TR15 ....60 D4
Trevingey Rd RED TR15 ....60 D5
Trevissome FAL TR11 ....53 G5
Trevithick Av TOR PL11 ....80 D3
Trevithick Cl CAMBORNE TR14 ....15 E4
    NEWQ TR7 ....46 C5
    TRU TR1 ....85 G2

Trevithick Ct *CAMBORNE* TR14......14 B3
TRU TR1 ....85 G1
Trevithick Crs *HAYLE* TR27 ....27 E4
Trevithick Rd *CAMBORNE* TR14......14 C3
FAL TR11 ....22 A1
STAUS PL25 ....64 B4
TRU TR1 ....85 G1
Trevoarn *HAYLE* TR27 ....26 D4
Trevol Pl *TOR* PL11 ....80 D4
Trevol Rd *TOR* PL11 ....80 B4
Trevone Crs *STAUS* PL25 ....63 F3
Trevorder Cl *TOR* PL11 ....81 E5
Trevorder Rd *TOR* PL11 ....81 E5
Trevose Av *NEWQ* TR7 ....21 H2
Trevose Rd *TRU* TR1 ....84 A2
Trevu Rd *CAMBORNE* TR14 ....14 D4
Trewans Ter *RED* TR15......................60 D2
Trewartha Cl *STIVES* TR26 ....71 F2
Trewartha Est *STIVES* TR26 * 71 F3
Trewartha Ter *STIVES* TR18 * 71 F2
Trewarton Rd *PENRYN* TR10 ....52 B2
Trewarveneth St *PENZ* TR18 ....45 C3
Trewavas Crs *HELS* TR13 ....29 G4
Trewavas Rd *PENZ* TR18 ....45 G3
Treweath Rd *PENZ* TR18 ....54 D3
Trewen Br *CAMEL* PL32 ....16 C5
Trewhiddle Rd *STAUS* PL25 ....63 H5
Trewidden Cl *TRU* TR1 ....85 G2
Trewidden Ct *TRU* TR1 * 85 G2
Trewidden Rd *STIVES* TR26 ....69 F3
Trewince La *LOST* PL22 ....37 F3
Trewinnard Gv *TRU* TR1 ....84 D1
Trewinnard La *HAYLE* TR27 ....66 D5
Trewinnard Rd *RTRUS* TR3 ....18 A5
Trewint Crs *LOOE* PL13.....................35 F2
Trewirgie Gdns *RED* TR15................61 E4
Trewirgie HI *RED* TR15.....................61 E4
Trewirgie Rd *RED* TR15 ....61 E4
Trewirgie Vean *RED* TR15 ....61 E4
Trewithan Parc *LOST* PL22 ....37 G4
Trewithen Rd *PENZ* TR18 ....54 D4
Treworden Cl *BUDE* EX23 ....13 C3
Treworder La *WADE* PL27 ....87 C3
Treworder Rd *TRU* TR1 ....84 D3
Treworlis Cl *HELS* TR13 ....29 H1
Treworthal Rd *RTRUS* TR3 ....18 A5
Treworvenneth Dr
  MARAZ TR17 ....38 D3
Treyew Rd *TRU* TR1 ....84 C3
Trezela Rd *PENZ* TR18 ....54 D3
Trinity St *STAUS* PL25 ....63 H4
Tristan Rd *TRU* TR1 ....85 H2
Troubridge Rd *HELS* TR13 ....29 C5
Troy Ct *FOW* PL23 * 24 C2
Trungle *LANDS* TR19 ....45 G5
Trungle Parc *LANDS* TR19 ....45 G5
Trungle Ter *LANDS* TR19 ....45 G5
Truro HI *PENRYN* TR10 ....52 D3
Truro La *PENRYN* TR10 ....52 D3
Truro Lanes *TRU* TR1 * 85 E3
Truro Rd *STAUS* PL25 ....63 F5
Truro Vean Ter *TRU* TR1 ....85 F2
Truthwall La *LANDS* TR19 ....72 B2
Tryhornek *STIVES* TR26 ....71 F3
Trythogga HI *PENZ* TR18 ....55 F2
Trythogga Rd *PENZ* TR18 ....55 F1
Tuckers Cl *RNEWQ* TR8 ....47 E5
Tuke Cl *FAL* TR11 ....22 A1
Turf St *BODM* PL31 ....10 D2
Turnaware Rd *STAUS* PL25 ....63 F3
Turnaware Rd *FAL* TR11 ....22 A4
Turnpike *HELS* TR13 ....29 G2
Turnpike HI *MARAZ* TR17 ....38 C3
Turnpike Pl *LISK* PL14 ....33 E4
Turnpike Quarry *RED* TR15 * 61 G2
Turnpike Rd *MARAZ* TR17 ....38 D3
The Turnpike *LANDS* TR19 ....72 C5
Two Hills Pk *SALT* PL12 ....76 B3
Two Trees *WADE* PL27 ....86 C4
Two Trees Est *WADE* PL27 ....86 C4
Two Trees Rd *LOST* PL22 ....37 H5
Tyacke Rd *HELS* TR13 ....29 F4
Tye Hill Cl *STAUS* PL25 ....63 E3
Tyland Rd *CAMEL* PL32 ....17 C4
Tyringham Pl *STIVES* TR26 ....26 A4
Tyringham Rd *STIVES* TR26 ....71 G2
Tyringham Rw *STIVES* TR26 ....26 A4
Tywardreath HI *PAR* PL24 ....51 C4
Tywarnhayle Rd *PERRAN* TR6 ....56 A3
Tywarnhayle Sq *PERRAN* TR6 * 56 B3

U

Uglow Cl *CAMBORNE* TR14 ....14 B3
Ulalia Rd *NEWQ* TR7 * 46 C3
Umfula Pl *STIVES* TR26 * 69 F3
Under Chapel Yd *PENZ* TR18 ....55 F5
Undercliff *HAYLE* TR27 ....27 F2
Underhayes La *LANDS* PL15 ....30 D3
Under La *LANDS* PL15 ....30 B3
Union HI *BUDE* EX23 ....13 C3
Union Pl *FOW* PL23 * 24 D2
TRU TR1 ....85 H3
Union Rd *FAL* TR11 ....53 E5
Union St *CAMBORNE* TR14 ....14 C4
PENZ TR18 ....55 E4
TRU TR1 ....85 H3
Unity Rd *HELS* TR13 ....58 B2
Upland Cl *TRU* TR1 ....85 H2

Upland Crs *TRU* TR1 ....85 G1
Uplands *SALT* PL12 ....76 D4
The Uplands *LOST* PL22 ....37 E4
Uplands Vean *TRU* TR1 ....85 G1
Upper Castle Rd
  RTRUE/STMW TR2 ....74 B2
Upper Chapel *LAUN* PL15 ....30 D5
Upper Eastcliffe Rd *PAR* PL24 ....51 F4
Upper Hillcrest *PERRAN* TR6 ....56 A4
Upper School La *TRU* TR1 ....85 H3
Upper Tredrea *RTRUS* TR3 ....18 B5
Upton Mdw *BUDE* EX23 ....12 A5
Upton Slip *FAL* TR11 * 22 D2
Uzella Pk *LOST* PL22 ....37 F4

V

Valley Cl *TRU* TR1 ....84 A1
Valley Gdns *RTRUNW* TR4 ....60 A3
Valley La *RTRUS* TR3 ....19 F1
Valley Pk *MEVA* PL26 ....41 G3
Valley Park La *MEVA* PL26 ....41 G3
Valley Rd *BUDE* EX23 ....12 A4
MEVA PL26 ....41 G2
SALT PL12 ....76 D4
STIVES TR26 ....71 E1
The Valley *STIVES* TR26 * 71 E1
Valley Vw *BODM* PL31 ....10 D4
WADE PL27 ....86 D2
Valley View Dr *TRU* TR1 ....84 A3
Vancouver Pl *LAUN* PL15 ....31 F4
Varley La *LISK* PL14 ....33 E3
Varley Ter *LISK* PL14 ....33 E3
Vean Rd *CAMBORNE* TR14 ....14 D4
Vean Ter *CAMBORNE* TR14 * 14 D4
Vellanhoggan *PENZ* TR18 * 55 G2
Vensloое HI *LISK* PL14 ....33 E1
Ventnor Ter *STIVES* TR26 * 69 E2
Venton East Sq *LANDS* TR19............72 C3
Ventonleague HI *HAYLE* TR27 ....27 C2
Ventonleague Rw *HAYLE* TR27 ....27 C2
Venton Rd *FAL* TR11 ....22 A2
STIVES TR26 ....69 C5
Veor Rd *NEWQ* TR7 ....47 F2
Vernon Pl *FAL* TR11 ....22 D2
Vernon Vis *PAR* PL24 ....50 B4
Viaduct Rd *HAYLE* TR27 ....27 C3
Vicarage Gdns *PLYNW* PL5 ....77 H4
Vicarage Ga *HAYLE* TR27 ....67 F3
Vicarage HI *MEVA* PL26 ....41 G2
STAUS PL25 ....63 H4
TINT PL34 ....78 B4
Vicarage Meadow *FOW* PL23 ....24 C2
Vicarage Rd *BUDE* EX23 ....12 B1
PAR PL24 ....51 F4
TOR PL11 ....81 C5
Vicarage Row *LANDS* TR19 ....72 B4
Victoria Cl *LISK* PL14 ....33 F2
Victoria Ct *PENZ* TR18 * 55 E4
Victoria Gdns *RTRUS* TR3 ....18 B5
Victoria La *SALT* PL12 ....77 E3
Victoria Ms *PENZ* TR18 * 55 E3
Victoria Pk *WADE* PL27 ....86 D2
Victoria Pl *PENZ* TR18 * 55 E4
STAUS PL25 * 63 H4
STIVES TR26 ....69 F2
Victoria Quay *FAL* TR11 ....22 D1
Victoria Rw *LANDS* TR19 * 72 B4
Victoria Sq *BODM* PL31 ....11 E4
PENZ TR18 ....55 E3
TRU TR1 ....85 E3
Victoria St *CAMBORNE* TR14 ....14 C4
TOR PL11 ....81 G4
Victoria Ter *LISK* PL14 * 33 E3
Vincent Wy *SALT* PL12 ....77 E3
Vine Pl *PAR* PL24 ....51 G3
Vingoe's La *RPENZ* TR20 ....54 A1
Virgin HI *MARAZ* TR17 ....38 B2
Virgin St *STIVES* TR26 ....69 F2
Vivian Cl *BODM* PL31 ....10 A3
NEWQ TR7 ....46 B4
Vivian Dr *TRU* TR1 * 85 E4
Vivian Pk *CAMBORNE* TR14.............15 E4
Vivian Rd *BODM* PL31 ....10 A3
Vorfield Cl *RED* TR15 ....61 C2
Vosporth HI *RNEWQ* TR8 ....21 F5
Vosporth Rd *RNEWQ* TR8 ....21 F4
Vounder Glaze *LANDS* TR19.............72 A4
Voundervour La *PENZ* TR18..............55 E4
Vyvyan Pl *HELS* TR13 ....29 G4
Vyvyan St *CAMBORNE* TR14.............14 C3

W

Wadeland Ter *LISK* PL14 ....32 C3
Wadham Cl *LISK* PL14 ....33 F3
Wadham Dr *LISK* PL14 ....33 F3
Wadham Rd *LISK* PL14 ....33 F3
Wainsway *PERRAN* TR6 ....56 B4
Walk Ter *FOW* PL23 ....24 C3

The Walk *LAUN* PL15 ....31 F3
Wallace Rd *BODM* PL31 ....10 C2
The Walled Gdn *PENRYN* TR10.........52 B5
Walsingham Pl *TRU* TR1 * 85 E3
Walters Rd *PLYNW* PL5 ....77 H4
Warburton Gdns *PLYNW* PL5 ....77 H4
Ward Cl *BUDE* EX23 ....13 F3
Warfelton Crs *SALT* PL12 ....76 D3
Warfelton Gdns *SALT* PL12 ....76 D2
Warfelton Ter *SALT* PL12 ....76 D2
Warraton Cl *SALT* PL12 ....76 C2
Warraton Gn *SALT* PL12 ....76 C2
Warraton Rd *SALT* PL12 ....76 C2
Warren *STIVES* TR26 ....69 F3
Warren Cl *HELS* TR13 ....58 B2
Warrens Fld *CAMEL* PL32 ....17 C3
The Warren *STIVES* TR26 * 69 F3
Warwick Dr *STAUS* PL25 ....65 E3
Warwick Rd *FAL* TR11 ....22 C4
Watering Hill Cl *STAUS* PL25 ....64 B4
Water La *HAYLE* TR27 ....67 F1
RNEWQ TR8 ....21 F5
Waterloo *TRU* TR1 * 85 G2
Waterloo Cl *RTRUE/STMW* TR2 ......74 C1
Waterloo Rd *FAL* TR11 * 22 D2
Waterloo Rd *FAL* TR11 * 22 D2
Water-ma-Trout *HELS* TR13 ....29 C1
Watermill Wk *CAMEL* PL32 * 17 C5
Watersedge Cl *STAUS* PL25 ....63 G5
Waterside Ct *PENRYN* TR10 * 53 F4
Watery La *BODM* PL31 ....10 C3
Wavish Pk *TOR* PL11 ....81 F5
Wearde Rd *SALT* PL12 ....76 D5
Webber Rd *FAL* TR11 * 22 C2
Webber St *FAL* TR11 ....22 C2
Webb St *FOW* PL23 ....24 D2
Wedgewood Rd *STAUS* PL25 ....64 D3
Weeth Cl *CAMBORNE* TR14 ....14 B3
Weeth La *CAMBORNE* TR14 ....14 A2
Weeth Rd *CAMBORNE* TR14.............14 B3
Wellington *CAMBORNE* TR14 ....14 B3
Wellington Gdns *FAL* TR11 * 22 C2
Wellington Pl *FAL* TR11 * 22 D2
PENZ TR18 ....54 D4
WADE PL27 ....86 D4
Wellington Rd
  CAMBORNE TR14 ....14 B3
Wellington St *TOR* PL11 ....81 C5
Wellington Ter *FAL* TR11 * 22 D2
PENZ TR18 * 54 D4
TRU TR1 * 85 E3
Well La *FAL* TR11 * 22 D2
LISK PL14 ....33 F2
LOOE PL13 ....35 E2
Well Park Rd *TOR* PL11 ....81 G4
Wells Ct *MBRK/KGSD* PL10 ....43 F2
Well St *PAR* PL24 ....51 G3
Well Wy *NEWQ* TR7 ....47 F2
Welway *PERRAN* TR6 ....56 B4
Wendron St *HELS* TR13 ....29 F4
Wendron Ter *HELS* TR13 * 29 C3
Went Worth Cl *BUDE* EX23 ....12 A5
Wentworth Cl *RTRUNW* TR4.............61 F5
Wentworth Wy *SALT* PL12 ....76 B3
Wesley Ct *MEVA* PL26 * 41 C3
TOR PL11 ....81 H4
Wesley La *SALT* PL12 ....77 E3
Wesley Pl *PENZ* TR18 ....45 C2
STAUS PL25 ....64 C4
STIVES TR26 ....69 F3
Wesley St *CAMBORNE* TR14 ....14 D4
PENZ TR18 ....54 C2
RED TR15 ....61 F3
Wesley Ter *LOOE* PL13 * 35 E2
Wesley Yd *NEWQ* TR7 ....46 A3
Westborne Hts *RED* TR15 ....61 E5
Westborne Rd
  CAMBORNE TR14 ....14 A2
Westbourne Dr *STAUS* PL25 ....63 G4
Westbourne La *LISK* PL14 ....33 F2
Westbourne Ter *SALT* PL12 ....77 E2
West Bridge Rd *LAUN* PL15 ....31 E2
Westbridge Rd *STAUS* PL25 ....62 D3
Westby Rd *BUDE* EX23 ....12 C3
West Charles St
  CAMBORNE TR14 ....14 C4
West Cl *HELS* TR13 ....29 H2
West Cnr *RTRUS* TR3 ....19 F1
Westcott Wadd *FAL* TR11 ....22 D2
Westcotts Quay *STIVES* TR26 * 69 F3
West Cs *NEWQ* TR7 ....21 H2
West Downs Cl *LOOE* PL13...............35 E2
West End *MARAZ* TR17 ....38 D3
PENRYN TR10 ....52 D3
RED TR15 ....60 D4
RPENZ TR20 ....39 G3
West End Cl *PENRYN* TR10 ....52 D3
West End Ter
  MBRK/KGSD PL10 * 43 F2
Western La *STIVES* TR26 ....69 E2
Western Pl *PENRYN* TR10 ....52 C3
Western Promenade Rd
  PENZ TR18 ....55 E5
Western Rd *LISK* PL14 ....31 E5
Western Ter *BODM* PL31 * 10 B3
FAL TR11 ....22 C3
LAUN PL15 ....31 E4
West Fairholme Rd *BUDE* EX23 ....12 C1
Westgate Ms *LAUN* PL15 * 31 F4
Westgate St *LAUN* PL15 ....31 E4

Westground Wy *TINT* PL34 ....78 D3
Westheath Rd *BODM* PL31 ....10 A4
West HI *STAUS* PL25 ....63 H4
WADE PL27 ....86 D2
Westlake Cl *TOR* PL11 ....81 E4
West Looe HI *LOOE* PL13..................34 D3
West Looe Sq *LOOE* PL13 ....35 E3
Westmoor Crs *RTRUS* TR3 ....18 A4
West Pk *RED* TR15 ....60 C4
RTRUS TR3 ....18 A4
WADE PL27 ....86 D2
West Park Rd *BUDE* EX23 ....12 B1
Westpark Rd *WADE* PL27 ....87 E4
West Pentire Rd *RNEWQ* TR8 ....20 C4
West Pl *FAL* TR11 ....22 C3
LANDS TR19 ....72 B4
STIVES TR26 * 69 F2
West Quay *MBRK/KGSD* PL10..........43 F1
West Ri *FAL* TR11 ....22 B3
West Rd *LOOE* PL13 ....35 E2
West St *FOW* PL23 ....24 C4
LISK PL14 ....33 E2
MBRK/KGSD PL10 ....43 F2
PENRYN TR10 ....52 D3
West Ter *HAYLE* TR27 ....26 D3
PENZ TR18 * 45 G1
West Tolgus *RED* TR15 ....60 A2
West Trevingey *RED* TR15 ....60 D4
West Trewirgie Rd *RED* TR15 ....61 E4
West Vw *HELS* TR13 ....40 A1
Westward Rd *STIVES* TR26 ....69 E2
West Whf *PENZ* TR18 ....41 H3
Westwood *LISK* PL14 ....33 E2
Wharf Rd *PENZ* TR18 ....55 F4
STIVES TR26 ....69 F2
The Wharf *BUDE* EX23 ....12 B3
STIVES TR26 ....69 F2
Wheal Perran *STIVES* TR26 ....56 B3
Wheal Alfred Rd *HAYLE* TR27 ....27 H4
Wheal-an-Wens *MARAZ* TR17 ....38 C3
Wheal Ayr Ter *STIVES* TR26 * 69 E2
Wheal Cunning *LANDS* TR19............72 A3
Wheal Dream *STIVES* TR26 ....69 G2
Wheal Eliza Cl *STAUS* PL25 ....65 E2
Wheal Fortune La *RED* TR15.............60 A4
Wheal Gerry *CAMBORNE* TR14.........14 D2
Wheal Harmony *RED* TR15 ....61 E1
Wheal Jane Mdw *RTRUNW* TR4.......82 D3
Wheal Leisure *PERRAN* TR6 ....56 B3
Wheal Leisure Cl *PERRAN* TR6.........56 B3
Wheal Margery *STIVES* TR26 ....69 G5
Wheal Montague *RTRUNW* TR4........60 D1
Wheal Northey *STAUS* PL25 ....65 E2
Wheal Oak *HELS* TR13 ....29 H1
Wheal Regent Pk *STAUS* PL25 ....65 C4
Wheal Rose *HELS* TR13 ....58 B2
Wheal Silver *RED* TR15 ....61 E3
Wheal Speed *STIVES* TR26 ....71 E1
Wheal Speed Rd *STIVES* TR26 ....71 E2
Wheal Tehidy *RED* TR15 ....60 B4
Wheal Tehidy La *RED* TR15 ....60 B4
Wheal Trelawney *RED* TR15 ....61 G5
Wheal Venture Rd *STIVES* TR26.......69 G5
Wheal Vor *RED* TR15 ....61 G5
Wheal Whidden *STIVES* TR26...........71 E1
Wheatfield Crs *NEWQ* TR7 ....46 D5
Wherry Pl *FOW* PL23 ....24 D4
Whieldon Rd *STAUS* PL25 ....64 D3
Whitcross HI *RED* TR15 ....15 H3
Whitegate Rd *NEWQ* TR7 ....46 D3
Whitehill Ter *HELS* TR13 * 29 G5
White House Cl *STIVES* TR26 ....71 E1
Whiterock Cl *WADE* PL27 ....86 C3
Whiterock Rd *WADE* PL27 ....86 C3
Whiterock Ter *WADE* PL27 ....86 C3
Whitestone Crs *BODM* PL31.............10 B4
Whitestone Rd *BODM* PL31 ....10 B4
Whitford Yd *FOW* PL23 * 24 D2
Whitley Cl *TRU* TR1 ....85 F3
Whitley Gra *LISK* PL14 ....32 D2
Wilcove Cl *TOR* PL11 ....80 D2
Wildflower La *NEWQ* TR7 ....85 E3
Wilkes Wk *TRU* TR1 ....85 F3
William Edwards Cl *BUDE* EX23.......12 C2
Williams Cl *TRU* TR1 ....85 E2
William St *CAMBORNE* TR14 ....14 C3
TRU TR1 ....85 F4
Willis La *STIVES* TR26 * 69 F2
Wilson Wy *PAR* PL24 ....50 A5
RED TR15 ....60 A5
Windmill Cl *BODM* PL31 ....10 D4
Windmill HI *LAUN* PL15 ....31 F4
SALT PL12 ....76 D3
Windmill Hill Ter *LAUN* PL15 * 31 F4
Windmill La *LAUN* PL15 ....31 F4
Windsor Ct *FAL* TR11 ....22 D3
NEWQ TR7 ....46 A4
Windsor Dr *STAUS* PL25 ....65 F3
Windsor Gv *BODM* PL31 ....11 E2
Windsor HI *STIVES* TR26 ....69 E2
Windsor La *SALT* PL12 ....76 D3
Windsor Ms *BODM* PL31 ....10 D2
Windsor Pl *PENZ* TR18 ....54 D3
Windsor Ter *FAL* TR11 ....22 C2
PENZ TR18 * 54 D3
STIVES TR26 * 69 E2
Wingfield *BODM* PL31 ....11 F2

Winslow Ter *RNEWQ* TR8 ....21 F5
Winwell Fld *WADE* PL27 ....87 E2
Woburn Rd *LAUN* PL15 ....31 E5
Wodehouse Ter *FAL* TR11 ....22 D2
Wolcocke Cl *MARAZ* TR17 ....38 D3
Wolseley Rd *PLYNW* PL5 ....77 G4
Wood Acre *SALT* PL12 ....76 A1
Wooda La *LAUN* PL15 ....31 E3
Wooda Rd *LAUN* PL15 ....31 E3
Wood Cl *SALT* PL12 ....76 A2
Woodfield Rd *BUDE* EX23 ....12 C1
Woodgate Rd *LISK* PL14 ....32 D3
Woodland Av *PAR* PL24 ....51 F3
Woodland Cl
    PENRYN TR10 ....52 C4
Woodland Cl *FAL* TR11 ....22 D3

STAUS PL25 ....64 B4
Woodland Ct *TRU* TR1 ....85 G2
Woodland Hts *TRU* TR1 ....85 G2
Woodland Ri *PENRYN* TR10 ....52 C4
Woodland Rd *STAUS* PL25 ....64 B4
Woodlands Vw *LOOE* PL13 ....34 D2
Woodland Wy *TOR* PL11 ....81 E4
Woodlane La *LAUN* 22 D3
Woodland La *PAR* PL24 ....51 F2
Woodlane Cl *FAL* TR11 * 22 D3
Woodlane Crs *FAL* TR11 ....22 D3
Woodlane Dr *FAL* TR11 ....22 D3
Woodley Cl *BUDE* EX23 ....13 F3
Wood Parc *STAUS* PL25 ....64 C4
Woodside *PENRYN* TR10 ....52 C4

Wood St *PENZ* TR18 * 55 E4
Woodvale Ter *LAUN* PL15 ....31 F4
Wood Vw *PENRYN* TR10 ....52 C5
Woodway *PENRYN* TR10 ....52 C5
Woon La *RTRUS* TR3 ....19 F1
Wrey Av *LISK* PL14 ....33 F1
Wych Hazel Wy *NEWQ* TR7 ....46 C5
Wyndhurst Orch *WADE* PL27 ....86 C3

Yeomans Cl *LISK* PL14 ....33 G3
York Rd *TOR* PL11 ....81 G4
York St *PENZ* TR18 ....54 D3

Y

Yellow Tor La *SALT* PL12 ....76 B3
Yellowtor Rd *SALT* PL12 ....76 A3

Index - featured places

Acorn Theatre
    PENZ TR18 ....55 E4
Albert Pier
    PENZ TR18 ....55 F4
Alverton CP School
    PENZ TR18 ....54 C5
Alverton Manor Hotel
    TRU TR1 ....85 G2
Antony House (NT)
    TOR PL11 ....80 C2
Archbishop Benson CE
    Primary School
    TRU TR1 ....85 F2
Atlantic House Hotel
    BUDE EX23 ....12 B2
Atlantic Road Cemetery
    NEWQ TR7 ....21 H2
Ayr Holiday Park
    STIVES TR26 ....69 E2
Balnoon Camping Site
    STIVES TR26 ....70 B2
Barbara Hepworth Museum
    & Sculpture Garden
    STIVES TR26 ....69 E2
Barbican Rise
    Industrial Estate
    LOOE PL13 ....35 G1
Barncoose Industrial Estate
    RED TR15 ....60 B5
Barnoon Cemetery
    STIVES TR26 ....69 F2
Barrowfield Hotel
    NEWQ TR7 ....46 D3
Barties Industrial Estate
    RED TR15 ....61 E2
The Beacon Infant School
    BODM PL31 ....10 C3
Benbole Gardens
    LOST PL22 ....37 F4
Berrycoombe
    Primary School
    BODM PL31 ....10 A2
Best Western Hotel Bristol
    NEWQ TR7 ....46 C2
Best Western
    Penmere Manor Hotel
    FAL TR11 ....22 A3
Best Western
    Restormel Lodge Hotel
    LOST PL22 ....37 E4
Biscovey Infant School
    PAR PL24 ....50 B5
Biscovey Junior School
    PAR PL24 ....50 B5
Bishop Bronescombe CE
    Primary School
    STAUS PL25 ....65 E2
Bishop Cornish CE
    Primary School
    SALT PL12 ....77 E4
The Bishops CE
    Primary School
    NEWQ TR7 ....46 C5
Blue Lagoon Leisure Centre
    NEWQ TR7 ....46 B3
Blue Reef Aquarium
    NEWQ TR7 ....46 A3
Bodmin Business Centre
    BODM PL31 ....10 D4
Bodmin Business Park
    BODM PL31 ....11 E3
Bodmin Care &
    Learning Centre
    BODM PL31 ....11 E5
Bodmin C & CC Site
    BODM PL31 ....11 F2
Bodmin Cemetery
    BODM PL31 ....10 D1
Bodmin College
    BODM PL31 ....11 E5
Bodmin Jail
    BODM PL31 ....10 C2
Bodmin Leisure Centre
    BODM PL31 ....11 E5
Bodmin Town Museum
    BODM PL31 ....10 D3
Bodmin & Wenford Railway
    RBODM PL30 ....10 C5

Bodriggy Health Centre
    HAYLE TR27 ....27 E4
Bodriggy Primary School
    HAYLE TR27 ....27 F4
The Bolitho School
    PENZ TR18 ....54 C4
Bone Valley Caravan &
    Camping Park
    RPENZ TR20 ....54 B1
Boscundle Manor
    Country House Hotel
    STAUS PL25 ....65 G2
Boskerris Hotel
    STIVES TR26 ....71 F1
Bossiney House Hotel
    TINT PL34 ....78 D3
Bosvigo Garden
    TRU TR1 ....84 C2
Bridge Medical Centre
    WADE PL27 ....86 D2
Broadmead Hotel
    FAL TR11 ....22 C2
Brookdale Hotel
    TRU TR1 ....85 G2
Brunel Primary School
    SALT PL12 ....76 D2
Budehaven
    Community School
    BUDE EX23 ....12 D3
Budehaven Leisure Centre
    BUDE EX23 ....12 C3
Bude Industrial Estate
    BUDE EX23 ....12 D5
Bude J & I School
    BUDE EX23 ....12 C3
Bude Lifeboat Station
    BUDE EX23 ....12 B2
Bude & North Cornwall
    Golf Club
    BUDE EX23 ....12 B2
Bude Open
    Learning Centre
    BUDE EX23 ....13 C2
Bude RFC
    BUDE EX23 ....12 B4
Bude-Stratton
    Business Park
    BUDE EX23 ....13 E4
Bude Town FC
    BUDE EX23 ....12 D3
Bull Point Primary School
    PLYNW PL5 ....77 G4
Burraton Primary School
    SALT PL12 ....76 B2
Callywith Gate
    Industrial Estate
    BODM PL31 ....11 F1
Camborne Cemetery
    CAMBORNE TR14 ....14 A3
Camborne Museum
    CAMBORNE TR14 ....14 C4
Camborne Redruth
    Community Hospital
    RED TR15 ....60 C4
Camborne Retail Park
    RED TR15 ....15 F1
Camborne RFC
    CAMBORNE TR14 ....14 A4
Camborne Science &
    Community College
    CAMBORNE TR14 ....14 A3
Camelford Primary School
    CAMEL PL32 ....17 E5
Camelford Sports Centre
    CAMEL PL32 ....17 E4
Camelot Cinema
    NEWQ TR7 ....46 A3
Camelot Hotel
    BUDE EX23 ....12 C1
Campdowns Cemetery
    STAUS PL25 ....65 E4
Cape Cornwall
    Comprehensive School
    LANDS TR19 ....72 B3
Carbeile Junior School
    TOR PL11 ....81 F4
Carbis Bay Hotel
    STIVES TR26 ....71 F1

Carclaze Community
    Infant School
    STAUS PL25 ....64 B1
Carclaze Community
    Junior School
    STAUS PL25 ....64 B1
Cardrew Business Park
    RED TR15 ....61 F2
Cardrew Industrial Estate
    RED TR15 ....61 F2
Carew Wharf
    Business Centre
    TOR PL11 ....81 H5
Carlton Hotel
    TRU TR1 ....85 E4
Carlyon Bay Caravan &
    Camping Park
    STAUS PL25 ....65 H3
Carlyon Bay Hotel
    STAUS PL25 ....65 H4
Carminnow Road
    Industrial Estate
    BODM PL31 ....11 F5
Carn Brea Leisure Centre
    RED TR15 ....15 H1
Carnon Downs Caravan &
    Camping Park
    RTRUS TR3 ....19 G1
Carrick Business Centre
    PENRYN TR10 ....53 E4
Carrick Sports Centre
    TRU TR1 ....84 D2
Charlestown
    Primary School
    STAUS PL25 ....65 F4
Charlestown Shipwreck &
    Heritage Centre
    STAUS PL25 ....65 E5
Charlestown World Heritage
    Site (UNESCO)
    STAUS PL25 ....65 E4
Church Lane Cemetery
    STIVES TR26 ....26 B3
Chy-an-Albany Hotel
    STIVES TR26 ....69 F4
Cinedrome Cinema
    PADS PL28 ....48 B3
Cliff Head Hotel
    STAUS PL25 ....65 H4
Cooksland Business Park
    BODM PL31 ....11 F2
Cooksland Industrial Estate
    BODM PL31 ....11 F2
Cornwall College - Falmouth
    Marine School
    FAL TR11 ....22 D2
Cornwall College Newquay
    NEWQ TR7 ....46 D4
Cornwall College St Austell
    STAUS PL25 ....64 A3
Cornwall College Saltash
    SALT PL12 ....76 C3
Cottage Hotel
    STIVES TR26 ....71 F1
Country Sports Centre
    LAUN PL15 ....31 G4
County Wharf
    FAL TR11 ....23 E2
Crantock Bay Hotel
    RNEWQ TR8 ....20 C4
Crantock Street Cemetery
    NEWQ TR7 ....21 H3
The Curnow School
    RED TR15 ....61 E2
Custom House Quay
    FAL TR11 ....23 E2
Delabole Wind Farm
    DELAB PL33 ....16 B2
Dennis Cove Camping
    PADS PL28 ....48 C5
Devoran School
    RTRUS TR3 ....19 E4
Discovery Centre
    LOOE PL13 ....35 E2
Dolcoath Industrial Park
    CAMBORNE TR14 ....15 F2
Doubletrees Farm
    PAR PL24 ....50 A4

Duchy College
    CAMBORNE TR14 ....14 C1
The Duchy Hospital
    TRU TR1 ....83 H1
Duchy Wharf
    FAL TR11 ....23 F2
Eagle House Hotel
    LAUN PL15 ....31 E3
East Cornwall Hospital
    BODM PL31 ....10 D2
East Crinnis Camping &
    Caravan Park
    PAR PL24 ....50 B1
Eastern Breakwater
    FAL TR11 ....23 G2
Eastwood Park Estate
    PENRYN TR10 ....53 E4
Edward Hain Hospital
    STIVES TR26 ....69 F3
Efford Farm Business Park
    BUDE EX23 ....12 A4
Egloshayle Cemetery
    WADE PL27 ....87 F4
Eliot Hotel
    NEWQ TR7 ....46 C3
Empire Wharf
    FAL TR11 ....23 F2
Esplanade Hotel
    NEWQ TR7 ....21 G2
Fairbank Hotel
    RNEWQ TR8 ....21 E5
Fairpark Cemetery
    NEWQ TR7 ....47 H3
Falcon Hotel
    BUDE EX23 ....12 A3
Falmouth Art Gallery
    FAL TR11 ....22 D2
Falmouth Arts Centre
    FAL TR11 ....22 D2
Falmouth Beach Resort Hotel
    FAL TR11 ....22 D4
Falmouth Business Park
    FAL TR11 ....22 A3
Falmouth Cemetery
    FAL TR11 ....22 C4
Falmouth Coastguard &
    Lifeboat Station
    FAL TR11 ....23 F3
Falmouth & District Hospital
    FAL TR11 ....22 B2
Falmouth Golf Club
    FAL TR11 ....22 B5
Falmouth Hotel
    FAL TR11 ....23 F3
Falmouth Primary School
    FAL TR11 ....22 C1
Falmouth Tennis Club
    FAL TR11 ....22 C3
Fieldhead Hotel
    LOOE PL13 ....35 E4
Film Centre Cinema
    STAUS PL25 ....63 H4
Forge Industrial Park
    CAMBORNE TR14 ....14 D1
Formal Industrial Estate
    CAMBORNE TR14 ....14 A2
Fourlanesend CP School
    MBRK/KGSD PL10 ....43 H3
Fowey Coastguard Station
    FOW PL23 ....24 C4
Fowey Community College
    FOW PL23 ....24 B2
Fowey Hall Hotel
    FOW PL23 ....24 C2
Fowey Health Centre
    FOW PL23 ....24 D2
Fowey Hospital
    FOW PL23 ....24 C1
The Fowey Hotel
    FOW PL23 ....24 C2
Fowey Lifeboat Station
    FOW PL23 ....24 D1
Fowey Museum & Town Hall
    FOW PL23 ....24 D2
Fowey Primary School
    FOW PL23 ....24 B1
The Fun Factory
    NEWQ TR7 ....46 A3

Garrack Hotel
STIVES TR26 ....68 D2
Glendorgal Resort Hotel
NEWQ TR7 ....47 E1
Glynn Valley Crematorium
RBODM PL30 ....11 H5
Godolphin Arms Hotel
MARAZ TR17 ....38 B3
Golf Driving Range
NEWQ TR7 ....46 D4
Goonhavern
Primary School
RTRUNW TR4 ....57 H4
Great Mills Industrial Parc
PAR PL24 ....65 H2
Green Lane Cemetery
FOW PL23 ....24 C1
Green Lawns Hotel
FAL TR11 ....22 C3
Guildford Road
Industrial Estate
HAYLE TR27 ....27 G2
Gulval Primary School
PENZ TR18 ....55 G1
The Gwealdues Hotel
HELS TR13 ....29 H2
Gwel Avon Business Park
SALT PL12 ....76 C1
Hall For Cornwall
TRU TR1 ....85 F3
Hannafore Point Hotel
LOOE PL13 ....35 F4
Hartland Hotel
BUDE EX23 ....12 B2
Hayle Community School
HAYLE TR27 ....27 F4
Hayle Estuary RSPB Site
HAYLE TR27 ....67 E1
Hayle Industrial Park
HAYLE TR27 ....27 H2
Hayle RC
HAYLE TR27 ....27 H2
Hayle World Heritage Site
(UNESCO)
HAYLE TR27 ....27 E5
Headland Caravan &
Camping Park
TINT PL34 ....78 C3
Headland Gardens
FOW PL23 ....24 C4
Headland Hotel
NEWQ TR7 ....21 H1
The Health Centre
NEWQ TR7 ....46 B4
Heamoor Primary School
PENZ TR18 ....54 B3
Heathlands Business Park
LISK PL14 ....33 F3
Heathlands Industrial Estate
LISK PL14 ....33 F3
Helston Cemetery
HELS TR13 ....29 G5
Helston Community College
HELS TR13 ....29 F2
Helston Community Hospital
HELS TR13 ....59 H1
Helston Cricket & Rugby Club
HELS TR13 ....29 H3
Helston FC
HELS TR13 ....29 H3
Helston Health Centre
HELS TR13 ....29 G4
Helston Medical Centre
HELS TR13 ....29 G4
Helston School
HELS TR13 ....29 G2
Helston Sports Centre
HELS TR13 ....29 G1
High Cross Cemetery
STAUS PL25 ....64 A4
Higher Moor Holiday Park
RNEWQ TR8 ....20 D5
Highfield Road
Industrial Estate
CAMEL PL32 ....16 D5
Highfields Private School
RED TR15 ....61 E2
HMS Raleigh
TOR PL11 ....80 D5
Holmbush Industrial Estate
STAUS PL25 ....65 E3
Hotel Anacapri
FAL TR11 ....22 D4
Hotel California
NEWQ TR7 ....21 G3
Hotel Penarvor
BUDE EX23 ....12 A1
Hotel Penzance
PENZ TR18 ....55 F3
Hotel Riviera
NEWQ TR7 ....46 D2
Hotel St Eia
STIVES TR26 ....69 F4
Hotel Victoria
NEWQ TR7 ....46 B3
Huers Hut
NEWQ TR7 ....46 A2
Humphry Davy School
PENZ TR18 ....54 D2
Idle Rocks Hotel
RTRUE/STMW TR2 ....74 C2

The Industrial Estate
PERRAN TR6 ....56 C4
Jubilee Bathing Pool
PENZ TR18 ....55 F5
Kernick Business Park
PENRYN TR10 ....52 B5
Kernick Industrial Estate
PENRYN TR10 ....52 B4
Kilbirnie Hotel
NEWQ TR7 ....46 D2
King Charles CE
Primary School
FAL TR11 ....22 D3
King Charles Quay
FAL TR11 ....23 E2
Kings Acre
CAMEL PL32 ....17 E3
King's Hill Industrial Estate
BUDE EX23 ....12 D4
King's Wharf
FAL TR11 ....23 E2
Kneehigh Theatre
TRU TR1 ....85 E3
Lakefield Caravan Park
CAMEL PL32 ....16 D1
Lamellion Hospital
LISK PL14 ....33 E4
Lamorran House Gardens
RTRUE/STMW TR2 ....74 B2
Lands End Coastguard Station
LANDS TR19 ....72 A3
Lanlivery Primary School
RBODM PL30 ....36 B5
Launceston Castle
LAUN PL15 ....31 E3
Launceston Cemetery
LAUN PL15 ....30 C5
Launceston College
LAUN PL15 ....31 F5
Launceston Golf Club
LAUN PL15 ....30 D1
Launceston Hospital
LAUN PL15 ....31 F5
Launceston Primary School
LAUN PL15 ....31 F4
Launceston Steam Railway
LAUN PL15 ....30 C2
Lawrence House Museum
LAUN PL15 ....31 F3
Liskeard Business Park
LISK PL14 ....33 H2
Liskeard & District Museum
LISK PL14 ....33 F2
Liskeard General Cemetery
LISK PL14 ....33 E3
Liskeard Infant School
LISK PL14 ....33 E2
Liskeard Junior School
LISK PL14 ....32 D2
Liskeard Police Station
LISK PL14 ....33 F2
Liskeard School &
Community College
LISK PL14 ....33 F1
Liskey Holiday Park
RTRUNW TR4 ....82 C2
Little Bodieve Holiday Park
WADE PL27 ....87 E1
Little Trevarrack Tourist Park
STIVES TR26 ....71 F3
Longstones Cemetery
STIVES TR26 ....71 G2
Looe Health Centre
LOOE PL13 ....35 E2
Looe Lifeboat Station
LOOE PL13 ....35 F3
Looe Police Station
LOOE PL13 ....35 E2
Looe Primary School
LOOE PL13 ....35 G2
Lostwithiel Hotel, Golf &
Country Club
LOST PL22 ....37 G3
Lostwithiel Museum
LOST PL22 ....37 F4
Lostwithiel Primary School
LOST PL22 ....37 E4
Lux Park Leisure Centre
LISK PL14 ....33 F1
Mabe Primary School
PENRYN TR10 ....52 A4
Madeira Hotel
FAL TR11 ....23 E3
Marazion Blues AFC
MARAZ TR17 ....38 D3
Marazion Cemetery
MARAZ TR17 ....38 D3
Marazion Hotel
MARAZ TR17 ....38 B3
Marazion Marsh RSPB Reserve
MARAZ TR17 ....38 A2
Marazion School
MARAZ TR17 ....38 C3
Marina Hotel
FOW PL23 ....24 C2
Maritime Museum
PENZ TR18 ....55 E4
Maritime Rescue
Co-ordination Centre
(MRCC)
FAL TR11 ....23 H4

Market Street Clinic
LAUN PL15 ....31 F3
Marlborough School
FAL TR11 ....22 C3
Marsh Villa Gardens
PAR PL24 ....51 E2
Mary Newman's Cottage
SALT PL12 ....77 F3
Mary Williams Pier
PENZ TR18 ....45 H2
The Medical Centre
CAMEL PL32 ....17 F4
Membly Hall Hotel
FAL TR11 ....23 E4
The Metropole Hotel
PADS PL28 ....48 B3
Mevagissey Cemetery
MEVA PL26 ....41 G2
Mevagissey Harbour Marine
Aquarium
MEVA PL26 ....41 G3
Mevagissey Museum
MEVA PL26 ....41 H3
Mevagissey Primary School
MEVA PL26 ....41 G2
Mid Cornwall Business Centre
STAUS PL25 ....65 H3
Military Museum
BODM PL31 ....10 D4
Millbrook CE Primary School
MBRK/KGSD PL10 ....43 F1
Miller Business Park
LISK PL14 ....33 E4
Moorlands Trading Estate
SALT PL12 ....76 B1
Moorswater Industrial Estate
LISK PL14 ....32 B3
Morven Trading Estate
STAUS PL25 ....64 C4
Mount Charles School
STAUS PL25 ....64 C4
Mount Haven Hotel
MARAZ TR17 ....38 D3
Mounts Bay School
PENZ TR18 ....54 B2
Moyclare Gardens
LISK PL14 ....33 E5
Nancealverne Special School
PENZ TR18 ....54 C3
Nansloe Primary School
HELS TR13 ....29 G5
The National Lobster Factory
PADS PL28 ....48 C3
National Maritime Museum
Cornwall
FAL TR11 ....23 E3
Newham Industrial Estate
TRU TR1 ....85 F1
Newlyn Art Gallery
PENZ TR18 ....45 G1
Newlyn Primary School
PENZ TR18 ....45 G1
Newport Industrial Estate
LAUN PL15 ....31 F2
Newquay AFC
NEWQ TR7 ....46 A4
Newquay & District Hospital
NEWQ TR7 ....46 C4
Newquay Golf Club
NEWQ TR7 ....21 H2
Newquay Junior School
NEWQ TR7 ....46 C3
Newquay Lifeboat Station
NEWQ TR7 ....46 A3
Newquay Sports Centre
NEWQ TR7 ....47 E3
Newquay Tretherras
School
NEWQ TR7 ....47 E3
Newquay Youth Centre
NEWQ TR7 ....46 D3
Newquay Zoo
NEWQ TR7 ....46 D4
Newtons Margate
Industrial Estate
BODM PL31 ....11 F3
New Wheal Leisure Mine
PERRAN TR6 ....56 C4
North Arm
PENZ TR18 ....55 F4
North Cornwall Museum &
Gallery
CAMEL PL32 ....17 E4
Northern Wharf
FAL TR11 ....23 F1
North Grange
Industrial Estate
RTRUS TR3 ....19 E3
North Pier
PENZ TR18 ....45 G2
North Quay
FAL TR11 ....23 E2
Oaklands Industrial Estate
LISK PL14 ....33 H1
Oddfellows Hall, Library &
Museum
PERRAN TR6 ....56 B3
Old Custom House Inn
PADS PL28 ....48 C3
Old Post Office (NT)
TINT PL34 ....78 C4

The Old Ship Hotel
PADS PL28 ....48 B2
Padstow Harbour
Industrial Estate
PADS PL28 ....48 C3
Padstow School
PADS PL28 ....48 A4
Padstow Touring Park
PADS PL28 ....48 A5
Paradise Park (Wildlife
Conservation Sanctuary)
HAYLE TR27 ....26 C5
Parc Eglos School
HELS TR13 ....29 F3
Park Grove Hotel
FAL TR11 ....22 C2
The Park Medical Centre
STAUS PL25 ....63 G4
Passmore Edwards Hospital
LISK PL14 ....33 E2
Paul Cemetery
LANDS TR19 ....45 G5
Pedn-Olva Hotel
STIVES TR26 ....69 G3
Penbeagle Industrial Estate
STIVES TR26 ....68 C1
Pendennis Castle
FAL TR11 ....23 G4
Penlee House Gallery &
Museum
PENZ TR18 ....54 D4
Pennoweth Primary School
RED TR15 ....61 E3
Pennygillam
Industrial Estate
LAUN PL15 ....30 D5
Penpol Primary School
HAYLE TR27 ....26 D5
Penrice Community College
STAUS PL25 ....64 C4
Penryn CE Infant School
PENRYN TR10 ....52 C4
Penryn Cemetery
PENRYN TR10 ....53 F4
Penryn College
PENRYN TR10 ....52 C3
Penryn Junior School
PENRYN TR10 ....52 C3
Penryn RFC
PENRYN TR10 ....52 B4
Penventon Park Hotel
RED TR15 ....60 D3
Penwith College
PENZ TR18 ....54 D3
Penzance Cemetery
PENZ TR18 ....54 D2
Penzance Community
Primary School
RPENZ TR20 ....54 C3
Penzance Heliport
PENZ TR18 ....55 H2
Penzance Lifeboat Station
PENZ TR18 ....45 G2
Perran-ar-Worthial
Primary School
RTRUS TR3 ....18 A4
Perranporth Camping &
Touring Park
PERRAN TR6 ....56 D3
Perranporth Golf Club
PERRAN TR6 ....56 D2
Perranporth Primary School
PERRAN TR6 ....56 B4
Phillack Cemetery
HAYLE TR27 ....27 F1
Phoenix Leisure Centre
LAUN PL15 ....31 F5
The Pier House Hotel
STAUS PL25 ....65 E5
Pine Lodge Gardens &
Nursery
STAUS PL25 ....65 G3
Plaza Cinema
TRU TR1 ....85 F3
Polean Industrial Estate
LOOE PL13 ....34 D2
Polkyth Leisure Centre
STAUS PL25 ....64 B3
Polmanter Tourist Park
STIVES TR26 ....70 B1
Polruan Holidays Camping &
Caravanning
FOW PL23 ....25 E4
Polruan Primary School
FOW PL23 ....24 D4
Poltair Community School &
Sports College
STAUS PL25 ....64 A2
Poltair Hospital
RPENZ TR20 ....54 B1
Pondhu Primary School
STAUS PL25 ....63 G5
Ponsharden
Industrial Estate
FAL TR11 ....53 F5
Pool Health Centre
RED TR15 ....15 G1
Pool Industrial Estate
RED TR15 ....15 H1
Pool Trading Estate
RED TR15 ....15 G2

Porth Avallen Hotel
  STAUS PL25 ....65 G5
Porth Beach Tourist Park
  NEWQ TR7 ....47 F1
Porthleven CP School
  HELS TR13 ....58 B1
Porthminster Hotel
  STIVES TR26 ....69 F4
Porth Veor Manor Hotel
  NEWQ TR7 ....47 E1
Powderham Castle
  Tourist Park
  RBODM PL30 ....36 B5
Premier Inn
  BODM PL31 ....11 F2
  HAYLE TR27 ....27 H1
  RTRUS TR3 ....19 G1
Prideaux Place
  PADS PL28 ....48 A2
Princess Pavillion &
  Gyllyndune Gardens
  FAL TR11 ....23 E3
Priory Lodge Hotel
  NEWQ TR7 ....46 B4
Queens Hotel
  PENZ TR18 ....55 E5
Queen's Wharf
  FAL TR11 ....23 F1
Racquets Sports Club
  TOR PL11 ....81 G4
Radio & Telegraph Station
  LANDS TR19 ....72 D5
Redannick Theatre
  TRU TR1 ....85 E3
Red Moor & Southern Red
  Moor Nature Reserve
  RBODM PL30 ....36 A1
Redruth School
  RED TR15 ....60 D3
Regal Cinema
  RED TR15 ....61 E3
  WADE PL27 ....86 C3
Restormel Castle
  LOST PL22 ....37 F1
Restormel Industrial Estate
  LOST PL22 ....37 G3
Richard Lander School
  TRU TR1 ....83 F3
Rising Sun Hotel
  RTRUE/STMW TR2 ....74 C2
Rivercroft Hotel
  LOOE PL13 ....35 F2
Robartes Junior School
  BODM PL31 ....10 C3
Rose Hill Cemetery
  PAR PL24 ....50 C3
Roseland Visitor Centre
  RTRUE/STMW TR2 ....74 C2
Roselyon School
  PAR PL24 ....50 D4
Rosemellin Primary School
  CAMBORNE TR14 ....14 D2
Roseville Holiday Park
  RTRUNW TR4 ....57 G3
Roskear Primary School
  CAMBORNE TR14 ....14 D3
Rosslyn Hotel
  FAL TR11 ....22 B2
Royal Cinema
  STIVES TR26 ....69 F3
Royal Cornwall Hospital
  (Treliske)
  TRU TR1 ....83 H2
Royal Cornwall Museum
  TRU TR1 ....85 E3
Royal Cornwall Yacht Club
  FAL TR11 ....22 D1
Royal Duchy Hotel
  FAL TR11 ....23 E4
Royal Hotel
  TRU TR1 ....85 F3
St Austell Arts Theatre
  STAUS PL25 ....63 G5
St Austell Bay
  Business Park
  STAUS PL25 ....65 H3
St Austell Brewery
  STAUS PL25 ....64 A3
St Austell Cemetery
  STAUS PL25 ....64 B4
St Austell College
  STAUS PL25 ....63 H3
St Austell District Hospital
  STAUS PL25 ....63 F4
St Barnabas Hospital
  SALT PL12 ....77 E3
St Breock School
  WADE PL27 ....86 C3
St Catherine's Castle
  FOW PL23 ....24 C3
St Catherines CE
  Primary School
  LAUN PL15 ....30 D5
St Clare Swimming Pool
  PENZ TR18 ....54 D3
St Columb Minor School
  NEWQ TR7 ....47 G2
St Day Road Cemetery
  RED TR15 ....61 G3
St Enodoc Golf Club
  WADE PL27 ....49 E1

St Erth Cemetery
  HAYLE TR27 ....67 F3
St Erth Industrial Estate
  HAYLE TR27 ....66 D2
St Erth Primary School
  HAYLE TR27 ....67 F3
St Ia School
  STIVES TR26 ....71 F2
St Ives Coastguard Station
  STIVES TR26 ....69 G4
St Ives Holiday Village
  STIVES TR26 ....66 A1
St Ives Infant School
  STIVES TR26 ....69 E3
St Ives Junior School
  STIVES TR26 ....69 E3
St Ives Leisure Centre
  STIVES TR26 ....69 E3
St Ives Museum
  STIVES TR26 ....69 G2
St Ives RFC
  STIVES TR26 ....68 D3
St Ives School
  STIVES TR26 ....69 F5
St John's Ambulance
  TRU TR1 ....85 E3
St Johns Business Park
  HELS TR13 ....29 E3
St John the Baptist RC
  Primary School
  CAMBORNE TR14 ....14 C4
St Josephs School
  LAUN PL15 ....31 E2
St Just Mining District World
  Heritage Site (UNESCO)
  RPENZ TR20 ....73 F1
St Just Primary School
  LANDS TR19 ....72 B4
St Just Recreation Centre
  LANDS TR19 ....72 C4
St Just RFC
  LANDS TR19 ....72 C3
St Just Sports Centre
  LANDS TR19 ....72 B3
St Lawrence Hospital
  BODM PL31 ....10 A3
St Madderns CE School
  RPENZ TR20 ....54 A1
St Martins CE Primary School
  LISK PL14 ....33 G3
St Marys Catholic
  Primary School
  BODM PL31 ....10 B3
St Marys Catholic School
  PENZ TR18 ....55 E2
St Mary's Cemetery
  TRU TR1 ....85 E2
St Marys CE Primary School
  PENZ TR18 ....55 E5
  TRU TR1 ....85 E1
St Marys RC Primary School
  FAL TR11 ....22 A3
St Mawes Castle
  RTRUE/STMW TR2 ....74 B3
St Mawes Primary School
  RTRUE/STMW TR2 ....74 C2
St Mawes Sailing Club
  RTRUE/STMW TR2 ....74 C2
St Meriadoc CE
  Infant School
  CAMBORNE TR14 ....14 B4
St Meriadoc CE VA
  Junior School
  CAMBORNE TR14 ....14 A4
St Mewan Primary School
  MEVA PL26 ....63 E5
St Michael's Catholic
  Small School
  TRU TR1 ....85 E3
St Michaels CE
  Primary School
  HELS TR13 ....29 G4
St Michaels Hospital
  HAYLE TR27 ....26 C5
St Michaels Hotel
  FAL TR11 ....22 D4
St Michael's Mount &
  Gardens (NT)
  MARAZ TR17 ....38 A5
St Pauls RC Primary School
  PLYNW PL5 ....77 H4
St Petrocs Ceva
  Primary School
  BODM PL31 ....10 D3
St Petroc's Hotel
  PADS PL28 ....48 C3
St Petrocs School
  BUDE EX23 ....12 B1
St Pirans School
  HAYLE TR27 ....26 C5
St Stephens
  Primary School
  LAUN PL15 ....31 E1
  SALT PL12 ....76 C3
St Uny Cemetery
  RED TR15 ....60 D5
St Uny CE Primary School
  STIVES TR26 ....71 F2
St Winnow CE
  Primary School
  LOST PL22 ....37 H4

Saltash Business Park
  SALT PL12 ....76 B1
Saltash Community School
  SALT PL12 ....76 D4
Saltash Health Centre
  SALT PL12 ....76 D2
Saltash Industrial Estate
  SALT PL12 ....76 A1
Saltash RFC
  SALT PL12 ....76 B1
Sandy Hill Primary School
  STAUS PL25 ....64 C3
Sandy Lodge Hotel
  NEWQ TR7 ....46 D2
Savoy Cinema
  PENZ TR18 ....55 E4
The Seafood Restaurant
  (Hotel)
  PADS PL28 ....48 C3
Ships & Castles Leisure Pool
  FAL TR11 ....23 G3
The Shire Hall
  BODM PL31 ....10 D3
Silverbow Park
  RTRUNW TR4 ....57 G5
Sir James Smith
  Community School
  CAMEL PL32 ....17 E4
South Pier
  NEWQ TR7 ....46 A2
  PENZ TR18 ....45 H3
  PENZ TR18 ....55 F5
South Quay
  HAYLE TR27 ....26 C4
Splash Leisure Pool
  BUDE EX23 ....12 D3
Stable Hobba
  Industrial Estate
  RPENZ TR20 ....45 F1
Stadium Retail Park
  STAUS PL25 ....65 H2
Stratton Hospital
  BUDE EX23 ....13 F3
Stratton Medical Centre
  BUDE EX23 ....13 F3
Stratton Primary School
  BUDE EX23 ....13 F2
Sunny Meadows
  Tourist Park
  RTRUNW TR4 ....57 G3
TA Centre
  TRU TR1 ....85 F2
Tamar Business Park
  LAUN PL15 ....30 D5
The Tarbert Hotel
  PENZ TR18 ....55 E4
Tate St Ives
  STIVES TR26 ....69 F2
Tehidy Holiday Park
  RTRUNW TR4 ....60 B1
Tencreek Holiday Park
  LOOE PL13 ....34 A5
Threemilestone
  Industrial Estate
  RTRUNW TR4 ....82 C2
Threemilestone
  Primary School
  RTRUS TR3 ....83 E3
Threemilestone Retail Park
  RTRUNW TR4 ....82 C2
Tidal Observatory
  PENZ TR18 ....45 H2
Tintagel Castle
  TINT PL34 ....78 A2
Tintagel CC
  TINT PL34 ....78 D3
Tintagel Primary School
  TINT PL34 ....78 C5
Tintagel Toy Museum
  TINT PL34 ....78 C3
Tollgate Farm Caravan &
  Camping Park
  PERRAN TR6 ....56 C1
Torpoint Cemetery
  TOR PL11 ....80 C4
Torpoint
  Community School
  TOR PL11 ....81 E3
Torpoint Infant School
  TOR PL11 ....81 G4
Travelodge
  HAYLE TR27 ....27 G2
  STAUS PL25 ....63 H5
Trebarwith Hotel
  NEWQ TR7 ....46 B3
Tregenna Castle Gardens
  STIVES TR26 ....69 F4
Tregenna Castle Hotel,
  Golf & Country Club
  STIVES TR26 ....69 F4
Treglisson Camping &
  Caravan Park
  HAYLE TR27 ....27 H5
Tregolls Primary School
  TRU TR1 ....85 H2
Tregrehan Gardens
  PAR PL24 ....65 H1
Treleigh Industrial Estate
  RTRUNW TR4 ....61 F1
Treliske Industrial Estate
  TRU TR1 ....83 G2

Treliske Retail Park
  RTRUNW TR4 ....83 G2
Treliske School
  TRU TR1 ....84 A2
Treloan Coastal Farm
  Holidays
  RTRUE/STMW TR2 ....75 H1
Treloggan
  Industrial Estate
  NEWQ TR7 ....47 E5
Treloweth Community
  Primary School
  RED TR15 ....60 A3
Tremarne Hotel
  MEVA PL26 ....41 H4
Trenance Holiday Park
  NEWQ TR7 ....46 C4
Trenance Hotel
  NEWQ TR7 ....46 A3
Trenance Infant School
  NEWQ TR7 ....46 B4
Trenance Leisure Park &
  Gardens
  NEWQ TR7 ....46 C4
Trenant Industrial Estate
  WADE PL27 ....87 E3
Trencreek Holiday Park
  NEWQ TR7 ....47 E5
Trenethick Business Park
  HELS TR13 ....29 G1
Trengweath Hospital
  RED TR15 ....61 E4
Trevaylor Caravan &
  Camping Park
  LANDS TR19 ....72 B1
Treviglas
  Community College
  NEWQ TR7 ....47 G2
Trevillett Quarry
  TINT PL34 ....79 H4
Trevithick Cottage (NT)
  CAMBORNE TR14 ....14 A5
Trevithick J & I School
  CAMBORNE TR14 ....14 C5
Trevol Business Park
  TOR PL11 ....80 D4
Trewince Manor
  RTRUE/STMW TR2 ....75 G1
Trewirgie Infant School
  RED TR15 ....61 E4
Trewirgie Junior School
  RED TR15 ....61 E4
Treyew Primary School
  TRU TR1 ....84 C3
Trinity House National
  Lighthouse Museum
  PENZ TR18 ....55 E4
Truro Bowl
  TRU TR1 ....85 E2
Truro Cathedral
  TRU TR1 ....85 F2
Truro Cemetery
  TRU TR1 ....85 G3
Truro City AFC
  TRU TR1 ....84 D4
Truro College
  TRU TR1 ....83 G3
Truro Golf Club
  TRU TR1 ....84 A2
Truro High School for Girls
  TRU TR1 ....85 E4
Truro Leisure Centre
  TRU TR1 ....83 G2
Truro RFC
  TRU TR1 ....85 H3
Truro School
  TRU TR1 ....85 G3
Tunnels Through Time
  NEWQ TR7 ....46 A4
Tyacks Hotel
  CAMBORNE TR14 ....14 C3
Tywardreath Cemetery
  PAR PL24 ....51 E3
Tywardreath
  Primary School
  PAR PL24 ....51 F3
University College Falmouth
  (Tremough Campus)
  PENRYN TR10 ....52 A3
University College Falmouth
  (Woodlane Campus)
  FAL TR11 ....22 D3
Upper Lynstone
  Caravan Park
  BUDE EX23 ....12 A5
Victoria Gardens
  TRU TR1 ....85 E2
Wadebridge Community
  Primary School
  WADE PL27 ....86 D1
Wadebridge School
  WADE PL27 ....86 D2
Wadebridge
  Sports Centre
  WADE PL27 ....86 D1
Walker Lines
  Industrial Estate
  BODM PL31 ....10 D4
Waterworld
  (Pool & Squash Courts)
  NEWQ TR7 ....46 C4

Weeth Primary School
  CAMBORNE TR14 ....**14** B2
Westberry Hotel
  BODM PL31 ....**10** D2
West Cornwall Arts Centre
  PENZ TR18 ....**55** E4
West Cornwall Golf Club
  STIVES TR26 ....**26** B3
West Cornwall Hospital
  PENZ TR18 ....**54** D3
West Cornwall Retail Park
  HAYLE TR27 ....**27** H2

West End Industrial Estate
  PENRYN TR10 ....**52** C3
Western Pier
  STIVES TR26 ....**69** F2
Western Wharf
  FAL TR11 ....**23** F2
Westover Surgery
  FAL TR11 ....**22** C3
Wharfside Shopping Centre
  PENZ TR18 ....**55** F4
Wheal Rodney Holiday Park
  MARAZ TR17 ....**38** D1

Whitegate Shopping Complex
  NEWQ TR7 ....**46** D2
White Hart Hotel
  STAUS PL25 ....**63** H4
Whitsand Bay Lodge &
  Touring Park
  MBRK/KGSD PL10 ....**42** C2
Windmill
  Industrial Estate
  FOW PL23 ....**24** C2
Woodland Garden
  TOR PL11 ....**80** C2

Woods-Browning
  Industrial Estate
  BODM PL31 ....**11** E5
World of Model
  Railways
  MEVA PL26 ....**41** G3
Wren Industrial Estate
  TRU TR1 ....**83** G2

Acknowledgements

Schools address data provided by Education Direct.

Petrol station information supplied by Johnsons.

Garden centre information provided by:

Garden Centre Association   Britains best garden centres

Wyevale Garden Centres

The statement on the front cover of this atlas is sourced, selected and quoted
from a reader comment and feedback form received in 2004

Discover
Britain

with AA travel guides.

AA Travel Guides
Britain's largest travel publisher
order online at www.theAA.com/travel

AA

Street by Street — QUESTIONNAIRE

Dear Atlas User
Your comments, opinions and recommendations are very important to us. So please help us to improve our street atlases by taking a few minutes to complete this simple questionnaire.

You do not need a stamp (unless posted outside the UK). If you do not want to remove this page from your street atlas, then photocopy it or write your answers on a plain sheet of paper.

Send to: Marketing Assistant, AA Publishing, 14th Floor Fanum House, Freepost SCE 4598, Basingstoke RG21 4GY

ABOUT THE ATLAS...

Please state which city / town / county you bought:

_____

Where did you buy the atlas? (City, Town, County)

_____

For what purpose? (please tick all applicable)

To use in your local area ☐   To use on business or at work ☐

Visiting a strange place ☐   In the car ☐   On foot ☐

Other (please state)

_____

Have you ever used any street atlases other than AA Street by Street?

Yes ☐   No ☐

If so, which ones?

_____

Is there any aspect of our street atlases that could be improved?
(Please continue on a separate sheet if necessary)

_____
_____
_____
_____

ML221z

continued overleaf

Please list the features you found most useful:

_____

_____

_____

Please list the features you found least useful:

_____

_____

_____

LOCAL KNOWLEDGE...

Local knowledge is invaluable. Whilst every attempt has been made to make the information contained in this atlas as accurate as possible, should you notice any inaccuracies, please detail them below (if necessary, use a blank piece of paper) or e-mail us at *streetbystreet@theAA.com*

_____

_____

_____

ABOUT YOU...

Name (Mr/Mrs/Ms) _____

Address _____

                                      Postcode _____

Daytime tel no _____

E-mail address _____

Which age group are you in?

Under 25 ☐   **25-34** ☐   **35-44** ☐   **45-54** ☐   **55-64** ☐   **65+** ☐

Are you an AA member?   **YES** ☐   **NO** ☐

Do you have Internet access?   **YES** ☐   **NO** ☐

Thank you for taking the time to complete this questionnaire. Please send it to us as soon as possible, and remember, you do not need a stamp (unless posted outside the UK).

We may use information we hold about you to, telephone or email you about other products and services offered by the AA, we do NOT disclose this information to third parties.

Please tick here if you do not wish to hear about products and services from the AA. ☐

ML221z